IDEAS FOR INTERCULTURAL EDUCATION

IDEAS FOR INTERCULTURAL EDUCATION

Simon Marginson and Erlenawati Sawir

KH

IDEAS FOR INTERCULTURAL EDUCATION
Copyright © Simon Marginson and Erlenawati Sawir, 2011

First published in 2011 by PALGRAVE MACMILLAN®
in the United States—a division of St. Martin's Press
LLC, 175 Fifth Avenue, New York, NY 10010.

Where this book is distributed in the UK, Europe and the rest of
the world, this is by Palgrave Macmillan, a division of Macmillan
Publishers Limited, registered in England, company number 785998,
of Houndmills, Basingstoke, Hampshire RG21 6XS.

Palgrave Macmillan is the global academic imprint of the above
companies and has companies and representatives throughout the
world.

Palgrave® and Macmillan® are registered trademarks in the United
States, the United Kingdom, Europe, and other countries.

ISBN 13: 978–0–230–11793–8
ISBN 10: 0-230-11793-7

Library of Congress Cataloging-in-Publication Data

Marginson, Simon, 1951–
    Ideas for intercultural education / Simon Marginson and
Erlenawati Sawir.
        p. cm.
    Includes bibliographical references.
    ISBN 978-0-230-11793-8
        1. Multicultural education—Cross-cultural studies. I. Sawir,
Erlenawati, 1960– II. Title.

    LC1099.M37 2011
    370.117—dc23   2011017331

A catalogue record of the book is available from the British Library.

Design by Scribe Inc.

First edition: November 2011

10 9 8 7 6 5 4 3 2 1

Printed in the United States of America

3/19/12

CONTENTS

PREFACE

Like wind-blown grass
We feel the time

Graham Lowndes,
Till Time Brings Change, 1973

Ideas for Intercultural Education is the unplanned and welcome outcome of seven years of research on the social and economic security
of cross-border students in the global student market. It was a book
that burned to be written, on the basis of what we discovered about
cross-cultural relations in the course of that research.

The research began at Monash University in Melbourne, Australia, in 2003 and later spread to the University of Melbourne in the
same city where both authors of this book worked. More recently
it followed one of the authors to Central Queensland University's
Melbourne office. The research team working on this project con-
sisted of the two authors of the book and Chris Nyland, Gaby Ramia,
Helen Forbes-Mewett, and Sharon Smith, with contributions also
from Felicity Rawlings-Sanaei and Ly Tran. Between them the full
group has worked at seven different Australian universities in the
last half decade. During the project we collected extensive data on
cross-cultural relations between international students and local students and others, and on what happens inside classrooms with large
numbers of international students. We also prepared a critical literature study on all aspects of international student security, including
cross-cultural issues in international education and on cosmopolitan
approaches to education.

In preparing the summary book[1] arising from that study, we planned
to include a chapter on cross-cultural relations in international education and international student life. However, we found that the draft
chapter on cross-cultural relations was 75,000 words and still growing,
instead of the planned 10,000. We also found that much of the prior
literature was grossly inadequate for an understanding of intercultural
relations in international education. It was seriously at variance with

what our interviewees were saying. It was clear that many researchers were unable to understand international students from non-English-speaking backgrounds on the basis of equal respect, or even conceive of forms of international education in which the autonomy and rights of the students were a central element. We began to conceive international education as a process of *self-formation*, led by the students themselves, in contrast to the patronizing vision of other-formation that dominated some of the research (especially many studies in the field of counseling psychology).

It was also becoming obvious that the intercultural dimension, while crucial to student security issues, was also extending beyond the confines of a study focused on security. There was a larger story to be told about cross-cultural and intercultural relations in international education programs in the English-speaking countries, a story with both negative and positive aspects and one that we very much wanted to tell. We wanted to provide a detailed review of what the research literature was saying, drawing truths from some of it and critiquing other parts of it, and to explore the potentials for cross-cultural relations and for a more fulfilling international student experience for all parties. It was clear that the intercultural potentials of international education were as yet largely unrealized in Australia and apparent from the research literature that they were also largely unrealized in the United Kingdom (UK), New Zealand, United States, and Canada.

All of that led directly to the writing of *Ideas for Intercultural Education*. The bulk of the text was prepared immediately after the summary book on international student security was completed in 2009, with revisions and additions a year later.

Ideas for Intercultural Education does not set out to be the last word on intercultural issues in higher and international education. That would be too big a task for one book, and perhaps "being definitive" about something as large and important to human relations as intercultural education is not an appropriate task for any book. In the discussion of intercultural relations in education there is much good work and a number of unresolved issues. There are also too many people trying to lay down the law. We do not want to join them. Intercultural relations are an ongoing conversation that involves all of us. We can point to lessons learned, but we cannot be categorical about what the future might hold; and while some general principles (such as openness and responsiveness) hold in all sites, intercultural relations are *always* contextualized. Our educational connections with cultural "Others" are always located in space and time. They vary across the different sites and programs. This means that solely general formulas cannot solve all the issues involved here. Neither ethnocentric stereotypes based on one culture nor an abstract cosmopolitanism that treats all cultures as equivalent and interchangeable is adequate to the issues. Yet these barren alternatives have been the main options offered up to this point. As this book's title suggests, to move beyond the present limitations we need new *ideas* to inform research and practice, ideas that combine principles of human relations with action in particular contexts.

The objective of *Ideas for Intercultural Education* is to break open the debates to encourage fresh thinking, talk, and, through that, fresh educational practice. Practices and ideas are in continual interplay. This book was generated by problems we observed in the practical domain of international education. This practical orientation led us to a critical review of knowledge in the field. In turn, a forward move in the domain of knowledge and ideas is the precondition for better practices. As new ideas emerge and begin to colonize that practical domain—a domain in which improving the quality of intercultural engagement has become one of the ways of gaining a market edge—those ideas will be enriched by research-informed practitioners and lead to more fruitful strategies in higher education institutions in the English-speaking world, especially in their classrooms.

The book's argument is presented in three stages. First, Chapters 1–3 lay out the terrain of discussion and critically review the existing scholarship and research on intercultural aspects of international education and related fields. The book tackles the scholarship and research first because knowledge matters. Knowledge frames and limits our educational practices both directly and indirectly. Correspondingly, new knowledge also helps us to expand practice.

Second, Chapters 4–6 move beyond the realm of ideas to consider what happens in educational sites: in the lives of international students, in their classrooms, and in their relationships with locals. Again we review, summarize, and critique knowledge and insights from the published research literature and also include data we collected. Chapter 4 consists of stories of individual students. These stories have been taken from actual research interviews with students in Australia during 2005–2008 and are reported accurately, except that the names of the students have been altered to protect their privacy. Chapter 5 focuses on cross-cultural barriers and problems. Chapter 6 explores cross-cultural classrooms and relations between local and international students.

Third, the book concludes with Chapters 7–8. Chapter 7, "Conclusion 1: International Education as Self-Formation," summarizes our theory of international educational in the light of the book's discussion of intercultural relations. Chapter 8, "Conclusion 2: Toward Intercultural Education," draws together the ideas in the book and explores the practical implications in educational organization and classroom teaching and learning. We are sure that if international education is to move toward the located, relational cosmopolitanism that is needed, changes in theory, scholarship, research, and learning practices will all inform each other.

The stories about Zhao Mei at the beginning of Chapters 1 and 8 are fictional, a composite of several real-life East Asian student stories unearthed during the research.

This book makes a pair with the study of the social and economic security of international students published separately as *International Student Security* (Marginson et al., 2010). That book focuses on issues of social protection and personal empowerment affecting international students, the regulation of those issues, and gaps in that regulation, with reference to English-speaking nations in general while focusing on the Australian case. The two books are about different things but sympathetic to each other. The underlying ambition of both works is to rethink and remake international education in terms of universal humanism and global cosmopolitan intercultural exchange. *International Student Security* is about grounding the mobile noncitizen student securely in the country of education. *Ideas for Intercultural Education* is designed to open up the possibilities for mutual learning that are offered by the large-scale presence of international students. Both books are about our slow but essential progress toward a one-world society.

The research and literature review on which this study was based were initially funded by the Monash Institute for the Study of Global Movements at Monash University. The main support was from the Australian Research Council through an ARC Discovery Grant. The Australian Professorial Fellowship awarded to Simon Marginson provided reading and writing time. Erlenawati Sawir was helped by an Early Career Researcher Grant from the University of Melbourne. Erlenawati Sawir conducted the two hundred interviews used in the empirical studies that are drawn on in Chapters 4–6 and prepared early drafts of some materials from those studies used in Chapters 5–6. Simon Marginson did all final writing and editing.

The authors would like to thank their coresearchers in the international student project, who have been most kind and solid colleagues and a delight with whom to work. We would also like to thank the students and staff who generously participated in interviews and opened up as they did. We also acknowledge those working in Australia or elsewhere who helped to advance our thinking about intercultural education and related issues, especially Fazal Rizvi, who founded the Monash Centre for Research in International Education where this work began, and others including Chi Baik, Melissa Banks, Joe Lo Bianco, Brendan Cantwell, Dang Thi Kim Anh, Glyn Davis, Nadine Dolby, Paula Dunstan, Hiroko Hashimoto, Jane Kenway, Kazuhiro Kudo, Betty Leask, Jenny Lee, Allan Luke, Grant McBurnie, Peter McPhee, Dennis Murray, Rajani Naidoo, Thi Nhai Nguyen, Peter Ninnes, Imanol Ordorika, Hiroshi Ota, Yoko Ota, Phan Le Ha, Natt Pimpa, Michael Singh, Nishani Singh, Ravinder Sidhu, Hans de Wit, Simone Volet, Yang Rui and Chris Ziguras. Erlenawati Sawir would like to thank Paul Rodan at the International Education Research Centre of Central Queensland University. Simon Marginson would like to thank Richard James, Sophie Arkoudis, and Mirella Ozols at the Centre for the Study of Higher Education at the University of Melbourne, and Field Rickards, Dean of the Melbourne Graduate School of Education.

The first draft of the chapters was largely written in August to September 2009 while Simon Marginson was a visiting professor at the Research Institute for Higher Education (RIHE) at Hiroshima University in Japan. The scholarly atmosphere sustained by RIHE Director Yamamoto Shinichi and colleagues, and the daily walks between the university and the apartment in nearby Saijo, provided excellent conditions for this work. Special thanks go to Huang Futao, Oba Jun, and Araki Hiroko. The drafts were thoroughly revised in Melbourne in March 2011 on the basis of comments from colleagues and a wise Palgrave reviewer.

ABOUT THE AUTHORS

Simon Marginson is a professor of higher education at the Centre for the Study of Higher Education in the Melbourne Graduate School of Education at the University of Melbourne in Melbourne, Australia. He works on globalization and higher education, comparative and international education, knowledge economy policy, and issues of freedom and creativity, with some emphasis on the Asia-Pacific region. He is a coordinating editor of the world journal *Higher Education*, a member of 14 other international journal boards, and the author of over two hundred scholarly articles and chapters. His previous books include *Markets in Education* (1997); *The Enterprise University* (2000) with Mark Considine; and three books with Peter Murphy and Michael Peters: *Creativity and the Global Knowledge Economy* (2009), *Global Creation: Space, Mobility and Synchrony in the Age of the Knowledge Economy* (2010), and *Imagination: Three Models of the Imagination in the Age of the Knowledge Economy* (2010). In 2010 he also published *International Student Security* with Chris Nyland, Erlenawati Sawir, and Helen Forbes-Mewett. In 2011 his published work has included the collection *Higher Education in the Asia-Pacific: Strategic Responses to Globalization*, edited by Simon Marginson, Sarjit, Kaur and Erlenawati Sawir; and *Handbook of Higher Education and Globalization*, edited by Roger King, Simon Marginson, and Rajani Naidoo.

Erlenawati Sawir is research fellow at the International Education Research Centre of Central Queensland University in Melbourne. Previously she worked as research fellow at Monash University and the University of Melbourne, and prior to 2000 as a senior lecturer at the University of Jambi in Sumatra, Indonesia. A 2003 Monash PhD graduate in sociolinguistics and education, and specialist in international education, she has contributed to *Asian EFL Journal, Australian Journal of Education, International Education Journal, Higher Education, Journal of Studies in International Education, Journal of Asia Pacific Education, Higher Education Policy*, and

Global Social Policy. With Simon Marginson, Chris Nyland, and Helen Forbes-Mewett she was an author of *International Student Security* (2010), and in 2011 she has coedited *Higher Education in the Asia-Pacific: Strategic Responses to Globalization* with Simon Marginson and Sarjit Kaur.

Chapter 1

International and Intercultural Education

Ideas for Intercultural Education begins with a short story. We promise serious-minded readers that the serious-minded research and scholarship will follow. But perhaps the story of Zhao Mei will help to explain what this book is about.

Zhao Mei is 24 years old and comes from Zhejiang in Eastern China. She did well in her studies, especially at the end of secondary school, and a little to her surprise she performed even better in her first-degree program in science at Zhejiang University. She had enjoyed her studies at the university and had done well in her job in the construction company office after leaving the university. The idea of going abroad for study came gradually. Mei was a confident person though she had not had a big adventure on her own before. She always did well in English classes but had little opportunity to practice English language conversation. Her parents and older sister, who was married and had a baby daughter, had encouraged her. Fortunately her uncle's trading business was doing well, and he had lent the family enough money at low interest to cover Mei's airfare and first two years of tuition fees. The Australian masters program started in February, which was a different starting time from the university in China. So while waiting to go to Melbourne, she had worked for a few months and saved money for the trip and for the first interest payment for her uncle's loan. It was good she had paid that.

Mei likes Australia in some ways, especially the ways that don't involve people. The weather is nice, and everything is open and clean. There's so much space, especially outside the city. Mei loves going to the beach although she hasn't had much time for that. There are things to do in Melbourne, though lack of money is a problem. She feels free. She feels fairly safe walking around and when she is alone at night in her little apartment. She hasn't had any bad experiences (though she has heard stories about others who have been robbed in the home and abused in the street). Often she feels lonely and misses her mother. She has friends who came from Zhejiang and other places in China, but they are doing different study programs and have different interests than hers. She gets along well with a younger girl from Thailand who is in her masters class in environmental management. But no one is really close. The other students from China in her program are from the south. She is unlucky because some of the other students from Zhejiang at the university are sharing a study group and a few live together in the same house. Before she came to Melbourne, Mei decided not to live with people from home because she should get to know Australia, but she has no one with whom to share her feelings about her studies and all the problems she has been having. Lately she has been dreaming about her sister and the baby.

Mei is still not quite sure why she chose Australia. Some classmates and friends of the family knew people who had studied in Australia. The stories were mostly good. It seemed to be kinder and more welcoming than the United States, where nonwhites were not always treated well. The United Kingdom had interested her for a while, but it was colder, farther away, and more expensive. Australia seemed a good alternative. The universities were fine and there were many students from China studying there. A lot of families from eastern China had settled in Australia and seemed to be doing well. But she hadn't known much about the higher education before she came. She had not been well prepared.

The thing that she has been having most of her trouble with is the language. It was a terrible shock when she first arrived. She was confident about her English before she came, and she had done fine in the International English Language Testing System tests. She hadn't felt the need for any extra language classes. She had always been a quick learner. But in that first week at the university she just couldn't understand anything people were saying. It had been terrible. She had staggered through every day in complete confusion, and she had cried almost every night. While it is getting a bit better, she misses a lot in lectures and classes and when the Australian students speak to her, though the latter doesn't happen much. She doesn't like having to ask other people—even other Chinese students—for help because she doesn't want people to think she is stupid. She is not stupid. She has always been a good student. She knows that she is not especially beautiful or talented, just ordinary. But she has always been good at her studies and has won prizes in two university science subjects. Her communication problems are so humiliating. There is a language support unit (LSU), but it is really there to help with essay writing, not oral English. And each student is entitled to only a limited amount of help from the LSU per semester. There are no extra classes she can take to build her language skills. She never feels she is making progress and knows she is slipping behind the other students.

There have been some really bad moments. In Mei's third week, the tutor looked straight at her and said, loudly: "And what do you think, Zhang? Is it like that in China too?" She was flustered. The tutor had never spoken to her before. And he had got her name wrong, which was embarrassing. But the worst thing was that she hadn't understood what the class had been talking about before she was asked the question, so she had no idea what to say. She had just frozen, silent, while everyone waited. Finally the tutor stopped looking at her, said something, and the other students smiled. Then he asked someone else a question. Mei just wanted to sink through the floor and hide. She was shaking and felt cold. After that the Thai student, Araya, had spoken to her. She took Mei to have some tea and calm down and stop shaking. She was very kind.

A few days later, though, there was another bad experience. While they were waiting outside for the lecture to start, one of the Australian students, a man with curly blonde hair, looked at her and then said something rude about her to his friends. She knew it was about her because they all looked at her when they were laughing. He spoke about her as if she was not there even though she was standing quite close to him. It was always like that. There were two Australian students, a man and a woman, who sat at the back next to her in the lecture, holding hands. They never said anything to her. She knew their names, David and Mia. She felt she liked them the first time she saw them together and wanted to talk to Mia, but they were not interested in her. It was hopeless. They never noticed Mei. When she shared a work group with them they never looked into her eyes, although Mia said "thanks" one time when Mei handed out the equipment at practical class. Mei knows that some local students don't like the international students. She's picked that up from looks and body language. She knows that some local students complain that international students hang out with each other all the time. But if local students are unfriendly, what else can international students do? Araya wasn't Chinese, but she understood how Mei felt.

The only nice local people Mei sees regularly are in the international office, where she pays her semester fees and gets referrals for service use. Her lecturers said at the start of the program that all students would be treated the same and all would be expected to perform to the same standard. There would be no extra help for any individuals or any type of students. That would be unfair to others. At the time she had accepted this, but she had not known what it would mean for her.

To add to her problems with language, Mei is finding the course difficult as well. It is environmental management, but the main emphasis in the first year is on environmental science. She likes science, but her Zhejiang science degree had been mostly in physics and inorganic chemistry. The environmental management course discusses geology, meteorology, oceanography, and life sciences. It is all new to Mei. Her reading skills in English are OK and she has the textbooks, but the teachers don't always follow the textbooks. Because she was having so much trouble in class, Mei thought the best thing to do was to get to know the textbooks as well as she could. That way, she would improve her written English skills as well. Reading was the foundation for writing. But she hadn't done well in her long assignments and had been given a bare pass in the first semester. There had been a written warning that she would fail the year if her assignments and class participation did not improve. The tutor wrote harsh comments on the second assignment, for which Mei had been given a low mark—probably the lowest in the class. "This is all textbook. Any primary school student can copy a textbook. Just quoting a textbook won't solve practical problems, which is what you were asked to address in this assignment. What are your own ideas? You should be using the broader reading and Internet sources that were discussed in the lecture." Mei hadn't understood what the lecturer said.

In the next assignment Mei had tried to use her own ideas. She used as an example some material from the environmental impact report that she had prepared for the construction company in Zhejiang. The lecturer had marked this assignment. He said the example that she used was not relevant to the question. There were a lot of overseas examples in the teaching materials used in program, but they were mostly from North America and Europe, not China. The only time that China had come up was when the tutor asked Mei that question.

Mei does not know what to do. Her whole family is supporting her, but she cannot tell them how bad it is. They won't want her to drop out. They will just be upset, and there's nothing they can do to help. The teachers have a lot of students, including many internationals, so they don't have much time to help Mei. She will try to use the

Internet more in future, but she can't always get computer access when she needs it at the university. Only PhD students with scholarships have computer access at all times. Others have to book time and can use the computer only for a limited time in each session. She knows she needs her own laptop, like most students have, but it is expensive. Rent is higher than the agent had said it would be before she came to Melbourne. Mei is using up her savings faster than she expected. If she doesn't start to do better soon, she will have to go back to China.

DOES IT HAVE TO BE THIS WAY?

That is Zhao Mei's story. Does she give up her struggle to be educated in the foreign country and go back to her family to look for a local job again? Or do things get better? Does Mei's story have a happy ending? Does she make it?

Readers will have to wait until the final chapter of the book to see what might happen to Mei. But the point is that this is a typical international student story. We have not exaggerated the problems. As *Ideas for Intercultural Education* will show, and much other research confirms, many students from East Asia (especially), Southeast Asia, and elsewhere experience similar communication difficulties. Mei's academic program is not as helpful to international students as are the best of existing programs. But many programs are much the same as Mei's program according to the witness of students (and some teachers). Mei is more isolated than many Chinese students, who spend much time with same-culture friends in households and study groups. However, a large minority of international students are isolated and lonely.[1] Many international students, like Mei, are attracted to the openness and strange beauty of Australia, the ease of passage in its cities, and the freedoms it offers in daily life but are profoundly disappointed at their inability to integrate socially. Mei's nonexistent relations with local students are all too typical of the experience of nonwhite international students in all the English-speaking countries. So is the indifference to her own background, values, and language within the education system she encounters.

If an intercultural education is a mutual learning and exchange between international and local students, Mei has been denied an intercultural education, though she is paying what for her family is a great deal of money for the opportunity to become more cosmopolitan and culturally diverse. That is also what she offers to Australia and to local students, but the offer is being refused. Her presence in the English-speaking country is an opportunity missed, for herself and for the country of education. Unfortunately, that is exactly what is happening to many if not most international students in the English-speaking nations.

International education is global engagement on a vast scale. It is one of the factors that are shaping the future of the earth. More than three million students cross borders for tertiary education each year, most changing their language of daily use as they do so. Almost half these students travel from emerging Asian nations to the English-speaking education systems, particularly in the United States, United Kingdom, and Australia. At best, international education promises to integrate nations more closely and open up the "exporting" educational institutions to the world, so local and international students experience life-changing learning. Is it working out?

No, it is not. For local students the learning outcomes are just not there. For international students the experience is worse than it could and should be. Some internationals have much better experiences than Zhao Mei, but others have the same or even worse experiences. Positive outcomes can happen spontaneously under the direst conditions, but the matter should not be left to chance.

International education is business as normal, with emphasis on both words. In the United Kingdom, Australia, and New Zealand it is run as a no-frills business, managed on the basis of minimum cost per student for maximum financial return. The U. S. approach is less commercial, but there is a large measure of indifference to foreign students, who are marginal in aggregate terms with only 4 percent of the higher education enrollment. International education is also "normal" in that it is essentially local education that is largely unchanged; international students are normalized into the local mold during the process. Despite the marketing rhetoric, does anyone seriously believe that international education is an exploration of diversity? The ethnocentrism traditional to English-speaking nations has hardly been dinted. The language and cultural barriers seem as high as ever, and the teaching and curriculum that are on offer are mostly the same as when there were only local students in the classroom. International students are often frustrated, isolated, and disappointed. After they fail to make local friends or become integrated into the country of education, many form strong networks with each other and go back to more of the same. Most local students remain stubbornly indifferent to the visitors.

What are the obstacles to moving forward on the intercultural education project? How can we create a more mutual and cosmopolitan experience?

CONDITIONS

Perhaps it is not surprising that international education falls short of its potential. The conditions have not been right. Enrollments might have been opened up to the world, but higher education institutions in the English-speaking countries have been slow to discard the old insular habits, and governments have not helped. There are a number of reasons for this.

Globalization and their own commercial impulses have pushed the English-language higher education systems beyond their capacity and willingness to respond. Three decades ago most education systems were largely closed to foreign students, with the exception of a handful of institutions that specialized in foreign scholarship students. International education, powered by the globalization of labor market opportunities and the rollout of a worldwide communications environment, has grown much faster than anyone expected. Most of the growth has been in business studies, computer education programs, engineering and health sciences, all directly vocational fields of study. Between 1990 and 2007 the number of international students in Australian universities grew from 25,000 to 254,414, reaching 26 percent of enrollments including students enrolled outside Australia in branch campuses and distance learning programs.[2] This was the highest level of intentional enrollment in the developed world. The Organisation for Economic Co-operation and Development (OECD) data for 2006 found that onshore international students constituted 19.7 percent of degree-level students in Australia compared to 15.2 percent in the United Kingdom and 15.1 percent in New Zealand. The OECD country average was 7.3 percent, and the US level was 3.8 percent.[3]

The sudden growth in international student numbers occurred at a time when in the Westminster countries of the United Kingdom, Australia, and New Zealand—which follow similar policies in higher education—the public funding of universities and other institutions was highly constrained compared to earlier years. This remains the case. From the 1990s onward, international education has been a major source of revenues for higher education institutions in those countries. (It is less crucial a revenue source in the United States and Canada.) Instead of providing a new wave of public investment to equip institutions to meet the international challenge, governments withdrew part of their previous funding, forcing institutions to become more dependent on the international student dollar but leaving them unable to service that student properly. Instead of funneling international student fees back into international service improvement, they had to source those fees to pay for the education of local students and for research. In Australia international education provided 17 percent of higher education funding in 2009; in the United Kingdom the figure was 10 percent. It is not surprising that a no-frills approach has taken over: standardized education provided at minimum cost per student. To compound this problem the average age of teachers in higher education has risen. There has been little funding to bring in new young people. Many of those teaching mixed classes with large numbers of international students entered academic life before the Internet and before the surge in international student numbers. They did not work in non-English-speaking countries or train in English as a second language teaching. Suddenly this has become the role they are expected to play.

Teachers are the change agents in education. Their capacities must be continually developed if they are to sustain that role when circumstances change.

In the absence of teachers properly equipped for international education, higher education institutions have hoped that setting a firm English language standard at the point of entry would ensure that all students are ready to learn without needing extra resources. As will be discussed, this has proven impractical. An English language test designed to guarantee near native speaker competence would exclude many of the present international students. The market forces driving higher education institutions had to be fed with more students, not less. In fact the opposite has happened, and some institutions have dropped English entry standards too low to maintain numbers. But a language test cannot constitute an educational preparation. There is no substitute for language teaching and support that is provided alongside and within the program of degree or diploma study.

Lack of English language preparation and servicing is fundamental and feeds into many other problems, as *Ideas for Intercultural Education* will show. By the same token stronger language foundations are also essential to the kind of solution where Zhao Mei gets the intercultural education she deserves. The shared capacity to communicate provides the basis not only of learning but of all human sociability. It brings with it confidence to learn experientially as well as academically, both to speak up in class and to initiate friendships with locals. However, language alone is not enough to render international education a genuinely shared experience, an intercultural experience, in which international and local students learn from each other. That is what international students want. But if intercultural education is to happen, then local students too must want it to happen.

THIS BOOK

One early challenge is to persuade national system managers and institutional leaders to modify the commercial approach to international education that is taken by Westminster countries such as the United Kingdom and Australia. Currently this blocks large-scale pedagogical innovations that would absorb more teaching resources. However, modification is possible even within the commercial settings if national systems and leading institutions compete on quality as well as on price and efficiency. We also wonder how much longer the English language systems, including higher education in the United States, can go on serving up an ethnocentric product, premised on the universal superiority of local approaches to learning and culture. The bottom line assumption of this position is that English language educators have nothing to learn from any other teaching and learning tradition. In other words, there is no need for global exchange. In the long term this just does not seem to be a feasible stance to adopt. Either there will be buyer resistance to it, or certain providers will lift their market position by providing a more culturally plural and inclusive learning, and this will send a signal to everyone. However, while this suggests that different approaches are possible, it does not guarantee these would take an intercultural form; that is, a curriculum premised on the mutual transformation of local and international students.

Most people working in higher education agree that a more diverse student body is an educational resource in itself. It creates the opportunity to enrich the education of all students, preparing them to take their place in the more global era now emerging. It sounds fine in theory, but it does not happen spontaneously. Just placing different groups of students in the same institution does not mean they will mix. Still less does it mean that teaching and learning will transform to a more cosmopolitan experience, in which our common global connectedness becomes one of the central elements in how students learn. This goal, or something like it, is widely shared. The issue discussed in this book is how to achieve that goal.

There are no quick fixes. And there are obstacles along the way that will need to be dismantled. *Ideas for Intercultural Education* starts with the assumption that our approach to intercultural education needs to be rethought from the ground up.

Above all, international education programs need to rethink their approach to the students themselves. The foundation of *Ideas for Intercultural Education*—a foundation further developed in Chapter 7, one of two concluding chapters of the book—is that international students should be seen as self-determining human agents with the full set of human rights. *Agency* is a term used frequently here. A fundamental limitation in much (but not all) of the academic knowledge about international students is failure to grasp the central fact that international students make their own futures, under often-difficult circumstances. These are strong human agents, not weak, fragile, or dependent agents. Yet much of the research, many of the teaching strategies, and some local students fundamentally treat international students as if they are people in learning and cultural *deficit*. On the contrary; many international students are much further advanced in the capacity for intercultural learning than are their teachers and local student fellows.

The ethnocentric approach flows through much of the research on international education, especially research in cross-cultural psychology. In much of the research, as in many of the programs and welfare strategies, the objective is to fashion the "adjustment" of international students to unquestionable local norms. International students find themselves "Othered" by these educational strategies, more softly but in much the same way they are Othered by stereotyping and discrimination in the English-speaking communities in which they live while they are studying. If intercultural education is to become a reality, ideas of cultural superiority and one-way adjustment will need to be dismantled. This does not mean dismantling the strengths of English-speaking education systems, including the shared global English which makes educational cooperation possible. Rather it means opening up those systems and for a new mood of global and cosmopolitan learning to take root among local people.

However, intercultural learning in higher education is not going to happen simply because it is imagined in theory and asserted as a good idea. It is essential to consider with a careful and open mind what the research tells us about cross-cultural relations and intercultural education, especially in relation to international students. *Ideas for Intercultural Education* does not review all of the research on every aspect of international education. (For a fine summary of areas not covered here, including much of the research on globalization and education, see the review by Nadine Dolby and Aiya Rahman.)[4] Rather this book focuses specifically on research and scholarship that is focused on cross-cultural relations involving international students.

When looking at the existing research, we find that the assumptions that have guided cross-cultural research in psychology need critical examination. Chapter 2 does this. This body of research has influenced teaching and administrative practice and shares responsibility for the present limitations of international education programs, especially their ethnocentrism. But some research in cross-cultural psychology is also a source of new ideas for intercultural education.

Chapter 3 reviews another body of research and scholarship that has helped to shape approaches to intercultural relation in international education: the work on transformational and cosmopolitan learning.

In Chapters 4–6 the emphasis shifts to the practical world of intercultural education. We are particularly interested in research that foregrounds the voices of international students themselves. Chapter 4 steps out of the main set of research literature and into the lives of six individual international students. This chapter draws on data from a program of interviews conducted by Erlenawati Sawir in 2005–2007 with two hundred international students in nine public research universities in Australia.[5] Many of the potentials and problems of intercultural education are vividly apparent here as the six students talk about their struggles and achievements, opportunities, barriers, problems, and the excitement of the many changes in themselves and their lives. Chapter 5 returns to the larger field of knowledge, reviewing what the literature has to say about cross-cultural relations between on one hand international students and on the other hand local students, local communities, and higher education institutions. Chapter 6 looks at the cross-cultural classroom. Chapters 5–6 again draw on data from the interviews with two hundred international students in Australia, and they refer briefly to another program of interviews, conducted by Erlenawati Sawir in 2008, with 80 teaching staff responsible for large numbers of international students in one Australian research university. (This last study will be reported in more detail in other publications.)

Chapters 7 and 8 provide our summation and concluding thoughts about the further development of international and intercultural education. Chapter 7 expands on the idea of international education as self-formation. In Chapter 8, we return to Zhao Mei's story and also consider practical strategies for classroom teaching in higher education.

The rest of Chapter 1 provides a discussion of key terms in the book, such as *globalization, internationalization, cross-cultural, intercultural, language proficiency,* and *communicative competence.* These terms are used in varied ways by different scholars. We do not claim our definitions are the only possible ones. People choose their language. We just want to make it clear what we mean in the book. Before the definitions, however, a brief note about the Australian context.

THE AUSTRALIAN SETTING

This book was prepared from Australia and has been partly shaped by our own research in the Australian setting. At the same time *Ideas for Intercultural Education* draws extensively on research and scholarship from across the world, including the American literature. We believe the issues discussed in the book are relevant in all of the English-speaking education export countries and have resonance in other cross-cultural contexts.

The book is most closely attuned to the Westminster countries, where commercial international education programs operate on a mass scale. It is in the United Kingdom, Australia, and New Zealand that the intercultural potential of international education seems most advanced because of the scale of the populations. It is also in those countries that the pedagogical potentials of international education tend to be emptied out. Intercultural education is resource thick compared to standard teaching. There is no place for it in classrooms in which the objective is to provide a minimum cost standard product. So far, in the tension between commercial imperatives and intercultural imperatives, intercultural education has lost nearly all the way. Australia is a good place to think about this tension. One quarter of its students are international and its business model is especially effective.

This is not to say Australia is the worst English-speaking country in which to study. As well as attractions such as natural beauty and climate, and an open civic culture, Australia is consistently stronger than the United Kingdom and New Zealand in surveys of student service provision, though behind the United Kingdom in ratings of academic quality. Australia has its share of that sense of cultural superiority common to Anglo-American nations, but arguably, it provides a more benign civil environment than the United States and United Kingdom do. In 2007–2009 a wave of racially motivated attacks affected international students[6] and seemed to give the lie to Australia's reputation as a relatively open, tolerant, and safe society. But while these attacks exposed weaknesses in the regulation of international student security and highlighted the marginalization of parts of the local male population from the education or career tracks that international students experience, they were exceptional behaviors in Australia. Thus the assaults were highlighted and widely condemned. Australia is also a place where good critical research on international education is done, much of which is cited here. This provides the international education industry with a national capacity in critical reflexivity, if it wants to use it.

DEFINITIONS

Here we provide a brief summary of the main terms distinctive to *Ideas in Intercultural Education*. These terms may be hard to comprehend in abstract but will become clearer as their use develops in the chapters of the book. However, it may be useful to be able to refer back to the expanded glossary that follows.

Globalization

Global refers to a world level or planetary spatiality. It describes spaces, systems, relations, elements, agents, and identities constituting and constituted by the world as a whole or by large parts of it in pan-national regions such as Europe. It includes "global flows"[7] in communications, transport and financial systems, and elements like language and research exchange that integrate nations and agents across borders. *Global* rests on a particular configuration of general/particular. The global dimension does not mean total or universal; it does not necessarily include every national and local element. It includes only those elements that are part of the constitution of the world as an integrated world. (The term *worldwide* can be used for the wholly inclusive concept that takes in every global, national, or local element.) Higher education institutions typically operate in three dimensions at the same time: that of global relations, particularly in areas like research and cross-border international education; that of national policy, funding and system organization; and that of local communities, including those internal to the institution. Higher education institutions are "glonacal" institutions that must successfully configure together their global, national, and local practices.[8]

Globalization refers to the growing importance of the global dimension of action; including global spaces, systems, agencies such as the OECD or World Bank, agents, and identities. It is constituted by the processes of engagement, integration, and convergence associated with the "transformation in the organization of human affairs by linking together and expanding human activity across regions and continents."[9] The growth of international education is a good example. Held and colleagues define *globalization* in short as "the widening, deepening and speeding up of world wide interconnectedness."[10] As globalization advances, cross-border interactions become more extensive, intensified, regularized, and faster. Local and global dimensions are more intermeshed. Local events can be transmitted everywhere, and distant events have a magnified impact. Common world systems such as the research system and university rankings in higher education become more visible on a day-to-day level.

As this suggests, globalization is not necessarily about markets or capitalist economies. Still less is it merely an ideological proposition developed in neoliberal politics. There are different ideologies of globalization, but our focus here is on the actual processes of transformation, not on interest-based claims. Economic globalization is one influential form of global convergence, but there are many others. Perhaps the most important single element driving the growing interconnectedness of the world is the spread of global communications.

Internationalization

Internationalization is a familiar term but the most difficult one for this book because it is subjected to extensive and varied usage in research and discussion about international education and globalization in higher education. To name a few examples, *internationalization* is used to refer to international development aid and the transfer of expertise between national systems of education;[11] the international school movement that prepares students for employment anywhere in the world;[12] foreign affairs initiatives and the provision of aid for international students;[13] and student mobility as in foreign exchange students.[14] The conceptualization of internationalization is hotly contested and might remain so for a considerable time to come; although cross-border relations, however defined, are now widely seen as integral rather than marginal to higher education.[15]

In the most straightforward sense, *international* refers to a movement or relationship *between nations*. It does not presume anything about the contents or significance of the relationship. The term is neutral and open. Here international might refer to a comparison between nations in relation to a common quality. It might take the form of a movement of people across borders, as in "international students." It might refer to a gathering of people from two or more nations. Internationalization, then, means any process of creating or enhancing such cross-national relations, movements, or comparisons. For example, growth in the number of international students in UK higher education could be described as internationalization of the enrollment. Outside the discussion of higher education and international education, for example in the social sciences, and in some but not all of the popular usage, the term *internationalization* takes this neutral form. Often it is understood to refer to intergovernmental relations;[16] that is, relations conducted at the official level between sovereign states as separate legal entities.

However, much use of internationalization is not neutral but normative. That is, the term is defined to mean a preferred state or preferred actions of a particular kind. Here there are different views about which values to attach to internationalization. One important tradition of internationalization, which has had some impact in the popular usage of the term, has grown out of the efforts to achieve a peaceful and just international order through the League of Nations before World War II and the United Nations since that time. It is premised on twentieth-century nationalism. It assumes the sovereignty of nations, which are seen as separate entities, and focuses on improving the relationships between them in a multilateral setting. A key element is the improvement of mutual understanding through increased contact between persons. Much of the post–World War II evolution of international education, fostered by scholarships provided by particular countries, was seen in this light. Thus in the most influential definition in higher education, Knight describes internationalization as follows: "Internationalization at the national, sector and institutional levels is defined as the process of integrating an international, intercultural or global dimension into the purpose, functions or delivery of post-secondary education."[17]

In her work Knight has repeatedly emphasized the normative nature of this definition. "The term *process* is deliberately used to convey that internationalization is an on-going and continuing effort."[18] It is also a commitment, a set of values and attitudes. However, these can vary. "Internationalization is interpreted and used in different ways in different countries and by different stakeholders."[19]

Both the normative and variant character of Knight's *internationalization* generate difficulties. We agree it is vital to understand local variance and agent control. But when this is factored into the definitions, analytical precision is lost and a common understanding of terms becomes impossible. Participants in the conversation talk at cross-purposes. This also means that the understandings of the term internationalization in education circles bear little relationship to the usage by scholars in other social sciences. This is compounded by an inclusive, if not quasi-universal, use of the term, which Knight extends to include the "global" and "intercultural" aspects. Hence all of these elements also become subjected to the variant normative interpretations. It becomes difficult to use any of them.

A further problem with Knight's definition of *internationalization* is the implications for understandings of globalization, which have become crucially important for all actors in higher education institutions. Knight's original formulation of internationalization (1994) contrasted it with a globalization that was seen only as the extension of world capitalist markets. Globalization was understood as external to national education systems, something that necessarily called up a defensive response. The counterstrategy was seen as internationalization, which was said to be premised not on economic profit-making but on universal human rights, free cultural exchange, and respect for cultural others. This served as a rallying point for those who (with good reason) wanted to assert an aid-based and sharing-based approach to international education, not a profit-making approach.

However, one problem with the demonizing of globalization, which in essence meant accepting the neoliberal definition of *globalization* as world markets, was that the growing global systems entailed more than just capitalist world markets. Globalization also included communications and knowledge flows. Further, universities were strongly implicated as drivers of this kind of globalization, which arguably contributed to Knight's objectives of closer cultural exchange and more universal human understanding (though we can note here that there is global dominance in cultural and research knowledge, as well as in economics—both can be equally problematic). Thus in later formulations Knight has switched to a neutral definition of *globalization*, defining it not as economic markets but as global integration and convergence. Hence the reference in the definition quoted earlier to integrating a "global dimension" into educational activities while retaining the normative form of internationalization.

Arguably, however, the notion of United Nations–style internationalization is now obsolete. It assumes nations that are ontologically separate from each other. This is the foundation of both twentieth-century nationalism and multilateralism. But in a more globally interdependent era that kind of separation no longer exists. Nations are still an important factor, but individual universities connect to both global systems and national systems simultaneously, in relation to both research and students. In this context Knight's attempt to enfold "global" under her banner of a normative internationalization can be seen as a last-ditch attempt of twentieth-century multilateralism to secure control over global processes from the locations of nation and institution. That attempt—and all strategies premised on the global dimension as external to the local and national, rather than *implicated with them in a glonacal setting*—are doomed to fail. The global horse has already bolted.

For these reasons, in this book *international* and *internationalization* are understood as neutral spatial descriptors, which is the most common approach in both social sciences and popular usage. Thus *international* refers to a movement or relationship between nations. It does not presume anything about the contents or significance of the relationship. *Internationalization* means any process of creating or enhancing cross-national relations, movements, or comparisons. There is no particular or variant baggage attached to our use of these terms. Instead of using *international* as a synonym or container for "global or intercultural," as in Knight's definition, we use those terms (which in any case differ significantly in meaning from each other) in a direct manner with the definitions that follow.

Cross-Cultural and Intercultural

Both *cross-cultural* and *intercultural* are used frequently in this book. Their meanings are different. The use of one or the other is significant to the argument.

By *cross-cultural* we simply mean a move or a relationship between two separately identifiable cultural sets. We follow contemporary usage in allowing *culture* to refer to language groups, nations, self-identified groupings, and so on. The term *cross-cultural* is neutral as to the contents or the significance of the relationship. When people are involved in a cross-cultural comparison or relationship it does not necessarily mean that their cultural or other identities change during that interaction, though that is possible. (In that respect *cross-cultural* parallels our use of *international* as mentioned earlier for relations between nations.) In the case of a cross-cultural comparison, there is no necessary interaction at all. Cross-cultural relations can occur between groups that are friendly and groups that are hostile. All are included in the broad category of cross-cultural relations.

Within that broad category of cross-cultural relations, some relationships involve the potential for mutual transformation. These are *intercultural* relations. The conditions for intercultural relations involve both sameness and difference.[20] First, it is essential to have common elements (language, a shared mission or activity, etc.). Second, both or all parties need to be willing to open themselves up to some extent, allowing themselves to be influenced by the other(s). That is, both are prepared to change and to do so while self-referencing in relation to the other or allowing themselves to be referenced by the other. The elements of openness and reciprocity are key, distinguishing intercultural relations from all other cross-cultural relations.

Intercultural relations recognize that people live in an interdependent world and make that interdependency part of self-formation.

Cosmopolitanism

The notion of *cosmopolitanism* is contested, and various takes on it are discussed in Chapter 3. As used here, *cosmopolitanism* transfers the idea of intercultural relations as defined earlier to the level of the whole social space. In a cosmopolitan setting people are grounded in their own identities, which are both given and self-formed. Their identities are continually changing. Some elements may remain constant over long periods of time while others shift. People also acknowledge, explore, and develop their interconnectedness and interdependency within a common setting that is also continually moving and evolving. Thus a cosmopolitan intercultural education is an education that equips students for self-formation in a relational environment marked by both local grounding and interconnectedness. (For a fuller discussion of self-formation, which is the heart of our argument, see Chapter 7.)

Language and Communicative Competence

With the term *language proficiency* the book refers to the testable capability of individuals in domains of language use: listening, speaking, reading, and writing.

Language proficiency is not the same as the capacity to utilize language and other communicative media, including nonverbal modes, in practical situations. *Communicative competence* is about the capacity to use language and all other media in a situation so as to participate effectively in social relations and achieve desired objectives. Communicative competence is both inherently relational (more than individual attributes are needed: the setting must be sufficiently sympathetic) and also context based. It is not automatically transferable between contexts, for example national settings, and to some extent is learned anew in each situation.

Agency and Identity

By *identity* we mean what people understand themselves or others to be. Identity changes continually during a lifetime, and people often draw on more than one identity in composing a sense of themselves and what they do. There are various strategies for mixing and combining elements of identity (see Chapter 7).

Agency means the sum of a person's capacity to act. Agency is the seat of self-will, the "centralizing" part of the self through which we manage ourselves and our own continuing formation in education, work, and other zones of activity.

CONCLUSION

This chapter has outlined the contents of *Ideas for Intercultural Education* and introduced its problem. How can we make the transition from the present state of international education in the English-speaking countries—marked by separation between international and local students and failure to change local education—to a richer, more genuinely intercultural practice appropriate to the global setting? How can Zhao Mei gain access to the intercultural education she deserves?

To help facilitate this transition, we begin with a critical review of existing knowledge in this field (Chapters 2–3). Chapter 2 focuses on the ideas of cross-cultural psychology about international students and cross-cultural relations.

CHAPTER 2

———◆〇◆———

REFUSING THE OTHER

PSYCHOLOGY AND ETHNOCENTRISM

INTRODUCTION: CROSS-CULTURAL PSYCHOLOGY

Intercultural education in the English-speaking countries could be much better than it is. Large populations of international students, drawn from a diversity of cultural backgrounds, offer an excellent starting point in evolving intercultural approaches. After that, the potential starts to crumble. Local education systems and people have been very slow to respond to the opportunity created by the international student presence and to engage in their own process of intercultural transformation. It seems that only the visitors are expected to gain from adjusting. The locals have nothing to learn. There is more than just laziness here. At the bottom of local complacency, this refusal to step through the doorway marked "intercultural" indicates a deep-seated unexamined belief that Western education and Western ways of life are always inherently superior. *Ethnocentrism* privileges one particular cultural standpoint over all others. In this complacent view of the world—one that is all too widespread in English language education systems—relations based on equal cultural respect become impossible and local teachers, administrators, student servicing personnel, and students believe they have little or nothing to learn from other cultures or other education systems.

One reason why this ethnocentrism is reproduced and largely unchallenged is that it is repeatedly reinforced by much cross-cultural psychology, the main body of knowledge about international education used by institutions, teachers, and counselors. This is *not* to say that all cross-cultural psychology is ethnocentric, as this chapter will make clear. Even less is it to say that all educators and counselors are complicit in ethnocentrism and in the systemic "Othering" (negative referencing as different) of internationals from non-Western backgrounds. Psychology is both part of the problem and part of the solution. Some work in the discipline has generated valuable insights that inform the development of more cosmopolitan approaches, in which all parties to the relationship are open to each other. (Scholar-researchers using a more critical and open-ended approach to intercultural psychology are often themselves from plural cultural backgrounds.) But a large body of research in psychology feeds ethnocentric notions of cultural superiority.

What follows is a critical review of the scholarship and research in cross-cultural psychology that touches on international education. There is much literature to consider, and the chapter is selective and abbreviated. (The original draft was almost three times this length.) The main focus is on factors affecting the psychological and sociocultural "adjustment" or "acculturation"[1] of mobile students. Generally, this process of adjustment is *not* seen as a mutual one.

Psychology is a powerful social science. It reshapes identities. It reorders and standardizes behaviors. Applied psychology has a long-standing interest in normalization, that is, adjusting people to fit a given social system. But in intercultural relations, especially in the fully global setting, there is no one "normal" culture and society. If educational institutions pursue strategies of normalizing international students to fit the country of education, this shows little respect for their cultural backgrounds and human rights. Yet many welfare and teaching strategies used with international students are premised on the idea there is something wrong with them—that they, or their learning methods or social relations, are "in deficit." In this way of thinking, acculturation means not simply learning to cope but becoming part of the new setting: blending in invisibly with the locals, discarding the old self. When joined to quantitative psychological methods that objectify the students under study and diagnostic counseling, in which the student is automatically subordinated by the process, ethnocentric approaches can damage intercultural relations and inhibit liberal student self-formation. Where psychology has generated barriers to intercultural relations in higher education, those barriers need to be dismantled.

This Chapter

This chapter begins with early cross-cultural studies by Adler, Bochner, Berry, and others in the 1970s and 1980s and the first wave of research on international education summarized by Church and Pedersen. It then looks at two subsequent directions in psychological research: ethnocentric studies focused on the "cultural fit" of sojourners and premised on cultural determinism, and more enabling studies centered on the evolving capacity of international students themselves. The latter body of work highlights the interaction between three sets of factors that together shape the capacities and experiences of international students: language proficiency and communicative competence, cross-cultural encounters, and active agency.

FOUNDATIONS

After World War II, as the number of international students entering the English-speaking education systems increased, and as more and more American and British business executives and professionals worked abroad, there was a growing interest in the psychology of cross-cultural sojourners. In his influential "culture shock" thesis in 1960, Oberg argues that sojourners in a new country undergo a standard succession of experiences. First is a "honeymoon period" characterized by fascination, elation, and optimism. This is followed by hostility toward the host culture and retreat to the company of fellow sojourners, then a recovery phase characterized by growing knowledge of language and culture while maintaining a superior attitude to the host people, and a final stage in which "anxiety is largely gone, and new customs are accepted and enjoyed." "Culture shock" entered the English language lexicon after Oberg's work was published and is still widely used.

In another account of the trajectory of cross-cultural experience, Adler imagines the final stage as one of "independence" characterized by "a cherishing of cultural differences and relativism, behaviour that is expressive, creative, mutually trusting and sensitive, and, most important, increased self- and cultural awareness enabling the individual to undergo further life transitions and to discover additional ways to explore human diversity."[2] Like the culture shock thesis, the idea that a culturally relativist and reflexively cosmopolitan person is the highest level of cross-cultural development has proven an influential one.

Cultural Learning

In Bochner's cultural learning model cultural adaptation is less forced, proactive agency is more central, and there is more space for a non-hierarchical valuation of cultures. Sojourners experience the absence of familiar positive reinforcements such as approval and other social rewards, and the presence of new adverse stimuli such as unfamiliar situations, language difficulties, and anxious encounters. They develop new response-reinforcement patterns. Bochner and collaborators see this as a process of cultural learning.[3] The task for international students and other sojourners is not so much to absorb the new culture "but to learn its salient characteristics" so as to be able to work and learn in the host country.[4] The failures and problems of sojourners are understood not as symptoms of individual deficit but merely as the lack of the learned skills that are needed.[5] The previous values and behaviors are not "wrong" as such, and the relationship between home and host culture can be a positive-sum. These ideas are more enlightened than much of the work that followed Bochner. "Remedial action does not involve 'solving' the problems as much as training the international student in appropriate skills. By the same token, 'adjustment' implies cultural chauvinism, suggesting that the student should abandon the culture of origin and embrace these new values and customs. By contrast, 'learning' the customs and values of a new culture is less ethnocentric in its emphasis."[6]

Bochner also suggests that the extent of transfer of home-country learning depends on the similarity between the home and host culture. This pointed to studies in which cultural distance was one variable affecting sojourner learning.[7]

Acculturation Strategies

The work of Berry and colleagues on acculturation has been especially influential. According to Berry, "acculturation occurs when two independent cultural groups come into continuous first-hand contact over an extended period of time, resulting in changes to either or both cultural groups." He notes that "individual members of these groups also experience change, and this phenomenon has been termed 'psychological acculturation.'"[8] The process of change incorporates "adaptation," which Berry defines as "changes that take place in individuals or groups in response to environmental demands."[9] There are two fundamental dimensions of acculturation: maintenance of the original cultural group and maintenance of relations with other groups.[10] The two are heterogenous to each other, not zero-sum parts of a unitary set. Various combinations of these behaviors are possible. Not everyone is engaged in a journey of adjustment from original identity to host-culture identity, and it is possible to augment both one's original "identity and customs"[11] and shape new social interethnic relations at the same time. This is an important insight that resonates with observable international student behaviors.[12]

Using the two dimensions, Berry identifies four "acculturation attitudes"[13] or "strategies"[14] that combine the two dimensions in contrasting ways: assimilation, integration, separation/segregation, and marginalization. Assimilation is when the agent opts to relinquish the original cultural identity and move into the larger society. Integration means that the cultural identity of the group is maintained while it also becomes "an integral part of a larger societal framework."[15] Berry states that another possible term for this is *bi-cultural*.[16] He notes that "integration can only be 'freely' chosen and successfully pursued by non-dominant groups when the dominant society is open and inclusive in its orientation to cultural diversity."[17] Nondominant groups must adopt the values of the larger society, while the dominant group is required to adapt institutional practices such as health, education, and religious tolerance to meet the needs of all groups.[18] Here integration is conceptually akin to the policy framework of multiculturalism developed in Canada and Australia. Berry notes that both assimilation and integration constitute an increased "fit" between the acculturating individual and the new context.[19] Separation or segregation occurs when the original identity is maintained and there is no desire to form relations with other groups. Dominant groups engage in segregation while nondominant groups such as international student sojourners engage in separation. Finally, marginalization occurs when groups lose cultural and psychological contact with both their traditional culture and the larger society.[20] Berry and colleagues use scales for measuring each acculturation attitude[21] and acculturative stress. Marginalization and separation are associated with high levels of acculturative stress, integration is associated with low levels of stress, and assimilation with intermediate levels of stress.[22]

Berry also discusses the distinction between "psychological adaptation" and the concept of "sociocultural adaptation." Both are psychological concepts but refer to different spheres of life. Psychological adaptation concerns inner mental health. Sociocultural adaptation is about the relational competences of individuals. This models social connectivity using psychological methods. Lacking a sociology, psychology can focus only on individualized relational competencies. Context is over-externalized.

Zhang and Dixon remark on the fact that *acculturation, assimilation,* and *adaptation* are not clearly distinguished in the psychological literature (they could add *adjustment*). At times acculturation is treated as multidimensional, incorporating an orientation to both culture of origin and the culture being entered, as Berry states. At other times it is understood as a process whereby "individuals from one culture come into contact with another culture and gradually adopt the behaviours and values of the mainstream culture,"[23] and sociocultural adjustment becomes readily interpreted as "fitting in" culturally. At times Berry himself appears to endorse the ethnocentric interpretation.[24] In this respect his intellectual legacy is ambiguous. He cites with approval the work of Ward on sociocultural adaptation (discussed later in this chapter), though Ward discards the critique of adjustment as ethnocentric and despite Berry often treats cultural differences as homogenous for analytical purposes. In this field ethnocentric notions of adjustment have proven resilient.

PSYCHOLOGY OF INTERNATIONAL STUDENTS

In a landmark 1982 article in *Psychological Bulletin,* Church provides a summative analysis of research on "the psychological adjustment of relatively short-term visitors to new cultures," focusing on students.[25] This sets down most of the central themes of work in psychology on international education, then and after.

Church notes the term *adjustment* is ambiguous. Studies tend to focus on one or another aspect. They use a variety of measures but rarely integrate multiple methods within a single study. "Researchers should be sensitive to the possibility of interactions between cultural variables and measurement problems that make cross-cultural differences difficult to interpret."[26] There are few longitudinal studies and an overreliance on surveys of sojourners. "Such studies tend to be superficial and generally fail to relate sojourn behavior and adjustment difficulties to specific sojourn experiences or cultural differences."[27] Theories based on types or patterns of adjustment, premised on distinctions between sojourners who remain loyal to their home cultures and those who prove to be highly adaptive, tend to be "largely impressionistic," based on sojourners from just one cultural background, and belie the large range of stresses and types of coping strategies sojourners experience.[28] Noting "the danger of assuming the relevance or equivalence of theoretical concepts cross-culturally," he remarks that "studies of sojourner adjustment are almost invariably pseudoetic, using concepts drawn from the host culture and applying them to sojourners from other cultures. In such studies the criteria of adjustment may themselves be culture bound."[29] Church correctly cautions that "a single, comprehensive theory of sojourner adjustment is not likely to be found"[30]—which unfortunately has not stopped his successors from developing ethnocentric theories that are claimed to apply universally to all international education.

He remarks that few studies compare adjustment of local and foreign students. "Foreign students have many problems similar to those of other students, but in some cases they also experience problems that are more uniquely culture-based or at least aggravated by the stresses of the new cultural experience." Among foreign students there is significant variation by home and host country.[31] These variations are governed by the "actual conditions to which the individual is exposed in the new culture," including social interaction with host nationals, language, academic achievement, student health, place of living (rural or urban), and length of stay.[32] Church focuses on both communicative competence and social interaction with locals. He notes a positive relationship between them. "Beyond a certain minimal level of competence, the relationship between language fluency and social interaction is a reciprocal one with greater language confidence leading to greater participation that in turn leads to improved command of the host language," he states, and "many researchers consider positive social interaction with host nationals a necessary condition for effective sojourner adjustment."[33] According to Church, "Status differentials, ethnocentric attitudes and stereotypes, evaluative or judgmental perceptions, cultural ignorance, different definitions and norms for friendships, fear of rejection from conationals, and the high level of anxiety and threat to self-esteem frequently associated with intercultural encounters . . . inhibit positive social interaction with host nationals."[34]

There is much discussion of studies that focus on "enclaves of fellow nationals that largely determine the living arrangements, friendship patterns and organizational affiliations of the sojourners involved." Church finds that such networks provide protective security and the transfer of knowledge within the group but are probably less effective than relations with host nationals in transferring knowledge of the host country. "Most writers acknowledge the positive benefits of such enclaves, but the majority of these writers also feel that restricting social interaction with host nationals to superficial encounters is self-defeating in the long run because it inhibits learning the language, values, and customs of the new culture and can reinforce a sense of alienation."[35] He also notes that some studies report that the greater the cultural distance between home country and host country, the lower the level of interaction with host-country nationals. This lower level of intercultural contact is seen to imply a lower level of sojourner adjustment. On the other hand, the greater the cultural distance between sojourner and host country, the more likely there will be "the self-questioning and culture analysis required for increased self-awareness" in the sojourner.[36]

Despite levels of contact between student sojourners and host nationals that are "not very extensive," sojourners often want "more social interaction with host nationals." Politeness regimes can inhibit this. For example, sojourners from some cultures wait for host nationals to initiate contact.[37] However, Church cautions that a quantitative increase in contact does not necessarily in itself generate mutual understanding.[38] It may reinforce negative stereotyping. It can also create a conflict between "identification with home and host culture values."[39]

According to Church some sojourners abandon all or part of the home culture in a wholesale adaptation to host culture. This is seen as a problematic, agent-weak, conflicted strategy, perhaps driven by "unresolved emotional conflict with one's own social group at home." Others respond defensively by maintaining their culture of origin, rejecting elements of the host culture, and interacting "superficially and less effectively." A third group responds in an "objective, discriminating and balanced" manner, adopting selected elements of the host culture "into a self-image based on the values and behavior of the home culture."[40] Arguably, a limit of all these notions is that they treat the shaping "cultures" as fixed, and there is continued dependence on the notion of a singular or primary identity. Where new elements are taken in, they are integrated by the primary identity that is invariant. Arguably, these concepts leave insufficient room for multiplicity and hybridity in student identity. (This will be discussed in Chapter 7.) Instead Church draws from the literature notions of the "universal communicator" and the "multicultural" sojourner able to adjust freely and link between "multiple cultures." This abstract cosmopolitan figure is found also in Bochner and Adler[41] (see Chapter 3).

Church states that enhanced sociability, self-knowledge, and cultural relativism often figure as outcomes of the student sojourn. Many students also report "a more international outlook or enhanced international understanding," though control group studies show mixed results on this.[42] Overall, "personal growth in terms of self-reliance and self-awareness appears to be a more consistent sojourn outcome than do changes in more value-laden, culture-based ideologies and norms, at least as perceived by the sojourners themselves." It is common to find more ability to view problems from multiple perspectives, but "sojourners differ in how positively or negatively they come to see the two cultures," home and host.[43]

In another much-cited summation of the research in 1991, Pedersen, like Church, emphasizes cultural specificity and debunks the notion of a universal theory of intercultural or international education. While "the problems faced by international students are not so different from problems confronted by students in general," many "traditional student development theories may not apply to these foreign students." Because there is potential conflict between orthodox development theory and the values inherent in the home cultures of student sojourners, it is "necessary for counsellors to recognize each individual international student as a special case."[44] Like Church, Pedersen cites Bochner's cultural learning model. The task is "not to adjust to the new culture but to learn its salient characteristics." Failures and problems are not symptoms of an underlying deficit but just lack of learned skills. "By the same token, 'adjustment' implies cultural chauvinism, suggesting that the student should abandon the culture of origin and embrace these new values and customs. By contrast, 'learning' the customs and values of a new culture is less ethnocentric in its emphasis," leaving room for a variety of identity trajectories.[45] Nevertheless, remarks Pedersen, though the students are from widely diverse backgrounds, "they are expected to 'adjust' to a narrowly defined set of behaviors requiring them to learn their new and 'proper' roles very rapidly."[46] Training, counseling, and social support facilitate adjustment.[47] Pedersen does not mention the possibility that host institutions might adjust in reciprocal fashion.

Pedersen argues that there is no clear-cut relation between personality type and successful adjustment, and measurement of personality-related variables across cultures is problematic.[48] He leans to the notion of "bi-national or bicultural persons, who belong simultaneously to two different societies and maintain two identities as they relate to their respective societies from within the context of one or another culture." Such persons are "creatively adaptive in either of their two cultural identities."[49] However, the strategic choices that Pedersen imagines for international students are limited. Following Berry, these are identified as "assimilation, integration, rejection, or deculturation." *Deculturation* refers to loss of identity when the student loses contact with both home and host culture.[50]

"The greater the cultural differences between the student and the host culture, the greater likelihood that misunderstandings will occur," states Petersen, suggesting like Church that adjustment is inversely related to cultural distance.[51] This opens the way to the cultural fit argument discussed in the next section of this chapter. He endorses findings that students with greater contact with American nationals are likely to be more satisfied in both academic and nonacademic aspects of the sojourn. He also notes the study by Lee that finds that "the highest-ranked barriers to good relationships with U.S. nationals for international students were negative American attitudes to international students, lack of sensitivity by Americans to cultural differences, and the international students' own isolation as foreigners."[52]

ETHNOCENTRIC ADJUSTMENT

The proposition that the larger the cultural distance between the home country and country of education, the more difficult it is to learn, is an arguable one. It assumes that learning proceeds on the basis of incremental progression—on the basis of the extrapolation of similarities—rather than transformation and engagement with a new "Other" that enables a new way of seeing. In fact, in intercultural learning and probably in most education, it is likely that both kinds of learning are in play, though not always at the same time.

Cultural Fit

Ward and colleagues have conducted a series of studies premised on the idea that cultural closeness or "fit" is positively related to successful "adjustment" by international students—that is, the larger the cultural distance between home and host country, the more difficult it is for the student. This methodology privileges the culture of the English-speaking nations. Significantly, the attempt has been unsuccessful. This points to the limitations of an ethnocentric worldview when attempting to explain cross-cultural relations.

Ward and colleagues define sociocultural adaptation as "the ability to 'fit in' or negotiate interactive aspects of the host environment."[53] This generates a problem of tautology. When adjustment is defined in terms of cultural fit, it is automatic that the closer the cultural fit between sojourner and host culture, the more competences associated with successful adjustment will be observed. Using this approach it is impossible to map the effects of cultural distance on adjustment unless there are longitudinal data showing changes in adjustment since

arrival in the host country. Few studies have a longitudinal compo-
nent. Instead Ward and colleagues use comparisons between different
populations to secure an indirect, inferred measure of the effects of
cultural fit; map internal variation of cultural fit within a population
against degree of adjustment; or use a proxy variable for either adjustment or cultural fit, such as a personality characteristic. A problem
with using comparative data or internally differentiated populations is
that differences within populations or between different populations,
in the extent of sociocultural adjustment, may be affected by factors
other than cultural fit. Likewise a problem with using a single proxy
variable is that other, hidden factors may interact with that variable
and contaminate the data.

In their study of American sojourners in Singapore, Ward and
Chang (1997) use as the proxy variable for cultural fit the level of
difference between host and sojourner culture, using an extraversion
scale. It is hypothesized that this will explain variations between the
groups in sociocultural adaptation.[54] The findings of the study record
no correlation between cultural fit thus measured and the amount
of social difficulties reported by the American sojourners. Nevertheless, Ward and Chang find a "low to moderate" correlation between
cultural fit and psychological health[55] and also suggest that cultural
fit might be the mediating factor between personality and adjustment.[56] It seems this is sufficient to allow the researchers to confirm
the hypothesis about the efficacy of cultural fit in adjustment.

In their study of identity conflict among Chinese sojourners in Singapore, one of the variables investigated by Leong and Ward (2000) is
cultural distance, defined as "the subjective perception of differences
between the home and host cultures." Citing previous studies by Ward
and colleagues, the researchers claim that "empirical studies have consistently demonstrated a negative relationship between sojourners'
perceived cultural distance and their behavioral or sociocultural adaptation." The further the "external environment" is "differentiated from
one's culture of origin, the more adversities one would be expected
to experience." The researchers expect "greater cultural distance to
be associated with identity conflict."[57] But the hypothesis is not confirmed by the findings of the study. "Contrary to expectation, however,
cultural distance [was] unrelated to the outcome measure." Leong and
Ward also find to their surprise that "increased quantity of contact
with host nationals was associated with greater identity conflict" and
the quantity of conational relations did not reduce identity conflict,
having no effect, though identification with host nationals tended to
reduce identity conflict.[58] There is no discussion of the collapse of the

assumption about cultural distance. In later work on migrants, Ward restates without qualification assumptions that cultural distance is correlated to identity conflict and a source of social disequilibrium.[59]

In research by Ward and colleagues on paired samples of host nationals and sojourners in Singapore and Australia, one of two main objectives is "to test the 'cultural fit' hypothesis."[60] Citing the 1997 study by Ward and Chang, the researchers suggest that "in many cases, it is not personality per se that relates to cross-cultural adjustment but rather the cultural fit between the acculturating individual and host-culture norms." They note that "this is not to suggest that all personality traits must resemble host-culture norms and conventions to be adaptive" and also that "some characteristics may universally (or near universally) function as psychological resources" (i.e., regardless of the sojourner's original culture). For example there appears to be a "stable association" between internal locus of control and psychological well-being and satisfaction, regardless of nation of origin or sojourn.[61] Nonetheless, the study attempts to establish the personality-adjustment relationships mediated by cultural fit and whether the cultural fit proposition is viable in both Hofstede's individualist and collectivist cultures. "To date, research has only provided limited evidence in Singapore, a relatively collectivist society, where circumstances are conducive to the influence and manifestation of cultural fit."[62]

The researchers find that in the case of the Australian study, in relation to agreeableness and conscientiousness, "contrary to the logic of the cultural fit proposition, greater discrepancies were associated with *fewer* symptoms of depression."[63] Once again, a cultural fit has not been confirmed. The results do indicate that for Singapore students in Australia, the more extraverted students had higher levels of psychological adjustment.[64] This might appear to confirm cultural fit—more extraverted Singapore students are closer to the Australian norm—but extraversion was linked to successful adjustment in both the Singaporean and Australian studies. In other respects students in the Australian study did not conform to the cultural fit hypothesis. In the case of the Singapore study, cultural differences ("discrepancies") as measured by degrees of extraversion and openness were only weakly related to psychological adjustment, and again, contrary to expectations, "greater discrepancies were associated with fewer symptoms of depression."[65] Australians in Singapore who were more extraverted and therefore exhibited a lower level of cultural fit exhibited relatively high levels of adjustment. Ward and colleagues note that the last finding is inconsistent with the findings of the earlier study in relation to Americans in Singapore. "The results are particularly disappointing," they conclude, meaning that they are disappointing for the cultural fit thesis. The present research project "represents a methodological improvement over the earlier investigation; in particular, it relied on identical measures of extraversion, and the data were collected at the same point in time."[66] In summary, according to the researchers, "Neither the Australia- nor Singapore-based findings supported the cultural fit proposition. Congruence between sojourner and host personality traits was unrelated to psychological well-being as hypothesized in sojourning samples, and this was the case in both individualist and collectivist settings. In short, there was no support for the cultural fit proposition or its cross-cultural generalizability."[67]

"Where does this leave the notion of cultural fit?" ask the researchers. "Does this mean that acculturation researchers should abandon the cultural fit proposition? We believe the answer is 'not yet.'" They point to limitations in the present study and suggest that cultural fit is more likely to be confirmed where host cultures are relatively homogenous and also where there is pronounced interaction between sojourners and host-culture agents.[68] That combination of circumstances would be an unusual one. But once again, it seems that the ethnocentric assumption is resilient and not one to be easily discarded.

Other researchers have worked with cultural distance or cultural fit as an explanatory variable.[69] The work of Yang and colleagues[70] is discussed in the next section. Sam's study of international students in Norway focuses on their levels of "life satisfaction." Citing Ward and Kennedy, Sam states that "students from non-western countries in western countries tend to have the greatest adaptation difficulties."[71] The "sociocultural adaptation" of international students "is a function of their level of social skills, which in turn is a function of the cultural distance"; the exercise of social skills is associated also with academic satisfaction.[72] In addition, proficiency in English is closely related to academic success and overall adaptation. However, Sam's own results find that while having friends enhances life satisfaction and experiences of discrimination tend to diminish it, there is no relationship between life satisfaction and either having *host-national* friends or having proficiency in the host language of Norwegian or in English.[73] While life satisfaction was lower for African students than for the other students, possibly due to discrimination, the results provide no clear support for the cultural fit hypothesis. Indeed, not one single study read during the literature review for this book provided such support.

Critiques of Cultural Fit

Anderson sharply criticizes Ward's use of the notion of cultural fit in the context of New Zealand debates about the intake of students and migrants from Asian countries, especially China. Anderson demonstrates how although the notion of cultural fit has not proven robust in empirical studies, it is congruent with prevailing ethnocentric assumptions in New Zealand society, and so it is very readily translated from empirical studies into policy debates—despite its failure to meet the test of truth in explanation. In reporting her own interview-based study of international students in New Zealand, Anderson cites research by Ward and Masgoret, who refer to the "relatively poor integration of Chinese students" into New Zealand education and society. Ward and Masgoret state that "Chinese students expressed the most dissatisfaction with their time in New Zealand, and the highest perception of discrimination on the part of New Zealanders." They also note that students from "Asian" countries feel "less included" in classrooms than students from Europe and North America. To Ward and Masgoret "this is not surprising," as "the acceptance and adjustment of international students is a function of cultural distance."[74] "In response to these findings", states Anderson, "Ward and Masgoret propose that optimal numbers of international students should be determined in order to avoid 'feelings of threat in members of the receiving community' (p. 72). Ward and Masgoret are not explicit about *which* students should be limited in number, nor *which* New Zealanders perceive particular students as a threat. At the 2005 ISANA conference however, Ward argued that since Chinese students appear not to be integrating, consideration should be given to limiting their numbers in future."[75]

Here "adjustment" and "integration" are rendered *explicitly* as ethnocentric notions in public policy. They are defined exclusively in terms of the perspectives and interests of the "receiving" community. Ward's statement at ISANA recalls her earlier claims about cultural difference and the potential identity conflict between migrants and residents. The logic is to discriminate against people who are "different," using an ethnocentric standard. To generalize about groups in this manner and favor one group over another reproduces a culturally essentialist (if not racist) logic that locks into the stereotyping and segregation of sojourner populations. It also excuses local populations from any obligation to "adjust" to cultural difference:

To use "cultural difference" or "distance" as an explanation both for some international students' apparent lack of integration and their negative perceptions, is to simultaneously homogenise New Zealanders and the international students in question. From a critical theory perspective, assumptions of "difference" conveniently position the international students as deficient, and dismiss their perspectives. It is telling to note the convergence between racialised debates surrounding both international education and migration in New Zealand, in particular, the parallel calls to limit numbers of "Asian" international students and "Asian" migrants. As Butcher puts it, "the controversy over whom we educate, where we educate and how we educate may have less to do with our notions of education, and more to do with our notions of New Zealand and New Zealanders."[76]

The cultural fit argument is an a priori assumption in search of empirical manifestations of itself, yet it contains a built-in self-limitation. If adjustment is measured in terms of movement along a continuum between home culture and host culture, then the closer the cultural fit between international student and host culture, the lesser the quantity of observable adjustment. The further away cultural fit is, the larger the quantity of observable adjustment that can be observed. Students with less cultural fit will often exhibit larger quantities of adjustment. Cultural fit *must* overturn its own hypothesis, yet the cultural fit argument survives. We glimpse here a disciplinary imaginary more foundational than empirical truth and unshaken by repeated falsification. Cultural fit, together with assimilationist ("adjustment") or part assimilationist ("integration") concepts, reflect a deep desire for social equilibrium. Cultural fit automatically problematizes cultural distance. It "Others" the bearers of difference, in this case the international students from non-Western backgrounds, who are defined as threats to social order until they are "adjusted." Thus ethnocentrism provides the cultural content of the equilibrium. In this imagining, "cultures" are seen as static things within a normative realm, fixed in nature, zero sum in relation to each other, and thus always potentially in conflict.

We suggest the cultural fit hypothesis has been sustained primarily for these ideological and instrumental reasons rather than its capacity to explain sojourner "adjustment." Ethnocentrism is deeply grounded in Anglo-American cultures (and many others).[77] The cultural fit argument also coincides with the desires of educators and counselors to normalize this population of "Others" so as to manage them and process them in standardized ways. And perhaps the idea that cultural distance increases the difficulties of international education also matches the feelings of professional staff, wearied of the heavy efforts that cross-cultural traffic entails: the more unfamiliar the culture of the student, the more the staff member must work to understand it. It is not surprising that some become tired of adjusting to their clients, even to a limited extent, an adjustment rendered more challenging when the home-country language is unfamiliar and so the background of the student lies forever beyond their grasp.

Fortunately, people's identities are more complex than the cultural fit idea would suggest. The implication of a pure "adjustment" model is that students transform from one culture to another within a zero-sum set of cultures. But this is not what happens, as the original formulations by Bochner and Berry make clear. Sojourners do not *fully* "adjust" or "integrate." They partially change identities and in various complex ways. Even while many do not achieve full integration into host-country culture, they are on top of their own lives and are flourishing in the host country. Many succeed in communicating with and forming effective relationships with locals without adopting local customs and values holus-bolus. They make their own choices. They do so from a position of authority over their self-formation.

Hofstede's Cultural Essentialism

Another and more influential body of work in the study of cross-cultural relations is that of Hofstede. Hofstede's theorization is grounded in cultural essentialism: he sees "cultures" (imagined as fixed in character) as foundational explanations. This combined with his assumptions about the content of cultures rendered his theory as ethnocentric in the sense of pro-Western. This becomes more apparent in the work of some of the followers who make use of Hofstede's theoretical concepts.

For Hofstede, cultures vary by geographical region but "show strong continuity over time."[78] "The core elements in culture are values . . . broad tendencies to prefer certain states of affairs over others" such as notions of "what is evil and what is good."[79] Hofstede's cultural analysis turns in five binaries. Actual "cultures" vary in the way they combine elements of these binaries. The binaries are individualism/collectivism, large/small power distance, long-term/short-term orientation, masculinity/femininity, and yes/no uncertainty avoidance. These categories provide tools for Western interpretations of Asian countries and have become widely used in psychology. For Hofstede the differences between Asian and Western approaches turn on binaries of collectivism versus individualism, large versus small power distance, and long-term versus short-term orientation.[80]

Space does not permit a full discussion of Hofstede's five concepts.[81] The most prominent in the study of international education is individualism/collectivism. Hofstede's notion of individualism versus collectivism refers to variations in the degree to which individuals are integrated into groups. In collectivist cultures the "basic survival unit" is the group.[82] People from collectivist cultures—for example as attributed to much of Indonesia, China, Japan, and Vietnam—are integrated from birth onward into strong, cohesive in-groups, often constituted by an extended family that includes uncles, aunts, and grandparents, who protect them in exchange for unquestioning loyalty.[83] Working with Hofstede's concepts, Triandis argues that the desire to remain with parents and extended family is stronger in a collectivist culture than in an individualist culture. Collectivists enjoy close and supportive networks and actively share in the lives of others in the group. Support from others is very important to them.[84] Friendships in this kind of society are nonspecific and predetermined by stable social relationships.[85] In a culture where social cohesion is very strong, the need for social support is also strong, particularly in the context of an unpleasant event.[86] Given that collectivists place higher value on close and supportive social networks than do individualists,[87] with a larger number of close personal relationships in their lives, this suggests that collectivists will tend to suffer more deeply the absence of such networks. It is also implied that people from individualist cultures exhibit fewer skills of close interaction with others and are more emotionally detached from their groups. They are more likely to believe they can stand and survive on their own.[88] According to Triandis and colleagues,[89] research suggests that individuals from collectivist cultures are more likely than those from individualist cultures to subordinate their goals to a stable in-group based on bonding ties. In contrast, people from individualist cultures are more likely to have multiple affiliations, enter new groups, and move between groups, and more often exhibit detached and self-reliant behaviors.

Research focused on cross-border Asian or African students often concludes that for the most part they have distinctive group-oriented values.[90] Hofstede's framework suggests that international students from, for example, China or Vietnam would find the challenges of international education more difficult to meet on an individual basis and that they are more likely to depend on same-culture enclaves. Is that true? How determining is the collectivism/individualism distinction? To what extent are cultural identities fixed as Hofstede's narrative implies? Triandis and colleagues, working in Hofstede's framework, cast doubt on the stronger claims. They note also that in both individualist and collectivist cultures, individuals vary in the tendency to conform to group norms. In collectivist cultures the requirements generated by group norms differ between the collectivist cultures. People in individualist cultures are not less sociable than people in collectivist cultures. They do not necessarily conform more, feel more similar to fellow members of the culture, or always subordinate their goals to the goals of others, such as parents.[91]

As Siu and colleagues also remark, self-efficacy is not confined to Western cultures.[92] Yang and colleagues find that collectivist students are only marginally more likely to derive their self-construct on the basis of interdependence rather than independence and that the difference disappears when age and length of student stay are taken into account. And "contrary to expectation, international students had greater independent self-construals than Canadian students."[93] Many students from so-called collectivist Asian nations enrolled in Australian institutions make much use of same-culture networking.[94] But so do local students from the local "individualist" culture, and their networks, too, appear as relatively closed to outsiders and with weak bridges and poor connectivity across cultural boundaries. And many students from "collectivist" backgrounds, from small national groupings and without access to large same-culture enclaves, cope on an individual basis.

However, when cultural essentialism is joined to ethnocentrism, this readily leads to prejudicial formulations. In the late 1980s Triandis and colleagues developed an historical narrative based on three stages of "cultural complexity." First, there is "proto-individualism" in hunter-gather societies. Second, there is the collectivism of societies such as the Aztec, the Romans, and contemporary China in which individuals "subordinate their personal goals to the goals of some collective, which is usually a stable in-group." Third, there are "extremely complex cultures (e.g., modern industrial cultures) in which one can have many more in-groups and has a greater independence from all of them."[95] Triandis and colleagues note that "cultural elements change slowly. In societies with long traditions the collectivism elements may persist although the societies have become very complex (e.g., Japan). However, one ought to observe shifts toward individualism as complexity increases. It is likely that Gross National Product (GNP) is both an antecedent and a consequent of individualism. Affluence implies the ability to 'do one's own thing,' but 'doing one's own thing' implies more creativity for the society, hence more innovation and more economic development."[96]

Triandis and colleagues believe that in collectivist cultures, social behavior is a function of in-group norms to a greater extent than in individualist cultures. Ward and colleagues echo this: "Collectivists are inclined to perceive in-group norms as universally valid, whereas individualists are generally tolerant of diversity."[97] The degree to which cultural categories are seen as uniformly determining is again read through the ethnocentric prism. Asian collectivists are trapped in culture, it seems, while Western individualists have the personal tools to escape narrow determination and exercise the full range of human freedoms. In this teleological framework the "superiority" of Western education is unquestionable. The notion that Westerners have something to learn from the international students in their midst appears like an argument for turning back the clock of history.

Critiques of Cultural Essentialism

Triandis's cultural privileging of American and European societies on economic grounds makes a weaker argument after two decades of spectacular growth in China, Taiwan China, Singapore, and Korea. Presumably, to preserve their historical narrative and the hierarchy of societies that underlies it, Triandis and colleagues would claim that China has only achieved (rapid) economic modernization because it has (slowly?) adopted Western individualism. This argument would allow them to preserve the idea of fixed cultures with categorical boundaries. But such an implausible account could only be secured by underestimating modernization in China, or alternatively, by overestimating the degree of cultural transformation or Westernization that has taken place. This example illustrates how an account of culture as fixed, singular, and largely invariant is unable to imagine complex cultural hybridity and multiplicity in identity. It also shows how, notwithstanding all of the claims about respect for diversity and self-determination as primary aspects of liberty in the Western tradition, these democratic virtues are seen as valid only within that tradition, not in the choice between traditions. In this convoluted manner, the normalization of international students is represented as a movement toward freedom rather than away from it.

In this framework, the student who spends "too much" time in same-culture student networks is seen as an obstacle to "adjustment," to democracy, and to modernization itself. But Stephens questions this conception of culture[98] and the corresponding empirical reading of student practices. She notes that the idea of a distinctive Chinese "way of thinking" has wide currency in UK education but carries risks of stereotyping and concealment of individual differences.[99] Her interview data suggest students from China are diverse in outlook and exhibit both individualist and collectivist characteristics. "I have found independent-mindedness, liking for argument, cynicism about authority, and individual differences consistent with differing educational experiences and home environments. I have had a sense of cultural difference and discord within Chinese groups."[100]

> A broad brush view of the Chinese as collectively-oriented and the British as individualistic may say something about the historical development of ideology, but in relation to contemporary culture it may miss as much as it reveals. It misses the astonishment of one newly-arrived Chinese student at the orderliness of British society, from the behaviour of drivers on the roads to the tendency to accept authority in the absence of obvious sanctions. This student commented that order in China is maintained in much more explicit and authoritarian ways. He claimed that the rhetoric of this authoritarian order is maintained because individualistic chaos is never far from the surface and concluded that in British society conformity is more thoroughly internalised than in China.[101]

ADJUSTMENT AND STUDENT AGENCY

A more promising strand of research in cross-cultural psychology brings the agency of international students into the center of the frame, paving the way toward intercultural relations grounded in greater equality of respect.

Beyond Fixed Identity

In the concept of "adjustment" the process of change is modeled as malleable international student moving from fixed home-country identity to meet fixed local culture in the host country. The student changes; the host country does not. This asymmetrical relation of power sets a decisive limit on the agency of the international student, who emerges not only as impotent to transform the local culture and education system but as primarily Other determined, driven into adjustment by external environment and its dominant culture. As noted, it is not a democratic model. It is also unrealistic. Identity is more fluid than this suggests.

If identity is fixed and bounded as much psychological literature suggests, then international students are the site of cultural conflict. It is true that some studies identify tensions between home-country and host-country settings, associations, and values, for example the findings of Constantine and colleagues about female students and African students.[102] But a limitation of this kind of research is the imaginary of differing identities (or cultures or values) as fixed poles with the student pulled between them. This underestimates the continuing changeability of both home-country and host-country cultures, misses the potential for combining identities in various ways, and underplays the reflexive relationship between students and their systems of belief and action. Many are far from being victims of a clash of cultures or identities. They consciously manage their own constellations of values. (Chapter 7 explores this further.) And this breaks through in those studies in psychology—even some critiqued previously—that attempt to model aspects of self-directed personality, such as the capacity to manage plural identity.

One example is the study by Leong and Ward of "identity conflict" among Chinese sojourners in Singapore. They note that "tolerance of ambiguity" is often identified as "one of the key characteristics of a successful and well-adapted sojourner." Another characteristic is "attributional complexity"[103] among individuals who process causal information more thoughtfully and consider more in-depth and complicated explanations for events. Leong and Ward note that "research has revealed a consistent relationship between discrimination and a range of maladaptive outcomes for both immigrants and sojourners" and also that perceived discrimination is likely to reduce the degree of identification with host nationals.[104] Strong identification with the culture of origin was associated with less identity conflict: "It appears that strong co-national identification provides a significant ballast during cross-cultural transition and decreases the likelihood of identity problems."[105] Identification with the home-country and the host-country cultures emerged as independent and "not intrinsically conflicting."[106] These findings move beyond notions of fixed identities in conflict from which the researchers start.

Hullett and Witte investigate "the causal agents" in personality "that lead to adaptation."[107] They compare sojourners for whom "uncertainty control processes" are uppermost with those for whom "anxiety control processes" are dominant. Anxiety refers to the fear of negative consequences in a foreign cultural environment.[108] Uncertainty control is dominant when attributional confidence exceeds anxiety.[109] Those for whom uncertainty control was dominant were more likely to interact with the host culture so that "adaptation was significantly more prevalent." Those drawing primarily on anxiety control "exhibited greater tendencies towards isolation than adaptation."[110] The notion of "uncertainty control" points to the capacity for flexible management of the self.

Matsumoto and colleagues developed a 55-item Intercultural Adjustment Potential Scale (ICAPS) that measures constructs empirically related to adjustment, including emotion regulation, openness, flexibility, and critical thinking.[111] Reporting on three studies using the scale, the researchers find that "adjustment involves an active involvement of the self with others, a tolerance of differences among people including an absence of intolerance and bigotry, empathy for others, a healthy level of adjustment to one's own culture and a tendency to be task focused." They note that "openness" is associated with "strong internal ego control of impulsiveness, tolerance of differences among people including an absence of bigotry, keen social and intrapersonal insight, an intrinsic drive for achievement, flexibility and task orientation." Critical thinking is associated with "the ability to consider the effects of one's own behavior on others, flexibility, comfort with the rules and mores of one's own society, and an active seeking out of the company of others."[112] Like Matsumoto and colleagues, Savicki and colleagues focus on positive, agency-building factors associated with successful intercultural adjustment, rather than psychological stressors. They note that "potential for intercultural adjustment may increase over a sojourn, since individuals are being exposed to the broadening effects of exposure to a different culture."[113] The researchers compare students studying abroad with those who have remained at home. The study abroad students did not increase their overall ICAPS rating during the sojourn but did increase in flexibility and critical thinking.[114] Again, these qualities can be seen as contributing to the capacity for self-formation.

Li and Gasser examine sociocultural adjustment, contact with the hosts, ethnic identity, and cross-cultural self-efficacy among 117 international students from 17 countries in Asia. Notwithstanding Berry's argument that relations with same-culture and host-culture groups are heterogeneous, Li and Gasser start by assuming that "students who hold a greater sense of ethnic identity will be less likely to interact with the host country nationals," and that "this reduced contact may hamper their sociocultural adjustment."[115] Ethnic identity is measured by perceived ethnic identification, the sense of belonging to the ethnic group, attitudes toward the ethnic group, and involvement in "ethnic activities."[116] But they add that students with greater cross-cultural self-efficacy are more likely to engage with host-country nationals, enhancing sociocultural adjustment.[117] "Self-efficacy is the belief that one can perform certain functions in order to produce a desired outcome."[118] Self-efficacy is confidence in one's powers of self-determination.

Li and Gasser find the quantity of contact with host nationals is strongly correlated to sociocultural adjustment. Ethnic identity is negatively related to the level of contact with host nationals, but less strongly. Against expectations, "Asian students' ethnic identity was not significantly correlated with their sociocultural adjustment."[119] This contradicts the widely shared assumption that ethnic closure is disabling of student adaptability. "It is possible that Asian students in the present study received social support from their ethnic network that protected them from social and cultural difficulties during the adjustment process."[120] Li and Gasser find also that contact with host nationals is strongly correlated to cross-cultural self-efficacy and that the correlation between cross-cultural self-efficacy and sociocultural adjustment is almost as strong. Via the regression analysis, the researchers find that not surprisingly, the apparent effect of cross-cultural self-efficacy is partly mediated by contact with hosts.[121] The study points to the key role of active student agency, confirms the potential for multiple affiliations in which international students manage a range of formative experiences in different cultural domains rather than moving from home to host culture, and points to the relationship between self-determining agency and intercultural mixing.

AGENCY VERSUS CULTURAL FIT

In a study of students in Canada, Yang and colleagues work with the notion of cultural fit and Hofstede's categories of individualism/collectivism but are also interested in active agency. They find themselves pushing against the limits of the cultural fit hypothesis and, like Ward, they are puzzled by the fact it does not work.

The researchers note earlier work that finds "Asian international students with high independent self-construals had better psychological adjustment," and also better sociological adjustment, which is "contrary to Ward's assumption that psychological and sociocultural adjustment are predicted by distinct variables unique to each adjustment dimension." Previous research also suggests that "Asian international students' use of direct, open, and prototypical communication styles (i.e., styles that match with the host society) were related to better sociocultural adjustment." These studies all emphasize "the importance of a match between individuals' internalized attributes and characteristics of the host society."[122] Accordingly, they hypothesize that self-construals, particularly the fit between the sojourner's profile and normative tendency of the host society, would predict better adaptation. Self-construals are defined as "the conceptualization of the self and behavior shaped through the primary culture."[123] Here Yang and colleagues distinguish their approach from the "invariable and universal aspects of personality assumed and understood in [the] traditional Western psychological framework."[124] They note that Ward studies cultural fit "from a stable, universal, and consistent personality traits framework (in contrast to the self-ways approach)." But they understand personality in terms of "culturally shaped self views."[125] Drawing on research related to intercultural communication they also focus on self-confidence and low anxiety in second language use. They note research has yet to examine "the link between communicative self-confidence and sociocultural adjustment, despite the straightforward rationale that ease in using the language of the host society would reduce the number of difficulties experienced in that society."[126] According to Yang and colleagues, "there may be distinct pathways to cross-cultural adaptation. Not only should researchers consider the 'fit' between international students' internalized self-views or ways of being, and those of the host society, they must also consider how confidence in using English mediates the impact of intercultural contact on cross-cultural adaptation."[127]

The researchers hypothesize that frequent intercultural contact contributes to adaptation and the link is mediated by English language self-confidence. Given their points that there is a strong connection between communicative competence and agency, and between both of these factors and cross-cultural efficacy, their work suggests a study of the flows between (1) communications, (2) agency, and (3) cross-cultural contact can tell us much about intercultural relations.

The findings provide no support for the cultural fit argument, encourage more work on the link between self-construal and language use, and overturn orthodox expectations about the forms of agency characteristic of internationals. The hypothesis that international students have greater sociocultural difficulties than local Canadian students is supported.[128] However, the notion that collectivist international students have greater psychological difficulty than Canadian students is not supported. "It may be the case that these international students may have unique personality characteristics (perhaps their independent self-construal) that moderate the effects . . . on their psychological adjustment."[129] "Contrary to expectation, international students were found to be more independent than Canadian students, even after controlling for age and length of residence."[130]

The researchers suggest a number of possible explanations for "these unexpected findings." First, international students from collectivist cultures may be more independent-minded than most people in collectivist cultures. A second possible explanation is that the students become more independent minded as a result of their exposure to Canadian culture. Another is that the "increased globalization of communication and cultural interactions in this group" have left their mark.[131] All of these explanations go to the notion of independent agency. Yang and colleagues show that whether international students are from individualist or collectivist cultures, they must learn to survive and succeed independently in an unfamiliar environment and in the absence of many if not all the familiar resources and supports. They also suggest that both independent agency and "collectivist" social relations can be pursued (and enhanced) by students simultaneously—in other words, independent agency/identity/personality should not be equated simply with Western individualism. These insights are an important corrective to Hofstedian and other research in which the conjunction of "Western" and "individualism" is universalized as a normative ideal, and implicitly or explicitly held to be superior to all other identities.

The second hypothesis of Yang and colleagues posited that the higher the international students' independent self-construal, and the closer it matched the normative tendency of the host society (cultural fit), the better their psychological adjustment. They find that an independent self-construal was positively associated with self-esteem and negatively associated with adjustment difficulty. In that respect the cultural fit hypothesis is supported. But as in the case of the 2004 study by Ward and colleagues, who found that extraversion was positively correlated to adjustment whether or not extraversion was consistent with cultural fit, this can be explained by the effect of independent agency and communicability on adjustment outcomes rather than the effect of the level of cultural fit.[132] This again confirms that being from a so-called collectivist society does not in itself handicap adjustment. Greater cultural fit in that respect does not help. But independent agency *does* help. Also, the international student can remain collectivist but also be independent. "Having an independent self-construal itself, regardless of the match with the host society, is conducive to better cross-cultural adaptation . . . This is not to suggest that they are necessarily low in interdependence or connectedness with others, but rather that independent aspect of themselves buffers them from the stressors of dealing with a different culture."[133]

Despite producing these findings, Yang and colleagues, echoing Ward, state that "this failure to find evidence for the cultural-fit hypothesis does not mean that we feel that the notion should be abandoned altogether." Remarkably, they still want to resurrect cultural fit. They suggest it should be tested for students moving in the culturally reverse direction, from individualist to collectivist cultures (even while noting that using just this method, Ward and colleagues had again failed to confirm the cultural fit hypothesis).[134] They also float several unconvincing explanations for the failure of the hypothesis.[135]

The researchers find no relation between contact with conationals and the level of psychological adjustment.[136] However "language self-confidence" is an explanatory element. It mediated the relation between contact with Canadians and both psychological adjustment and sociocultural difficulty. They also find that "independent self-construals were found to positively predict greater English self-confidence."[137] They conclude that the findings overall support the existence of "two important pathways" to adjustment. One pathway is via independent self-construal, which predicts better psychological adjustment, and through the link between psychological adjustment and sociocultural difficulty also predicts better sociocultural adjustment. The second pathway is via language self-confidence, which plays a pivotal role in "mediating the influence of intercultural contact on cross-cultural adaptation."[138] Using the agency-like notion of "self-ways," the researchers state that "some people with particular self-ways are more likely to experience better cross-cultural adaptation during international student sojourns." At the same time, "communicative competence and comfort in the host language plays a pivotal role . . . Not only do language and communication processes (indexed by self-confidence) mediate the relations between host cultural contact and psychological and sociocultural difficulty, but they also mediate the influence of self-construals on adaptation."[139]

The overall picture is of a range of outcomes determined by three elements in interaction: agency, communicative competence, and cross-cultural practices.

OPENNESS AND RESPONSIVENESS

Kashima and Loh researched a sample of two hundred international students in Melbourne, Australia.[140] More than two-thirds were from Southeast Asia and 61 percent from Singapore and Malaysia.[141] The researchers focused on socially active agency and the relational competences it exercises. Specifically, they investigated the need for

"cognitive closure" as a factor in intercultural relationships and acculturation. "An individual difference in need for cognitive closure . . .
reflects the degrees to which one desires a clear and firm solution over
uncertainty, confusion, and ambiguity."[142] Students with low need for
cognitive closure are those able to tolerate a degree of ambiguity in
identity and not prone to either/or binary thinking about identity
that forces them to make choices between bounded singular identities. Here cognitive closure is especially interesting because it would
seem that low cognitive closure would facilitate a conscious, reflexive
process of self-management.

Kashima and Loh considered the need for cognitive closure in
conjunction with their patterns of interpersonal relationships with
same-culture international students, local students, and other international students. Kashima and Loh remark that previous research
suggests that greater social ties with and social support from both
locals and conational students tend to facilitate psychological adjustment, while for sociocultural adjustment the benefits of social ties
with locals tend to outweigh those of ties with conationals. They note
also that in their 1970s and 1980s studies of international students,
Bochner and his colleagues established the importance of ties with the
third category of students, other international students, but that this
"has been a neglected topic in the acculturation literature which tends
to focus more on effects of conational and host cultural contacts . . . it
seems plausible that newcomers of different cultural backgrounds also
help facilitate each others' psychological adjustment in multicultural
environments."[143] Kashima and Loh expected to find that all forms of
tie contribute to psychological adjustment and both local and international ties contribute to sociocultural adjustment. They also looked at
these factors in conjunction with acquisition of host-cultural knowledge, students' orientation to home-culture ("heritage") identity,
and the Australian "university identity" they acquire. The researchers found that patterns of personal ties across the three groups, and
individual differences in the need for cognitive closure, "significantly
influence" acculturation, and "international students' social identities
may change dynamically during their acculturation."[144]

The researchers state that "newcomers inevitably find substantial
degrees of uncertainty and ambiguity in the new cultural environment. Yet, some cope with such conditions better than others."[145]
Ties with local and other international students predict psychological
adjustment. Ties with conational students do not. Cognitive closure
is negatively correlated with psychological adjustment: the higher
the level of cognitive closure, the lower the adjustment. To the extent

that "adjustment" involves self-change, this makes sense. However, among students requiring high cognitive closure, those with strong local ties tended to have higher psychological adjustment. In contrast, among students with a low requirement for cognitive closure, the pattern of local ties made little difference to psychological adjustment.[146] In other words cross-cultural interaction may "loosen" the agency of a student who finds flexibility difficult. On sociocultural adjustment, the researchers were surprised to find that none of the three types of networking predicted it. Factors that are positively correlated to sociocultural adjustment are English-speaking background and, encouragingly, the length of time in Australia. Cognitive closure also affects sociocultural adjustment. Students who need high cognitive closure tend to experience lower sociocultural adjustment. In general, high cognitive closure is associated with lower psychological adjustment and lower sociocultural adjustment. This suggests that a capacity for flexible self-formation sustains happier student sojourners who exhibit a higher rate of cultural learning (and much research suggests those with greater adjustment are more likely to succeed academically). The study also highlights the role of networks with international students other than those from the same country.[147]

As expected, ties with local students contributed positively to Australian cultural knowledge, as did English language background and time in Australia. Interestingly, the degree of cognitive closure did not affect the acquisition of local cultural knowledge.[148] In relation to heritage cultural identity, Kashima and Loh found that it is strengthened by ties with other international students, marginally strengthened by conational ties, and unaffected by the extent of local ties. The degree of cognitive closure has no effect on heritage cultural identity

Significantly, the researchers also found that language background, and time in Australia, made no difference to heritage cultural identity.[149] In other words, while international students might develop changing and especially more complex configurations of identity during the sojourn, they do not tend to discard their heritage culture over time. This again stymies the notion underlying much of the adjustment literature, of adjustment or acculturation as a journey from home-country identity toward host-country identity, in other words as a binary either/or process of transformation in which the more the student has discarded heritage identity to achieve cultural fit with the host culture, the greater the adjustment. In relation to Australian university identity, this was enhanced by all three types of network, including ties with conationals, and by English-speaking background.[150]

CONCLUSION

To the extent cross-cultural psychology employs static and normalizing concepts, it retards the advance of the more open and fluid methods that are needed in intercultural education, methods that take us into more intellectually challenging and socially generative territory. But the larger problem lies in the particular norms that have been employed. The cultural essentialism and ethnocentrism that run through much of the discipline—attributes that are continually reproduced in the institutional settings in which the psychology is applied—are a major handicap. More generally, the "adjustment" paradigm, which is modeled on the outer-in external determination of unfree human subjects rather than the inner-out self-determination of free human subjects, denies respect to international students and obscures and weakens their self-realization. The "adjustment" paradigm validates systems of other-formation and top-down professional control using devices like deficit modeling. It is essential to move beyond these frameworks.

The problem is both methodological and political, or rather, to take the point about power/knowledge made famous by Foucault,[151] it lies in the conjunction of the two. The method of orthodox psychology is that of bounded and static category analysis using mathematical modeling of complex relational processes. The intention is to freeze-frame that ever-moving complexity with an unreflexive form and certainty that enables the regression-based modeling. Even something as organic, fluid, and open ended as "culture" becomes defined as a tightly bound category. The goal of orthodox psychology is individual and social equilibrium within a philosophical framework in which the individual is treated as prior to the social. Too often in orthodox cross-cultural psychology, fixed cultural categories are deployed as static elements within a normative realm. The method privileges cultural determination and cultural uniformity while problematizing cultural difference. It does so from the viewpoint of one particular culture. When "cultures" are seen as primary and invariant, differences between them are read as sources of intrapersonal tension and disruptive of social order. The practical solution is to order recalcitrant "Other" cultures into line with the preferred culture—hence the "adjustment" paradigm in international education. Theories of cultural fit provide an apparently plausible intellectual justification for the normalizing project.

Three elements in the real world undermine the notion of cultural fit and all other theorizations based on cultural essentialism. First, students and other cross-border sojourners are often highly flexible people who do whatever they need to do, including developing and changing themselves in often quite conscious ways, for example by acquiring language competence, discovering new interests they can share with locals, or simply making themselves more aware and responsive. These students do want to adjust in the country of education; they want to learn and part-integrate in the new society and draw educational and personal benefits from social engagement—while retaining control over themselves as their own project. Second, identity is a complex matter and students arrange home-country and host-country identities, both of which are also constantly changing in different ways, mixing and matching. Research finds that individuals in sojourner populations vary considerably in their responses to questions about identity. These variations appear to cut across simple measures based on origins. Third, the influence of cultural origins is qualified by many other elements, especially but not only those related to the agency of students and their communicative competence.

However, ethnocentrism is not essential to psychology and it stymies what cross-cultural psychology can do. Some theorists of cross-cultural psychology are profoundly antiethnocentric, and the best work acknowledges the mobile character of social relations, deploying mathematical models to generate valuable insights while at the same time highlighting their limits. It is expanding our understanding of international student agency and of the relational space in which it plays out. That best work has also been frank in acknowledging the limits of ethnocentric analysis.

The strong finding from the psychological research is of three-way interaction among agency, communicative competence, and cross-cultural practices. In this interaction, each element provides favorable conditions for the development of the others. The potent interface between agency and communicative competence returns repeatedly in this book. Individuals are not solely individualized; they are also social beings and manage themselves in relational contexts. Both language and interaction with others are essential elements for survival and growth in the country of education. There is also a strong suggestion that the agency/communicative competence dyad both facilitates cross-cultural relations and is enhanced by them. Here lie the beginnings of an explanation of relations between international students and locals (including local students) and of the potential contribution of such relations to the capacity of international students to run their own lives.

Chapter 3 will further develop the picture of the relational intercultural context largely hidden from psychology. It explores different notions of cosmopolitan intercultural education, the attributes required to be effective in intercultural relations, and the potentials of mutuality in "adjustment."

CHAPTER 3

---·—:≫●≪:—·---

ENGAGING THE OTHER
IDEAS ABOUT COSMOPOLITANISM

INTRODUCTION: BEYOND "ADJUSTMENT"

Globalization is the process of worldwide convergence and intergration.[1] In the last 20 years it has been powered above all by the rollout of cheaper air travel and synchronous global communications and by the slower and more partial coming together of world economic activities. Its hallmarks are ecology, mobility, and connectivity. Globalization had driven the expansion of international education at twice the worldwide rate of growth of tertiary education enrolments as a whole. In this more global era, worldwide systems, forces, and relationships have become more important than before. This has changed the settings in which individual localities and nations operate, transforming human actions in many ways.

Global systems and forces loom larger in our lives, bringing us into contact with a more diverse range of cultures and educational forms. But individual outlooks do not *automatically* become more globally oriented.[2] Other ways of seeing continue to govern behavior and sustain institutional forms. Globalization calls up the need for new social relations that have yet to be created; these could take a wide variety of forms and serve many different interests. International education is at the forefront of these developments. The questions are, What will be the main kinds of cross-cultural relations in future? What will be the principal ideas that will shape those emerging cross-cultural relations in education?

Psychology does not hold the whole field of cross-cultural relations. There is a large and heterogeneous body of work focused on international education that derives from other traditions. Much of this work is critical of notions of "adjustment" and "cultural fit," and of Hofstedian cultural analysis. Some of it rejects Western ethnocentrism and wants to engage with the cultural Other on more equal terms. Some of this work is philosophical and conceptual in form; some of it is primarily empirical; and some of it is practical, focused on better teaching and learning. The most promising lines of argument can be described as "cosmopolitan" because of their worldwide sweep and notions of plural identity. Nevertheless, there is more than one kind of cosmopolitanism, a term that is explored further later in this chapter.

This body of work rarely connects in an effective manner with cross-cultural psychology, either to critique it or complement it. In the manner of separated intellectual disciplines, cross-cultural psychology and cosmopolitan cultural analysis push ahead regardless as if the other never existed, though often they talk about the same phenomena. But the cosmopolitan work is not framed as an alternative to psychology. Its project is rather different. It focuses not simply on individual persons but on the larger relational space in which individual personality and behavior, which are the core preoccupations of psychology, are played out. While not every cosmopolitan thought in international education is helpful—oddly, some of the ideas are culturally essentialist and Western-centric—the importance of the best cosmopolitan thinking for international education lies in its potential to support wider and deeper forms of intercultural engagement, in which student sojourners have greater freedoms to make their lives as they want.

This Chapter

The chapter outlines two strands of cosmopolitan thought with different implications for international education. In *Ideas for Intercultural Education*, these are termed "globalism" and "relational cosmopolitanism." It then applies the preferred strand, relational cosmopolitanism, to issues in international education. There is a brief return to the critique of decifit models and to Western-centric models, followed by discussion of implications for teaching and learning.

THE COSMOPOLITAN SPACE

The founding text in discussion of cosmopolitanism is Immanuel Kant's essay "Perpetual peace."[3] Kant sought a world moral order based on universal rules for managing human conduct. This moral order would guarantee all persons "hospitality" within the cosmopolitan setting of a "universal civil society" in which states were constrained. As he saw it, this was the only the alternative to perpetual war between nations. Kant disagreed with Hobbes's position that conflict was inevitable.

But Kantian liberal universalism, like all forms of cosmopolitanism since, was grounded in a particular worldview and one that was ill equipped to accommodate a plurality of positions. It "neither acknowledges cultural diversity as a permanent feature of modern life nor seriously addresses the historically inherited inequalities in power relations." Its humanism "presupposes that all cultural groups share similar moral outlooks."[4] Citing Stuart Hall,[5] Rizvi notes that where cosmopolitanism is based on universal principles this "assumes a fixed notion of moral tradition as already constituted in authority, as well as a view of culture as static, and not as something that is continuously changing, responding to the new circumstances in which it is embedded and encountered." This universalism assumes a world "segmented in terms of specific, well-bounded, tightly knit, organic communities." But this is no longer the world we inhabit. In today's global context, groups are "culturally marked" but never entirely separate from each other. They "are constantly re-shaped by cross-cultural encounters."[6]

Liberal universalism also assumes a state neutral as to cultural contents—yet states are always implicated in relations of power, and in the ordering of culture. Hall's argument against liberal universalism as a cosmopolitan framework is that it is unable to provide a medium for an open dialogue between differing traditions. The authority of the framework is doctrinal and exclusive of other traditions.[7] This is cosmopolitanism solely in Western liberal terms. And so it cannot work.

Globalism

One response to this problem has been the evolution of a utopian globalism claiming to be independent of *all* particular national and cultural traditions. The underlying vision, facilitated by the ecological imaginary[8] and continually powered by globalization, is the world as a single zone crisscrossed by diverse relations and inhabited by freely moving intercultural persons. Adept in cultural mixing and evolving their own identities, they pursue their life trajectories from outside specific cultures. Here, as Yuval-Davis says, "cosmopolitanism is frequently seen as an alternative to any exclusionary politics of belonging." For the global theorist Ulrich Beck, "to belong or not to belong is *the* cosmopolitan question."[9] In its full expression globalism not only advocates cultural neutrality and negates national identity but also tends toward the abolition of both cultural viewpoint and place.

These assumptions have shaped one part of the literature on intercultural education, particularly discussion about the preparation of "global citizens" and "global competences" in education. Thus Allan states the essence of intercultural-as-global attributes is the capacity to "feel comfortable and communicate effectively with people of any culture encountered," without privileging any culture.[10] On place, Bradley argues that the enhancement of global mobility has changed one of the premises of identity, which is the necessity for a single place-identity or "home." "Many have become adept at moving and are more 'at home' in movement; identity is less linked to a home which is located in a community in a fixed geographical space." For many travelers "home" is less in one place than in routine practices and social interactions often conducted across distances via communications media. "International students may be seen to be part of the shift towards cultural globalization in the way they sojourn in another place. Those who adapt more quickly and more readily may be the ones who are most able to carry their worlds with them," including habitual "behaviours and perceptions of self."[11]

The argument is grounded not so much in empirical studies but in normative exhortation to a kind of global setting, which is asserted at one and the same time as already true to life, and a goal to be brought into being. The vision rests less on persons without place or cultural home, as a particular kind of mobile English-speaking professional adept in using the airport and the Internet and able to leave and return at will while often continuing to draw sustenance from the original identity. Calhoun refers to it as "the class consciousness of frequent travellers."[12] Advocates of globalism in the literature on international education set out to transform whole educational institutions and systems according to the blueprint of the ideal "global citizen"—though only a handful of the users of those education systems will ever share the highly mobile and culturally polyglot globalist lifestyle.

Forming "global citizens" is a matter of inculcating generic skills that facilitate connectedness and mobility, such as communications, openness, tolerance, and flexibility, and combining these with a metanational outlook. The global dimension is understood not so much as an addition to the national and local dimensions as a substitute for them. The expected change in outlook is profound. The goal is a vantage point elevated above all particularities of identity. In globalist arguments, reflexive awareness and self-formation are seen as essential to globalism. The capacity to engage deeply with other cultures is seen as dependent on willingness to engage in self-change, though how far self-change needs to go is not always clear. Yet most globalist scholars pursue their abstract globalism in English and draw on a universal humanism. Without acknowledging that their own language and ideas constitute a specific standpoint, they relegate all other possible standpoints to the status of being merely particular. It is an ethnocentric antiethnocentrism.

There are echoes here of long-standing religious practices and the notions of higher consciousness developed in the 1960s counterculture. Part of the literature offers blueprints for self-formation as a "true" intercultural or global being. Olson and Kroeger envision intercultural education as a journey from its beginnings in communicative openness to the achievement of a fully global outlook. In their paper and others there is a hint of the Buddhist progression through successive stages of higher and higher enlightenment. Stone outlines a progression from "accommodating cultural difference" to becoming a "world citizen" aware of global trends and responsibilities.[13] More prosaically, according to Olson and Kroeger, the skills of intercultural communication are adaptability, empathy, cross-cultural awareness, intercultural relations, and cultural mediation. Empathy is "the ability to treat someone as they would wish to be treated." Cross-cultural awareness is "the ability to understand how another culture feels from the standpoint of the insider." Intercultural relations depend on the "ability to develop interpersonal relationships." Cultural mediation requires "the ability to serve as a bridge between cultures."[14]

There is much of value in these ideas, and in many of the globalist arguments it is emphasized that the scope for specific cultural positions is retained. But it seems that at the 'higher' stages of globalism, the globalist abandons specific positions, and the globalist standpoint is defined by the "bridge" between cultures, not culture itself. For example, Olson and Kroeger cite Bennett's influential model of "six stages of intercultural sensitivity."[15] Three of the stages are stated by Bennett to be "ethnocentric," described as "denial, defense, and minimization," and three stages are "ethnorelative," described as "acceptance, adaptation, integration."

Bennett defines ethnocentrism as the concept that the worldview of one's own culture is central to all reality. To be ethnocentric means that you make life choices and act based on the assumption that your worldview is superior. Ethnorelativism, in contrast, assumes that cultures can only be understood relative to one another and that behaviour can only be understood within a cultural context. The state of ethnorelativism does not imply an ethical agreement with all difference nor a disavowal of stating (and acting on) a preference for one worldview over another. The position does imply, however, that ethical choices will be made on grounds other than the protection of one's own worldview or in the name of absolute principles. As we become more interculturally sensitive and forge intercultural communication skills, we are able to move through the ethnocentric stages and progress toward more ethnorelativist stages.[16]

Olson and Kroeger note that Bennett distinguishes adaptation from "assimilation." Assimilation is replacing one worldview for another. "Adaptation . . . is an 'additive' process; new skills or ways of being are added to one's original 'repertoire.' Bennett argues that the most important intercultural communication skill at this stage is empathy; in his words 'the ability to experience some aspect of reality differently from what is "given" by one's own culture.'"[17] As the "adapted" individual becomes more competent she or he acquires "pluralism," the capacity to sustain bicultural or multicultural worldviews while also being sensitive to other cultures. At this stage there is still potential for internal tensions and "culture shocks." However, once the ultimate stage of enlightenment, that of "integration," is reached, individuals "are working to integrate their multiple aspects of identity into a coherent whole." At the same time, they are of no specific culture and are "culturally marginal" and "constantly creating their own reality." This is seen as a difficult but potentially powerful position. Such people are often brokers between cultures.[18]

Here Bennett's notion is ambiguous, on one hand suggesting in utopian fashion that "integrated" persons can be without a standpoint of their own, and on the other hand, more plausibly, that they create their own identity on a changing continuous basis, from the cultural resources available to them. Thus the enlightened globalist becomes elevated to universal Master Umpire, while ordinary mortals remain locked in particularist games supervised by the Master. It is a creed for the scholar-guru rather than for the follower. "For the ethnorelativist, difference is no longer threatening. It is no longer a question of preserving one's cultural reality but rather of creating new categories that allow for the coexistence of diverse cultural realities."[19]

Gunesch models personal cultural identity using a notion of cosmopolitanism that "could constitute an alternative to or complement for 'international education' in theory or practice."[20] His strategy for global relations is not based on multiplicity or hybridity, but "meta-culturality," simultaneously an engagement with all cultures and disengagement with all cultural particularity. This self-negating double move is the signature strategy of the utopian globalist. The globalist is universally relational and nonrelational in the same moment, thereby maximizing both influence and strategic flexibility. For Gunesch, enhanced global mobility drives the need for the model and creates its conception of identity.[21] Increasingly, the national dimension is seen as an obsolete distraction. Gunesch states that all cosmopolitans regret the privileging of national identities in political life,[22] though they diverge between those who continue to reconcile the nation-state with a global identity and those who "seek forms of attachment and identity only beyond the nation state."[23]

Yet we continue to live in a world of nation-states. While culture is part globalized and the economy follows more slowly, politics has scarcely begun the journey. As Held notes, "national institutions remain central to public life" while mass education institutions are central to state-coordinated modernization.[24] How many people have the option of opting out of nation-states? At its heart the globalist position is unreal. It negates itself and cannot be implemented. The position of no position is a nonposition. Globalism is the individual solution of a few, not a relational solution. The difficulty invoked by the globalist position—especially as a creed for education systems— becomes apparent in this point by Yuval-Davis: "(Ulrich Beck's question) implies that belonging is a choice that can always be made, and that one makes it solely for oneself. An alternative question to pose for cosmopolitans would be whether it is capable of including all 'others' (not just selves) as having the choice of belonging. Moreover, a politics based around the idea of belonging as voluntary risks [misses a] key aspect of the systems of social relations that sustain racism, which always involve boundaries that exclude or exploit 'the other.'"[25]

Yuval-Davis remarks on "two broad trends within cosmopolitanism." One approach, the globalist approach, "sees cosmopolitanism as a form of belonging which is detached and fluid, avoiding any fixed notions of boundaries." The other approach "remains based on local attachments, but conceptualizes the national as expanding into the international and the transnational"[26] (and global). The same point is made by Marginson and Rhoades where they argue that higher education systems and institutions, and human mentalities and actions in higher education, are simultaneously engaged in global, national, and local dimensions of life.[27] We now turn to this second and more connected notion of cosmopolitanism.

Relational Cosmopolitanism

The alternate line of argument draws on a relational cosmopolitanism in which locality, nationality, changing cultural identity, and global systems and imaginings are all at play. As with globalism, "cosmopolitanism" describes the manner in which the different cultures and identities are joined to each other. But it is not so much a personal creed as a descriptor of the relational space itself. It is a collective concept, like "democracy." The cosmopolitan (like the democrat) is a person with attributes and actions that sustain the common cosmopolitan (democratic) order.

For Rizvi both the scope for and the need for relational cosmopolitanism are continually expanded by globalization. The world is becoming more integrated and more globally interdependent. Most problems "are global in nature requiring global solutions." Both students and teachers need to know how their lives are being reshaped by "global processes and connections" and also how they might steer these economic, political, and cultural transformations.[28] These global processes are marked by steep inequalities. Many people cannot order their lives even at the local level let alone contribute to the shaping of global relations. Nevertheless, "global connectivity is neither systematic nor structured around some central locus of power" but is defined through the heightened role of forms of social imagination that are constituted organically in "popular consciousness."[29]

The question of how people steer global transformations is also the question of how they relate to each other, the question of how "to develop a conception of cosmopolitanism" both "empirically informed" and "ethically grounded."[30] This is not easy. Intercultural relations are "inherently unstable . . . looking and working across cultural differences." Such relationships involve "fluidity, indeterminacy and open-endedness."[31] As argued also by Amartya Sen[32] and noted in Chapter 2, identity is seen as plural and potentially hybridized. People now have multiple personal affiliations, including cross-border linkages.

> No one today is purely *one* thing. Labels like Indian, or woman, or Muslim, or American are not more than starting points, which if followed into actual experience for only a moment are quickly left behind . . . just as human beings make their own history, they also make their cultures and ethnic identities. No one can deny the persisting continuities of long traditions, sustained habitations, national languages, and cultural geographies, but there seems no reason except fear and prejudice to keep insisting on their separation and distinctiveness, as if

that was all human life was about. Survival in fact is about connections between things . . . It is more rewarding – on more difficult—to think concretely and sympathetically, contrapuntally, about others than only about "us."[33]

Vertovec and Cohen remark that "people are no longer inspired by a single culture that is coherent, integrated and organic."[34] They draw on multiple reservoirs of identity. A person may choose a reified singular identity but as a conscious choice, not an organic necessity, and as noted in Chapter 2, identities change—especially in the case of globally mobile persons. Likewise culture is creative and "always in the state of *becoming* . . . rather than something that is entirely inherited within clearly definable boundaries and norms" or a "redis-covery of lost roots."[35] Rizvi notes that the very concept of "culture" presupposes interculturality. People are only conscious of their lives as an identifiable set of practices, a culture, when they contrast them with practices that are different. It is necessary to understand and revalue "traditions and inheritances of cultural expressions in new and creative ways because the context in which they are expressed is continually changing."[36] "Local and national attachments" continue to be important but in a more dynamic manner. They are articu-lated in new ways, in a setting in which both problems and solutions "are inter-connected and transcend national boundaries."[37] Cos-mopolitanism provides the tools for this. Held states that "Cultural cosmopolitanism should be understood as the capacity to mediate between national cultures, communities of fate and alternative styles of life."[38] "While the 'globalists' can present convincing evidence of the leap in global connectivity and cultural pursuits, national cultures remain robust and capable of adapting and reinterpreting foreign imports. Cosmopolitanism, therefore, becomes a means whereby national and global cultures can be mediated, where dialogues can be initiated and transboundary issues resolved by those who can see above their national parapets."[39]

This suggests that the role of educators is to help to form in stu-dents that capacity for imaginative mediation between the zones of existence. As noted by Rizvi, a curriculum that enables students to enter into direct relations with different perspectives and contexts helps them to undertake their own formation.

CONTENTS OF COSMOPOLITANISM

Cosmopolitanism can follow many different paths. "Notions of global connectivity and interdependence have always been both located within particular historical contexts and informed by various political interests."[40] In the past, particular values or interests have dominated certain cosmopolitan orders, using the relational framework to lock subordinates into control from the metropolitan center.

Historically, the first cosmopolitan regimes were hegemonic empires: the Persians and Alexander, the Romans, Tang China, the Mongols, the Ottomans, and the British and French. Often these Empires were more cosmopolitan—some of the time at least—than many nation-states today, though they were usually presided over by dominant groups that were defined in cultural, locational, religious, and/or racial terms. Following Edward Said, Rizvi remarks that in the European colonial period, imperial cosmopolitanism had an educational agenda. "The colonial consciousness was above all a mode of thinking, a system of knowledge with which to exercise power over colonized people," one that justified global connectivity while maintaining the notion that the colonizers were the morally correct bearers of a superior way of life. "Education had to play a major role in the dissemination of colonial ideas," not only to "buttress the exercise of power" but also to legitimate it both in the colonies and at home. Both Britain and France funded extensive educational systems in their countries of rule. "Schools were established to educate the masses" while "universities were created to develop a local administrative elite beholden to colonial powers," and patterned along the lines of the higher education systems at the colonial center, with the same curricula and systems of examination.[41] "Universities in both Britain and the colonies encouraged students to imagine the British Empire as a seamless entity, built around a core set of values and interests often viewed as 'cosmopolitan.' Students were encouraged to learn the languages and cultures of the Empire, even if this knowledge was constructed in a particular way, which portrayed the native as simple, exotic or inferior, in need of 'civilizational' development.'"[42]

This was the origin of today's ethnocentrism in Anglo-American international education, which profits from perceptions of cultural superiority. Direct colonial control has been replaced by neocolonial systems in which educational trade feeds back revenues and cultural domination. Australia was itself a British colonial foundation, but it secures referred neoimperial benefits via the British forms of its educational institutions.

In sum, "differing accounts of cosmopolitanism are grounded in varying accounts of the ways in which the world is interconnected, that foreground different aspects of this connectivity,"[43] be it global economic markets, the universalizing projects of world religions, the claims of empire to install a globally metropolitan culture in subject peoples, horizontal encounters and exchange between diverse nations and cultures, or the flow of ideas and communications within common systems. Rizvi suggests that now, "corporate cosmopolitanism" might be hegemonic. Drawing together political, economic, and cultural ideas often referred to as "neoliberal," the corporate vision imagines the world as "a single global sphere of free trade and economic exchange." Cosmopolitanism becomes seen as the outcome of the market economy, which allegedly rests on and produces individual freedoms and tends to generate greater human mobility, innovation, and "cultural tolerance."[44]

Corporate cosmopolitanism does not foreground political democracy. In the neoliberal account, political forms are confined to the nation-state that is losing authority vis-à-vis the market. Corporate cosmopolitanism celebrates individuals who use mobility, cultural adaptability, and flexible citizenship as tactics to broaden their career options and accumulate capital, beyond the realm of politics. Rizvi suggests many international students, alive to the strategic economic possibilities offered by global mobility in education, share this perspective. Their outlook "is framed by the role they believe international education to play in better positioning them within the changing structures of the global economy, which increasingly prizes the skills of intercultural experiences and a cosmopolitan outlook."[45] In the corporate imagining, "cultural exchange" is seen as producing new hybrid global forms transmitted by global communications as a form of global consumption.[46] But corporate cosmopolitans are too quick to dismiss the continuing potentials of the nation-state and unable to explain how tensions between global systems and particularist nation-states are resolved. And corporate cosmopolitanism's notion that globalization opens up "new emancipatory possibilities" seems absurd given the evidence of continuing and probably increasing inequalities.[47]

Corporate cosmopolitanism is the creed of globally imperial countries and of globally mobile individuals with the full menu of personal options. In that respect it is not so different from the globalism that some of its practitioners adopt.

In the face of corporate cosmopolitanism, some advocate nationally based multicultural approaches to cross-cultural relations. Under multiculturalism, nondominant communities retain their identity on a subordinate basis while being integrated into dominant national forms. The equivalent in international education is Berry's notion of "integration," in which minority groups maintain their cultural integrity and the "dominant society" accepts diversity, but the minorities become "an integral part" of the larger social network.[48] However, as Anderson notes, this indicates an asymmetrical relationship in which international students are positioned as "deficient in some way" in relation to the primary culture.[49] "While lip-service is paid to the notion of integration as involving both international and local students, the burden of integration tends to fall on visible international students."[50] But, remarks Anderson, international students do not become integrated as imagined. She cites Babha, who refers to "jarring" and "grappling" within contexts of uneven power.[51] Her own empirical studies of changing international student identities "highlight ongoing movement, complexity and tension rather than endpoints and neat resolutions." Multiculturalism is not just asymmetrical; it is culturally essentialist.

Rizvi makes the point that cultures are dynamic and interpenetrated rather than demarcated.[52] "Cultural identities can no longer be assumed as static and nation-bound, and are created instead in deterritorialized spaces." Cultures are not pure but contaminated with each other. Migrant communities use communications and media to maintain active homeland links. "Multiculturalism takes its moral universe to be the nation. If it is to survive then it needs to interpret the local and the national within the wider global context."[53] The antidote to corporate globalism is not multiculturalism but another kind of relational cosmopolitanism. In fact, as Vertovec and Cohen state, "in contrast to multiculturalism, cosmopolitanism is now increasingly invoked to avoid the pitfalls of essentialism or some kind of zero-sum, all or nothing understanding of identity issues within a nation-state framework."[54]

What then is the desired form of relational cosmopolitanism? Hall suggests that in the more globally "open" spaces that constitute the contemporary world: "We witness the situation of communities that are not simply isolated, atomistic individuals, nor are they well-bounded, singular, separated communities. We are in that open space that requires a kind of vernacular cosmopolitanism that is aware of the limitations of any one culture or any one identity and that is radically aware of its insufficiency in governing a wider society, but which nevertheless is not prepared to rescind its claims to the traces of difference, which make its life important."[55]

Rizvi notes that people always interpret the world from particular standpoints.[56] Global negotiations take place between these different standpoints. It is possible to engage with other societies without approving or adopting their values and practices. "Cosmopolitanism can be a worthy goal" only if it is "historically informed" and open to the diverse range of traditions manifest in cross-cultural relations. It can be understood as "an ethical attitude to global connectedness,"[57] human relations amid swirling changes, with identity free to range over many possible contents. Vertovec and Cohen cite Kwame Anthony Appiah, who suggests being a "cosmopolitan patriot" by "celebrating different human ways of being while sharing commitment to the political culture of a single nation-state."[58] An alternative approach is to celebrate one's country where and to the extent that it contributes to the global common good, the standpoint of the patriotic cosmopolitan. There are many other possible positions.

Global Attributes

What are the desired attributes of the cosmopolitan person? Psychological research on international education provides one set of answers. Almost 30 years ago Church summed up the characteristics of the "potentially good adjuster" as follows:

> Early investigators of sojourner adjustment hypothesized that attitudes reflecting a closed mind and the ethnocentric tendencies described in the authoritarian studies would inhibit the sojourner in coping effectively with new social norms, values, and language forms. Gardner described the "universal communicator" as having a well-integrated personality, a central organization of the extroverted type, a value system that includes the "values of all", a socialization of cultural universals, and a high degree of sensitivity toward others. He suggested that the universal communicator would have the least difficulty in adjusting to another culture. More recently, the "multi-cultural" (Adler) or "mediating" person (Bochner) has been described as having the cultural sensitivity, resiliency, and pattern of identity that allows him or her to adjust to and serve as a link between multiple cultures.[59]

Though there are few empirical data to support it, Church is sure that "more positive sojourner adjustment or favorability of attitudes has been related to less authoritarianism, increased personal flexibility, increased modernism, sociability and assertiveness, and more realistic sojourn goals and expectations."[60] Pedersen suggests that "attitudes favouring open-mindedness, the value of knowledge, and greater freedom in the relationship between the sexes become much more important" during the student sojourn.[61] He finds there is no clear-cut relation between personality type and successful adjustment, and measurement of personality-related variables across cultures is problematic.[62] However, he cites cosmopolitan virtues such as "empathy, interest in local culture, flexibility, tolerance" and leans to Adler's idea of "multicultural man," a malleable, polymorphous person who is "skilled in constant adaptation to new values, whatever they may be, rather than knowledgeable about any particular culture. The multicultural person is always recreating an identity as roles are learned, modified or discarded in each discontinuous situation."[63] Here Pedersen moves close to the globalists. He also notes that managing plural identity is key: "There are also research studies on bi-national or bicultural persons, who belong simultaneously to two different societies and maintain two identities as they relate to their respective societies from within the context of one or another culture. Bicultural individuals have the potential to function with cognitive flexibility and are creatively adaptive in either of their two cultural identities."[64]

Other work in psychology emphasizes communicative competence; "sensitivity" to other cultures;[65] social decentring, the empathetic-like ability to take into consideration another person's perspectives, feelings, and thoughts;[66] an absence of bigotry; openness and critical thinking; and tolerance of ambiguity[67] and uncertainty management. Ward and colleagues discuss the sojourner fluent in moving through different cultural domains, the ideal mobile subject, which they identify with the Singaporean.[68] But these notions are limited to an individual adjustment paradigm and unsupported by theorization of the relational space.

The globalist literature provides another guide. Gunesch focuses on encounters with and a valuing of cultural diversity, against tendencies to global cultural homogenization,[69] and on "interconnectedness itself."[70] The cosmopolitan is a metacultural broker and network maker. Following Hannerz,[71] Gunesch's cosmopolitan knows the local but does not become local. Above all, the cosmopolitan engages with the Other. It is "an intellectual and ethical stand of openness to divergent cultural experiences."[72] In these imaginings, the cosmopolitan person displays many fluencies and functions of observing, connecting, communicating, participating, sharing, engaging, and understanding.

Rizvi notes many of the globalist formulations of intercultural education, internationalization, and the skills or values needed for "global citizenship" are presented "in a highly generalized and abstract manner making it difficult to infer implications for specific practices of curricular and pedagogic reform."[73] These are positioned alongside a variety of more mundane, practical notions. Deardorff attempts to determine the desired "intercultural" attributes using two methods: a Delphi-style inquiry to establish consensus among scholars of interculturality, and a questionnaire sent to "U.S. institutional administrators of internationalization strategies."[74] The scholars embodied "Western and mostly U.S.-centric view of intercultural competence, a view in which such competence resides largely within the individual."[75] Both scholars and administrators used a variety of generic terminology. The consensus formed primarily around notions of intercultural communicability and behavior rather than the metalevel global perspective.

Among the scholars the popular definition of intercultural competence was "the ability to communicate effectively and appropriately in intercultural situations based on one's intercultural knowledge, skills, and attitudes." The components of intercultural competence included generic personal attributes "such as curiosity, general openness, and respect for other cultures" and "the ability to shift one's frame of reference appropriately."[76] Among administrators, the highest ranked definitions were "knowledge of others; knowledge of self; skills to interpret and relate; skills to discover and/or to interact; valuing others' values, beliefs, and behaviors; and relativizing one's self." Linguistic competence was key. Several participant schools had institutional definitions of intercultural competence. "The top three common elements were the awareness, valuing, and understanding of cultural differences; experiencing other cultures; and self-awareness of one's own culture." All three "stress the underlying importance of cultural awareness, both of one's own as well as others' cultures."[77] The administrators were more enthusiastic than the scholars about measuring and testing intercultural competence.[78]

In a practical approach to defining cosmopolitan competences, described as "transnational," Vertovec talks of managing a diversity of interpretations and meanings. This includes knowledge of "the central beliefs, values, practices and paradoxes of counterpart cultures and societies"; the capacity to interpret one's own society in the light of others and vice versa; "the ability to manage multiple identities"; an emotional stance of willingness to open up and curiosity about the Other; "a capacity to foresee the synergistic potential of diverse cultural perspectives in problem solving"; an ability to envision mutually acceptable solutions; poly-linguistic abilities; code-switching and the capacity to read a range of messages; functionality in global relationships; and working across borders.[79]

Schuerholz-Lehr defines "intercultural competence" as "a set of congruent behaviors, attitudes, and policies displayed and applied by individuals that enable these individuals to interact effectively in cross-cultural situations." "Global awareness" is understood to mean "the extent to which a person is cognizant of the fact that experiences and events are part of an international, global, or world society, and his [sic] understanding of himself as a member of that society."[80] Likewise, Olson and Kroeger assert that "to be globally competent a person should have enough substantive knowledge, perceptual understanding and intercultural communication skills to effectively interact in our globally interdependent world."[81] We note here that the terms "global" and "intercultural" (and "international") are sometimes used interchangeably in the research literature, and more so in the policy statements of governments and educational institutions. But to what extent is "global" tied to global systems that are potentially homogenizing; to what extent is the term a signifier of international and intercultural engagement premised on diversity? Internationalization strategies often gesture to diversity without achieving cultural engagement. It must be specifically structured into the program.

For Fennes and Hapgood intercultural learning means greater openness to other cultures and overcoming of cultural bias and ethnocentrism.[82] For Otten, "The outcome of intercultural learning is intercultural competence, a long-term change of a person's knowledge (cognition), attitudes (emotions), and skills (behaviour) to enable positive and effective interaction with members of other cultures . . . it results from the experience of differences that cause cognitive irritation, emotional unbalance, and a disruption of one's own cultural worldview."[83]

Lasonen argues that "the task of international education is to guide citizens into continuous cultural interpretation, which is part of cultural competence."[84] For Lasonen intercultural education should emphasize "knowledge, skills, attitudes and responsibilities linked with perceiving and understanding the world as a single interconnected entity"; that is, it should be global in orientation.[85] Graduates should have learned to "tolerate diversity and to embrace alteration and differences without feeling a major threat to their own shared cultural identity."[86]

COSMOPOLITAN RESPONSES

Cosmopolitan perspectives (variously defined) have shaped on one hand research and scholarship and on the other hand intercultural teaching in international education.

The cosmopolitan standpoint drives sharp criticism of ethnocentrism in international programs, for example the assumptions that Western or English language ways of life and educational practice are either (1) universal to education or (2) manifestly superior to other cultural sets. One response has been to subject the ethnocentric narratives about both "Asian learning" and Western education to empirical scrutiny. Ninnes and colleagues note that learner autonomy and critical thinking are by no means universal in Western and Australian higher education. They investigate the stereotype of the Asian learner in relation to postgraduate students from India. In the cultural-deficit approach Asian students in Australia are seen to have been formed by "rote, reproductive, surface, teacher-centered and dependent approaches to learning; which lack analytical and critical perspectives; and which have occurred in contexts dominated by examinations and substantially lacking in educational resources."[87] The researchers find that some of these notions do apply to undergraduate education in India. They cite an examination obsession within the system and "the general lack of an analytical and critical approach."[88] For the most part, however, the stereotype is problematic. It misunderstands the role of memorization and repetition, which are often used as an aid to deep learning. In India, phenomena of dependence, lack of autonomy, classroom formalism, and teacher-centeredness play out in complex and highly variable ways,[89] as they do also in Australia. Ninnes and colleagues suggest that instead of a "culture-deficit" approach, it is more helpful to use the "culture-proficiency" approach developed by Volet and collaborators. When using this approach it is acknowledged that "while there are variations in learning across cultures, the 'home-grown' strategies used by international students are to some extent useful in the Australian university context and that students are able to adapt their learning to the new context."[90] This broadens the cultural base of self-development.

Doherty and Singh examine foundation courses for international students in Australia. These programs are premised on a cultural deficit approach. They impose a "pristine" and "purified" notion of Western learning that excludes the prior foundations of international students' learning (and represses the memory of the often violent East-West cultural entanglement). By emptying out the students' prior knowledge—or attempting to—they impair cognitive development. Unless the prior education and self-formation of each international student is taken into account, no teaching and learning strategy will be fully effective. The scope for incremental learning becomes reduced because the early foundations are removed from sight and the scaffolding kicked away. Learning becomes more dependent on transformational leaps in learning, which steepens the slope in front of non-English-speaking international students and renders their learning more fraught and pressured.

These foundation programs subordinate the students, even while promising to empower them as self-actualizing agents. With unconscious irony, one teacher talked of how she felt obliged to impose on the students a student-centered pedagogy to "try to force them to do things that they should be doing all the time in the tutorial situation."[91] Remarkably, the foundation programs emphasize the need for internationals to become empowered self-forming learners while subordinating the students and denying their prior capacity in self-formation! It is not simply that the ethnocentric impulse is stronger than the commitment to self-determination, it is that self-determination is seen as *only* valid in an Anglo-American framework. It seems that people from certain cultures are, or should be seen as, "more free" than people from other cultures; and "Asian learners" are only valued when they become, for all purposes, Australian learners.

A related strand in the cosmopolitan critique emphasizes cultural relativism. For example, in a comparison of the United States and four European countries, Harkness and colleagues find that "cognitive competence is relevant to specific cultures, to the social and physical contexts in which the child participates in organized activities, and to the cultural and societal demands."[92] Educational traditions are divergent within the Western family. Teekens remarks that "in spite of the fact that teaching is universal in nature, it tends to be very national in character. This applies in particular to higher education, despite the claim that knowledge is international and knows no borders. Even when the curriculum is more or less the same in terms of content, the method of delivery will differ according to national cultural background."[93]

In other words, the relational environment involves not just multiple and divergent identities, it involves contrasting ways of seeing, as Yuval-Davis points out. Some of this critical work focuses on the specific character of Anglo-American education. In an issue of *Comparative Education* focused on "Western-centrism," Elliott and Grigorenko note that while academic proponents of Anglo-American and European theories and practices often recognize their ideas are "culturally situated" and resist the idea their theories and practices can be directly transferred into other cultural contexts without negative effects, the same constraint is not shared by reform-minded policy makers and consultants for international agencies such as the World Bank.[94] In the same journal, Sternberg applies the critique of ethnocentrism to assessment practices.[95] Singh states that the failure of Anglo-Australians students to understand themselves in a relativist framework and imagine themselves as a culture is a major constraint on intercultural approaches. Local students are "yet to think of themselves as Others."[96] They are protected from this reflexivity by Australian "isolationism" (which parallels American isolationism and exceptionalism, though at a lesser level of hubris). To understand relations between international and local students, it is necessary to problematize not just international student identity but also "the power of Anglo-ethnicity."[97]

Lee and Rice make a similar point in the United States. "Some of the more serious challenges are due to inadequacies within the host society . . . the responsibility is often left to the student to 'adjust' or 'adapt' to the host culture rather than for institutions to understand and try to accommodate their unique needs."[98] This is a particular problem for certain students, such as nonwhite students in the United States, who must deal with heightened cultural obstacles. Where the problems move from communication to difficulties involving prejudice, it is the host society that is in question. Yet "most of the literature concerning international student experiences describes their difficulties as issues of adapting or coping, which embodies the assumption that international students bear the responsibility to persist, overcome their discomfort, and integrate into the host society." The assumption underlying this is that "host institutions are impartial and without fault." Few studies consider the manner in which institutions and individuals tend to marginalize international students, whether intentionally or not.[99]

Empirical studies of international student satisfaction find that the level of satisfaction is lowest in those areas in which respect for international students' own cultural backgrounds is integral, indicating the absence of reciprocity. These include Selvadurai's survey of international students at New York Technical College, Trice and Yoo's survey of international graduate students at another American university, and the 2006 Australian Education International survey.[100]

Implications for Teaching and Learning

For Rizvi, cosmopolitanism in education should be interpreted "not as a universal moral principle, nor a prescription recommending a form of political configuration, but as a mode of learning about, and ethically engaging with, new cultural formations," especially cultural formations vectored by "global interconnectivity."[101] Therefore, intercultural education should build students both a "critical global imagination"[102] and a sense of "situatedness" in the world, including "positionality in relation to the social networks, political institutions and social relations that are no longer confined to particular communities and nations, but potentially connect up with the rest of the world."[103] Following Said, Rizvi argues that grasping a sense of contingency is also important.[104] A cosmopolitan education will develop in students a set of "epistemic virtues." The desired approach is historical and critical. In learning, emphasizes Rizvi, knowing is always partial and tentative, and entails continuing "critical exploration and imagination." A cosmopolitan education should emphasize "understanding relationalities" and imagining alternatives.[105]

Simply, intercultural education should equip students to make their lives in a relational environment marked both by local grounding and interconnectedness, in which each person's position and affiliations are both given and chosen. "Cosmopolitanism is only worth pursuing if we are able to use it as an instrument of critical understanding and moral improvement." In other words, the cosmopolitan agenda in education is "at once empirical and normative." Empirically, it offers understanding of the effects of global transformations in people's lives. It also opens the question of "how we *should* work with these transformations, creatively and in ways that are potentially progressive," and in such a way that education diminishes rather than increases inequalities.[106]

This also requires evolution of "a critical global imagination" and a "de-parochialization of the processes of learning and teaching"[107] by restraining the extent to which national interest frames the curriculum and taking an open stance toward other nations and cultures. Here there is much to be gained in collaborative cross-border projects between groups of students, in which local problems can be examined on a cooperative basis while being linked to global processes. Even without the collaborative dimension, students can learn to "interrogate how things are done differently in different places."[108] Sanderson takes a similar position. For him a cosmopolitan outlook is "underpinned more by attitudes of openness, interconnectivity, interdependence, reciprocity and plurality" than particular cultural contents.[109] He argues for "a *rooted* cosmopolitanism as an arrangement that requires both the local and everything beyond the local to constitute its meaning." Again the argument for a multidimensional approach to the global setting is contrasted with an abstract globalism. Sanderson remarks that the alternative is to abandon the local in favor of universal moral cosmopolitanism (a hyperglobalist worldview), which would be "both illogical and undesirable."[110] Multidimensionality does not guarantee cosmopolitanism, but it is one of the necessary conditions for a practice of relational cosmopolitanism. Along the same lines Luke states that "What is needed is . . . the re-envisioning of a transcultural and cosmopolitan teacher: a teacher with the capacity to shunt between the local and the global, to explicate and engage with the broad flows of knowledge and information, technologies and populations, artefacts and practices that characterize the present historical moment."[111]

Luke joins the notion of cosmopolitan teaching to a critique of the narrow take on cross-border relations embodied in neoliberal policies. Likewise, in their notion of cosmopolitanism Matthews and Sidhu contrast cosmopolitanism with an international education dominated primarily by economic interests. They combine prior commitment to a place with reflexive distancing from that place. As with Rizvi, this suggests classrooms that simulate the relational global setting.[112]

CONCLUSION

A cosmopolitan education sets out to foster the human capacity in multiple relations across the three dimensions of global connectivity, national culture and government, and local day-to-day life, while at the same time building the capacity to understand and manage a diversity of cultural positions.

Exactly what constitutes the cosmopolitan relational order is difficult finally to pin down because it changes. Cosmopolitanism is a process rather than a goal. All universal rights-based orders are temporary, being open to replacement by another particular that masquerades as a universal. Yuval-Davis argues that "We cannot—and should not attempt to—construct a homogenous, or even unified, political order. Rather, we should engage in a transversal politics, bound by common political values, informed by recognitions of our differential locations and identifications, and led by a global discourse in which translation, rather than a unitary language, is seen as the cosmopolitan tool."[113]

A transversal politics has three features. First, "standpoint episte-mology, which recognises that from each positioning the world is seen differently." Any knowledge based on one position is "unfinished" or incomplete. Second, notions of difference encompass rather than replace notions of equality. This assumes a priori respect for other people's positionings. Third, transversal politics distinguishes between social position, group identity, and values, noting that one cannot necessarily be read from another.[114] The task is to create a zone for negotiation and within it to secure active cooperation based on mutual willingness to listen and perhaps to change. Within the cosmopolitan order there is a plurality of positions without privileging any one posi-tion, as under globalism. But the cosmopolitan is a participant in that order with her or his own social position, group identity, and values. This offers a far richer environment for personal development than does mainstream psychology, always handicapped by the absence of a sociology, and provides a stronger grounding in the real world than does globalism.

Teaching and learning strategies produce relational cosmopoli-tanism by creating conditions in the classroom that enable students to imagine that relational setting and evolve the attributes required to function within it. The next task is to dismantle the barriers that inhibit local student participation in the cosmopolitan project. Those barriers are discussed in Chapters 5 and 6. The implications of cosmo-politanism for teaching and learning are explored again in Chapter 8.

CHAPTER 4

——✦◉✦——

INTERNATIONAL STUDENT LIVES

INTRODUCTION: THE STUDENT INTERVIEWS

It is time to turn to the practical substance of notions such as agency, ethnocentrism, and cosmopolitanism in international and cross-cultural education. Let us look at what they mean in the day-to-day lives of international students.

In 2003–2009 the authors of this book, together with colleagues, investigated international student security.[1] The core of the empirical research was a program of two hundred semistructured interviews of 30–60 minutes with individual international students. These interviews were conducted in the years 2005–2007 at nine public research universities in Australia as follows: the Universities of Ballarat (Melbourne city campus), Deakin, Melbourne, RMIT, Swinburne, and Victoria in the city of Melbourne; Deakin University in Geelong; the University of Ballarat in Ballarat; New South Wales and Sydney Universities in Sydney; and the provincial Rockhampton campus of Central Queensland University. The students were drawn from 34 countries with 86 percent from Asia. Just over half were women, approximating the gender split in the source international student population.

In the semistructured interviews a standard set of 63 "stem" questions were used, covering all aspects of international student security. The interview format generated a large volume of valuable data, providing substantial insights into cross-cultural relations, not all of which had been anticipated by the researchers (and many of which have yet to be published). This is the virtue of interview-based studies. Most studies involving international students are not interview-based; they are sample surveys structured to represent the source population.

Surveys generate an impressive amount of information that can then be quantified ("crunched") for analytical purposes but are limited to preset questions and so confined by the researchers' prior assumptions. There is no opportunity for those under study to put things in their own words or explore new issues arising. In contrast, semistructured interviews are like a conversation. The researcher asks a stem question on a topic and follows with impromptu questions based on the answers. Depending on the answers some later stem questions are unnecessary and omitted, while long exchanges can develop in areas relevant to inquiry. This interactive method enables wholly new issues to emerge, and in a handful of cases the interviewees themselves contribute to modifying the overall research inquiry.

The interview questions focused on a range of aspects of the human security of international students studying in Australia. In the research *human security* was defined as "maintenance of a stable capacity for self-determining human agency." Security was seen as having two aspects: protected and proactive. This extends beyond a subsistence, protective, or welfare model of human security and beyond the model of students as consumers in a market, to encompass the notion of international students as active self-determining agents with "capability."[2] This is a more advanced notion of human security than in current policies on globally mobile refugees, who are modeled as persons needing protection without much emphasis on proactive agency. The United Nations Development Programme formalizes human security as "protection from sudden and hurtful disruptions in the patterns of daily life; whether in homes, jobs or in communities"; and "safety from chronic threats such as hunger, disease and repression."[3] This encompasses security in relation to food, health, personal safety, and the political economic order. It suggests active human agency only in relation to economic sustenance. In contrast, the definition of human security used in the study in which the interviews were conducted encompassed the capacity for agency in all spheres, enabling the exercise of all human rights (aside from rights exclusive to national citizens, such as voting). This is also consistent with the mission of education in forming self-developing individuals. In this larger view the security of international students is affected by language proficiency, personal safety, freedom from discrimination and abuse, consumer information, financial viability, safety at work, housing, health and welfare services, personal and social networks, relations with public and university authorities, and all forms of cross-cultural relationship in the country of education. There were interview questions in all of these areas.

What follows are the stories of six of the student interviewees, as explained in their own words. The implications of these student lives for the larger issues involved in intercultural education are reviewed at the end of the chapter.

CINDI FROM MALAYSIA

"Often white people are surprised when I open my mouth and start speaking English to them."

Cindi[4] is a medical student in the late stages of her program. She comes from a Chinese family in Malaysia. Her parents, who are English-speaking Christians (Cindi can speak Malay but no Chinese language), believe that the standard of education in Australia is "certainly higher than Malaysia" and "overseas education in a Western country is preferable because by and large Malays are given more support in Malaysia." It is hard for "Chinese and aliens" to get into a university. Cindi arrived in Australia at the age of 16 for the final two years of secondary education. She was a boarder at a private school, one of only two Asian students. In the initial period it was difficult for her to make friends because "I didn't understand any of the slang" and "we have very different sense of humour." She found herself confronted by the peer culture of the school, which required a major cross-cultural adaptation that was entirely on the terms of the locals:

> I was one of two Asian kids in the entire school, which was a bit daunting. The other one went to parties and drank with the others. So I didn't really fit in there. But I learnt very quickly that to fit in, you have to not be an achiever. When I was in school, I tried very hard to be mediocre . . . to try not to stand out. You already stand out physically, and they expect [you] as an Asian to be hardworking. Everyone says, oh, you Asians, you're so hardworking, I get it in hospitals all the time [from] patients. Well the reason why we're here is that our parents are really struggling to make ends meet to keep us here, so we can't afford to slack. (laughs) Yeah, so I used to study in the toilet, in the middle of the night in the bathroom. So nobody knew I was doing work. Which probably didn't help because they thought I was naturally a freak, which was not quite true. It was actually quite difficult in the beginning. If I could go back now, I would do a lot of things differently. (female, 26, medicine, Malaysia)

Like others, Cindi wanted to fit in and be part of the "cool crowd." "I think every female wants to be cool." But whether it was because of being Chinese, being good at studies, or not drinking at parties, that didn't happen. She became comfortable about her identity in Australia though, learning to manage it for herself rather than taking it from established groups. In retrospect she realized, "I was largely right. I had some friends eventually, they weren't the cool crowd. I never really thought about it, but now that I do . . . I used to think to myself about Australians, I don't respect them even though they are cool. And if I had hung out with the cool crowd I would have been an extremely boring person, without personality, who just basically fit to mould."

At school, exclusion on the basis of cultural identity had overlapped with exclusion on the basis of in-school culture. However, being good at studies could be turned into a personal positive that it made it easier to bear the lack of coolness and opened up empowering options for the future. And the potential for Othering (being excluded on the basis of ascribed difference) could be modified by the way one handled oneself.

After leaving school, Cindi's pathway had opened up. The university environment is both more cosmopolitan than the school's and more accepting of academic prowess. At university she shares accommodation in the staff section of the hospital with other international students. The housing is basic, and there have been five break ins. Cindi lost her camera and gifts from her parents, but her laptop has survived each time. She mixes freely with local students in classes. Just as she was unwilling to conform fully to the local peer culture at school, at university she refuses to identify primarily as a student from Malaysia.

> I have a lot of contempt for some of the things that happen at uni. I do a lot of stuff with my boyfriend . . . we organize things with friends, a bit quirky and a bit different. I don't go for a lot of mainstream stuff that the university offers. I go to the gym a lot but you don't meet a lot of friends there. I don't generally like clubs especially the nationality clubs. In my first year I was a member of the Malaysian Students Association and I found that it just sets you aside from other people . . . If you join a student organisation that is about that particular race or that particular nationality, you've just labelled yourself, you've just put yourself in that group of people.

After almost ten years in Australia none of Cindi's friends, who are mostly fellow medical students, are Asian. She has traveled a long way toward integration in Australian society while sustaining her own inner-defined identity. Her boyfriend, who has already graduated as a doctor, is a local. "It's nice to have him around. But of course he's white so he doesn't quite understand sometimes." In Australia there is "less racial and gender discrimination and less religious discrimination also" than in Malaysia, though Cindi says that as a Christian she is "part of the mainstream" in Australia and has not been through the experience of, for example, being Muslim. Like most nonwhite international students in the study, her experiences of discrimination and abuse, which have had a mild impact, have mostly occurred in the external community. There is an underlying stereotyping process that is always present, one she has learned to manage so that, as at school, she stands out less. She does not need to conform to the lowest common denominator in Australia but she has learned to blend in, and to use her wits when she is briefly Othered:

> When I was in Year 12, I was in a tram and a drunk man told me to go home. He didn't mean to school. I've heard patients say stuff to me, but nothing in a racist sort of way, more like, "Don't Asians have blue eyes?" A woman actually asked me that. Like, what planet are you from? (Laughs) "Blue eyes." So yeah, I do get some remarks that make you stand out. People have preconceptions when they see me. That's why I wear make-up, partly, because if I didn't wear make-up, I'd look like every other Asian person. And they immediately stereotype . . . often white people are surprised when I open my mouth and start speaking English to them. They can't believe I can speak English and I say to them, do you believe I just got here six months ago. (Laughing) They are actually gullible, some of them. I'm very quick . . . so yeah, do get some discriminatory remarks but they're not always said with a malicious intent.

Cindi has had one bad experience in the labor market. While she was working in a shop that sold coats and jackets, the shop owner used to make prejudicial comments. Cindi didn't tell her parents because they would have been very upset. "She was a bit racist (laughs). The boss. She was a particularly nasty old woman . . . she often gave me a very hard time. She'd make remarks [implying that] you people, you don't know how to clean up, or sweep the floor, this is how you sweep the floor. Things like that. Basically it just meant I wasn't doing things her way but she made generalizations that her way was the right way, culturally. But she was not representative of her culture. She was a nasty piece of job."

But Cindi likes Australia and has found her own accommodation and empowerment with it. "The good differences are freedom of speech, freedom to be creative and to express in art, in speech or in writing." People can find friends "with whom they feel safe to be themselves whatever country they come from" and "whatever nationality, whatever religion, whatever race." She wants to stay in Australia after graduation. Her advice to other international students is "keep an open mind and don't sequester yourself to friends of your own nationality," "be an individual," and "if you want to get to know Australia, live as an Australian," all of which by and large she has done herself. Helped by being fluent in English from day one and sure of her intellectual capacity, having learned to survive while being herself at school, having worked her way successfully through medicine to final year after initial difficulties, and despite occasional problems of loneliness as when her boyfriend is away, Cindi has plenty of agency. She has become fully confident in her capacity to fashion her own identity and the course of her life.

In transition, and closer to Australia than Malaysia as she is, the thing that Cindi finds most difficult is not being nonwhite or Malaysian or Chinese but being foreign. "I'm constantly aware that I'm not Australian, that I'm international . . . the basic assumption is that I'm going to go home." The only time during the interview when her confidence slipped, the laughter stopped, and more negative emotions surfaced, was when she talked about the immigration department. There, all of her strategies based on being herself, drawing on her intelligence, and casting off her old Malaysian skin while evading Australian pressures to conform, accommodating Australian culture flexibly by using its freedoms, are blocked.

> Oh the immigration department is the most frustrating thing ever. You go out to [location of an immigration office] which is quite far. You sit there and wait half a day or something. You go in to beg for an extension of your visa from someone who can't speak English as well as I can, who barely speaks English and who is a permanent resident of this country while I'm struggling just to stay here. It's extremely frustrating. I think I'm more Australian than some Australians. And it's really difficult to be in this state of limbo not knowing whether you're actually Australian or not. It's kind of degrading to go there and say, I need to extend my visa and this is why and just hope out of the kindness of their hearts they don't say, no you're not, you're going home. There's always that fear that he's going to say, doesn't check up, go home. Also I hate the fact that the immigration hotline is just a bunch of recorded messages, you'll never speak to a person. That is really annoying because every one is an individual. You have your own problem that has an individual twist to it and you've got your own case to make. One sweeping tape-recorded message cannot possibly solve

that problem. The Internet site is pretty useless. They make a lot of changes in immigration law. I would have liked to apply for permanent residency. What I didn't realize until too late, because I didn't know about it, was apparently I could have applied after my third year of medicine, because I got a BSc med degree in the first three years. I didn't realize there is a window period of a year between that time and applying. Now it is too late. I would've liked to have known that, but it's not made very obvious. I found out from somebody else who called them up and asked directly. She was too late as well and she was really upset. Immigration is one thing that really frustrates me. I hate it. It's based on an archaic white Australian policy.

Sitting waiting at the immigration office, Cindi is robbed of her personal agency, her hard-won capacity to manage herself and flourish in the world, as surely as the burglars that invaded the student apartments had once stolen her camera.

JABE FROM SINGAPORE

"A little bit segregated from the Australian community"

Jabe's family is also Chinese. He is from Singapore and had not experienced the same discrimination in the home country that Cindi's family faced in Malaysia. Since his high school days he has always been fascinated by Chinese literature and theater and he was very happy to find an Australian university where he could study them together. Before enrolling at the university in Australia he had completed the required period of citizen military service in Singapore. In fact his first impressions of Australia had been formed by that time in the national military, where service personnel were routinely warned of the dangers of racism:

One of the main things that was talked about in Singapore was the racism in Australia, especially when I was in the military. During my two and a half years in the military we came to Australia twice for training. Before we left for Australia we were briefed. They say, after you finished your training, when you have two or three days of rest and recreation in the cities of Australia, "please go out in groups. Don't go alone because you might be attacked" So [later when] I was going to come here alone without my fellow servicemen, as a university student, this fear struck me. (male, 23, humanities/performing arts, Singapore)

Initially, it seemed, the fear was justified. In his first week in Australia Jabe had a frightening experience while walking from the university to his residence 15 minutes away:

> I was in the first week, two years ago. Really scared. Everything was new. I was walking home one afternoon and approached a traffic light along the route. A car went past, with no top. There were four Australians inside, high school kids, shouting at me, "hey, hey, Chinese," and calling me many things. "Hey go back to your country!" I thought oh, it's terrible; the people here don't like me. They want me to go back, and I've just arrived here. What am I going to do? I am living here for three years. You're alone and you're really scared, in the middle of broad daylight. As the car approached the red light it stopped. I was thinking, should I turn and run or should I walk up to them and see what's going to happen. I decided to do the latter and walked slowly towards the traffic light. Luckily, when I was near the traffic light turned green and they sped off. I would now think that these are just high school students wanting to have a bit of fun, immature people. I would ignore it.

Since then Jabe's experience has improved. Australia is different from Singapore. His home city is more "fast paced" and competitive. Sydney is more "laid back . . . I think they enjoy the pace of life here." But that isn't a drawback for Jabe, though he misses the "supper culture"—the 10 pm snack for those who work late, which is part of life in Singapore. What makes Australia work for Jabe is his accommodation arrangements. He lives in a student residence on campus with 240 students, a mix of locals and internationals "from all over the world." He is very happy with residential college living. It feels safe and secure, it solves the problem of finding food, and there is more time to study. The scope of cross-cultural mixing is a major benefit. "It helped me integrate into Australian society in a very fast way." He continues, "You get to meet a lot of people from different backgrounds and you also assimilate very fast into the local culture because there are so many Australians there and you don't just meet them for class. You live with these people, you talk to them every day, you get to see them when you go for supper, so I think that helps, in assimilating me into Australian life in a shorter time."

But it is not a seamless integration. Like the larger student body does on Australian campuses, the college community separates into two broad groups. Jabe feels close to other Asian students in the college. The deeper intercultural experience is more with the other internationals than with the local students.

Basically in my college there are two [groups] . . . there is a relatively big Asian community in my college. A little bit segregated from the Australian community. But within ourselves we are quite united and close, and I see most of them, they are my close buddies, most of the time, so I go to them when I have problems. I go to them when I have no problems and we are like brothers and sisters.

Q. Have you experienced periods of loneliness or isolation?

A. Of course.

Q. Who did you talk to?

A. I think I was lucky to be in a college environment because I mean I'm not the only one who is new and lonely. There are other people out there, so I think when you are faced with that there are always two things you can do. One is you can hide in your room and cry alone, or you go out and try to meet people and talk to them, and say "hey, hello, how are you?" And then you say "I'm sad and lonely," and they say "hey I'm sad and lonely too, let's talk, OK." That is how I developed one of my closest friendships here. A Pakistani friend, totally from the other side of the world. I'd never really heard of Pakistan, he's Muslim. But we became really good friends and within a year we were the best of friends. I think I'm very lucky to be in the college environment.

Jabe feels that there is something of a barrier between him and the local students, however. Relations are friendly. The problem is not racism, not really, and it is not language. He can communicate easily, though he cannot always converse easily. The problem is cultural difference. It is a question of values. Compared with local students, he has different notions of what is significant.

Behind each culture there are different underlying assumptions. There are certain rules in each society which don't exist in another. I tend to put people on the spot most of the time. Unintentionally, but it happens. I don't really think it's the language issue, I think I speak really good English compared to Australians. But the problem is our underlying cultures are different. So when I sit in the dining hall with a group of Australians and just talk, sometimes I fail to strike conversation. And that never happens when I'm in a group of Asians. I don't think it's because they are particularly racist, we're just different I think.

The other problem that he has faced in Australia is in his theater activities. He is involved in the NSW Theatrical Society, but being Asian—and also not being Australian—seem to be a disadvantage when vying for theater parts, especially those focused on Australian news, politics, or history. Jabe feels it as a kind of unconscious discrimination. "They have an underlying assumption that they are less likely to use you." Sometimes, he says, "I feel a bit angry. It's like 'hey, you know, that's a simple act, I can do it, why are you not using me?'"

MIGUEL FROM SPAIN

"Racism is not such an issue here."

Miguel is working on a PhD in biotechnology. He originally came from the Basque country in Spain. His grandparents were immigrants into the Basque country from other parts of Spain and Portugal, and he spoke Spanish at home as a child. He had learned both Basque and English at school and is now fully fluent in English. Prior to coming to Australia he had completed a master's degree in business at Arizona State University. After graduation he worked in New York and in Tokyo for IBM. Aged 33, he is married to a Japanese woman he met when they were both studying in the United States. He could have studied in Tokyo but feels that "Japan is a bit kind of isolated" and sees Australia as a better starting point for later career moves. "Australia is a small country, a bit local too, but it's very well connected to the United States and the UK." Australia also has other advantages. "First of all, there are not some [of the issues] that you have in America. Racism is not such an issue here. Things are more cool and relaxed. People take it easy . . . you have to enjoy the education and the lifestyle. You have to smell the roses on the way. Second, this is more inexpensive. It's cheaper to live here. The fees [are cheaper]" (male, 33, PhD in medicine, Spain).

The cost gap might be narrowing, however. The costs of tuition and accommodation are rising, and there are charges for items like Internet use, which had been free in the United States.

It is notable that unlike many nonwhite students in the study, and unlike four of the students whose stories are told in this chapter, Miguel mentions no experiences of stereotyping, discrimination, or abuse. Nevertheless, cultural difference is a factor for him. Despite a long fluency in English it had taken time to learn to talk with people in Australia. Both the language and the politeness regime have surprised him. The politeness regime governs the way the language is used:

> I have communication problems with Australians. The way the Australian people speak and American people speak English is totally different. Maybe they are a bit more sincere here. Australian people are more

honest so they don't intend to be politically correct all the time. If they feel good, and they feel like being kind, they are kind and talkative. If they don't they [incomprehensible words] . . . At the beginning it was a bit of an assault. I was expecting somebody to come in and say "good morning, how are you, can I help you, blah, blah, blah." I thought there was something I was doing wrong. Three years in Tokyo: I probably had become too localized to the Japanese system. [With] Australian people, they tend not to explain everything. If you don't ask, they don't tell you. If you want them to give you information you have to ask, otherwise they don't tell you.

Miguel feels that Australians are also less engaged with each other than people are in Spain. In Spain people seem to find more time to live life socially.

Life here is more colourful than in other countries like Britain or the United States, but it's still a bit kind of monochrome. They deal more with the neighbours and so on and so forth in Australia. But the range of things they do seems limited. How do they engage all the members of the community? Barbeques? In Spain you go to the park also, and you go to soccer matches. You do your life in the street more in Spain. It's not just the day of the barbeque and the day of the festivity, it's on a more constant basis.

But Miguel has no difficulty in making friends from a variety of backgrounds. There are local citizens he sees regularly, not so much typical Australian suburban residents as people like him who are world aware and at ease in different cultural contexts while sharing a common English language. He has attended dance classes and taught others dancing, though at 33 years old and married he is no longer up to partying. And anyway, most international students are first degree students and much younger than him. He doesn't have much in common with them. But he is too busy to be lonely. His wife had been lonely until she started working with one of their friends from Tokyo in web design. She is OK now.

A period as president of the university postgraduate students' association had absorbed Miguel. He has many stories about internal difficulties in the organization—"it was rough and tough"—and about dealing with a complex university bureaucracy. He recounts several incidents in detail, emphatically and with strong feelings. One thing Miguel is very critical about in the university is the lack of postgraduate scholarship support for international students. For most kind of awards it is necessary to have citizenship or permanent residence status. Postgraduate students are not supported on academic merit. Miguel sees this as a form of discrimination. But despite his problems with university policy, Miguel has much respect for his academic teachers and for his department. He is worked hard but receives excellent support and advice whenever he needs it.

Miguel appreciates the scope to do what he wants in Australia but has not planted deep roots. He has mixed feelings about the formal institutions. He says he has found the Australian Tax Office good to deal with, but he is less kind about the immigration department. "With immigration, I understand that the people are there . . . to make the international students' life miserable. They do accomplish their task indeed. Also they are there to make the immigrants or alien residents of Australia miserable, too, and they accomplish that task. What do you expect them to be? I don't like them much, but they do very well indeed."

He talks about changes in the immigration regulations concerning permanent residence, which have caught many international students halfway through their programs—including students from underdeveloped countries for whom the fees are relatively high and whose families have sacrificed financially to give them the opportunity to study abroad. This kind of thing is to be expected, he says. The government is not going to help noncitizens. "They don't even help the first Australians, and many other Australians who come from underprivileged backgrounds. End of story." He is sharply critical of the Australian approach to international students. Miguel is not indignant so much for himself as for many others he has seen in difficulty. Australia is less welcoming of skilled labor than is the United States. "If you want to put that kind of money, and you want to open yourself to global markets, you'd rather go to America. It's as simple as that. In America with a master's you can find your way. I did. I just didn't go ahead at the time because I didn't think I wanted to live in America. It's easy to finish your master's and get that one-year visa to work in a company."

He again uses "rough and tough" to describe the local scene. Confident and energetic, and engaged and resourceful with much negotiating experience, Miguel is confident that he can deal with anything in Australia. "Don't trust the government; find hope in yourself," he says. If Australia is not working for him he can go elsewhere. Miguel is a global cosmopolitan. He and his wife have plenty of work and study options. He knows it is not the same for all internationals. Prospective students should "do their homework" and "get the best advice that you can." They should think carefully about coming to Australia if they want to migrate.

NYASHA FROM ZIMBABWE

"There was one incident that I'll never forget."

A 22-year-old business student from Zimbabwe, Nyasha is close to her family. At first she had found it very difficult to be away from home, though the university had been welcoming and supportive from the start. She is fluent in English, her second language, which she had used through her schooling in Zimbabwe, but when she arrived in Australia she knew very little about "the culture, the language, or the food" and had no friends or family in Australia. "Right at the beginning when I first got here, I didn't have anyone to talk to, that was the thing. It was really hard . . . who to approach, who to talk to? I had no clue. So I used to be on the phone every day with my Dad, 'I wanna go home.' Every single day, I'll call my dad and cry and cry on the phone and . . . there was a lot of loneliness" (female, 22, business, Zimbabwe).

Things eventually worked out well, for the most part. Her parents have visited her in Australia. Her little sister is studying in another part of the country, and they have visited each other also. She speaks to her parents and sister regularly by phone, though she has drifted a little from the family religion, Roman Catholic Christianity. She is not attending church regularly, though she tried to get there some Sundays. "As long as this doesn't get to my mother!" she laughs. Accommodation and budgeting were the main challenges early on, but she now feels on top of the situation. Her dealings with immigration have been fine, at least since a problem with her health coverage was straightened out. Nyasha has a one-bedroom apartment close to the university and a part-time job as a pharmacy assistant, which she quite enjoys; it is more pleasant and better paid than her previous work as a waitress. The university has helped her financially with loans when she has needed them. An early visit to student counseling when she was disorientated and depressed was unhelpful; the counselor avoided the emotional domain and just talked about time management. But the staff in her academic program have been good. If she had a problem she would speak to her boss at the pharmacy. "He's really good; he came out here when he was 17 from Malaysia. He understands what it's like to be an international student."

Articulate and empathetic, Nyasha is active in the university's peer support program for international students. Though she describes herself as "a very private person" with little need to socialize, she has made a variety of friends from different backgrounds, though to her regret she has no boyfriend yet. She is closest to two other students from Zimbabwe. In principle she believes in integrating locally as much as possible. She says, by way of advice to prospective students,

> Australia is such a lucky country. It really is, like, people here are so, so lucky, very lucky. Sometimes I don't think people realize that. It's a beautiful country and . . . it's very well-maintained, looked after. [There are] so many benefits, so many things the government does for people here . . . very easy lifestyle, compared to home where it's very tense. You've always got to be watching your back. You've got to lock the door and close the windows. There's no protection, there's no government funding or things like that. It's a beautiful place, Australia, [though] the winter is dreadful . . . [if] you are coming out all the way from another country to Australia, [you should] experience it and enjoy it. Embrace the culture here. Maybe do things the way it's done here, instead of always trying to hold back on to what you have. Really explore it and enjoy it.

Yet Nyasha has not carried out her own advice. She does not have a strong sense of Australian society. Competent in managing her life, once able to cope emotionally with the separation from home, she created for herself a stable world sufficient for the study period, linked by short car trips between home, university, work, and the services and government offices she deals with. It is low-risk, enclosed, and based on predictable and regular forms of cooperation. It does not require an open-ended local engagement. One early experience of racism in the Australian community has left a deep mark. As is often the case for students in this research study, the abuse occurred when Nyasha was using public transportation:

> Most of the time I would simply brush it aside. But there was one incident that I'll never forget. It happened to me when I was up in Melbourne, in my first six months here. I was at the South Yarra train station. I was standing next to this woman, and she turned round to me and started abusing me. "Why don't you just go back where you came from, we don't want you here!" It really took me aback. It was the last thing I expected . . . I was blind. I was walking into town . . . I just carried on walking. It was so embarrassing. Even since that, I've been more conscious about being different, about my colour, my nationality.

She has no thoughts of staying in Australia after she graduates. She is waiting to go home.

AREF FROM IRAN

"When you don't have any money, you don't live as a person."

Aref has turned 40 and is married with two young children. He has been in Australia for 18 months. An academic staff member at an Iranian university, with two master's degrees in physiotherapy and medical education from that country, he has been awarded a doctoral scholarship by the Iranian government. The scholarship conditions specified that the students could enroll only in the United States, Canada, Australia, or New Zealand. It was difficult to get a visa for the United States. Aref initially had chosen Canada but realized it was too cold there; he changed his mind and applied for an Australian visa through the Australian government website. His only prior concern had been "the tension between our countries."

He was unsatisfied with the teaching in one of the coursework units required for his doctoral degree in Australia. Though there were a majority of international students in the class, the lecturer spoke "as fast as possible." But otherwise his studies have worked out fine and his supervisor has provided generous help both with the academic program and with problems of day-to-day life. Language has not proved a great problem; although his family mainly spoke Farsi at home, he had learned English at school and at the university. He is fluent and his wife has considerably improved her English while in Australia.

But living in Australia has been quite difficult for the family. The scholarship covers nominal family expenses but is insufficient, and the standard of living is considerably lower than at home. Nevertheless, things have been a little easier since his wife obtained work as a teacher, which was her occupation in Iran. His wife found the transition to working in Australia difficult at first. She misses her mother badly and has experienced many changes and problems, but things are better now. Accommodations have been hard to find. Housing is much more expensive and of poorer quality than the subsidized housing provided to university academics in Iran. Aref and his wife are still not satisfied with their apartment. The Melbourne weather is changeable and unpredictable. Most seriously, the children have been frequently ill, with about fifty to sixty visits to the doctor and four periods of hospitalization. The unexpected difficulty was asthma or "an asthma-like condition" probably triggered by the different pollens in Australia. This in turn has triggered ongoing financial difficulties. Each visit to the medical clinic requires an extra ten dollars above the normal consultation fee. The private medical coverage taken out by all international students does not cover the family's pharmaceutical costs, and despite the fact that they have taken out extra health insurance for what is nominally "full coverage," they have paid out about $3,000 for drugs without any rebate. The medical crises have made it hard for the family to settle down.

The family has good relations with their proximate neighbors. All of their other regular friends are from Iran: Iranian students, Iranian relatives, and other Iranians resident in Australia. The family observes Muslim prayer and worships regularly at the mosque. There are two structured groups of fellow country people that they see regularly: a group of Melbourne-based friends and a student group. Each month they have a meeting, following by more informal conversation and something of a party. Aref is friendly with some non-Iranian students but sees them little outside university. When asked whether there are barriers in making cross-cultural friends, he says that the main barrier is time. It is easy to be friendly with people one meets in the park, but "I work too hard. I am too busy."

When asked if he has experienced discrimination or bad treatment, he says, "Sometimes yes, in public, but not too much. Sometimes we have problems because there is a difference, for example, between our religions. I think that in Australia, because so many groups live there, there isn't much problem [compared to] Western countries or European countries. Yes, maybe you feel sometimes there is discrimination, according to the behaviour of the person responsible. But about 90 percent we don't have any problems" (male, 40, PhD in physiotherapy, Iran).

Dealing with immigration has been fine in Australia. "They work totally well," Aref says. It is much better than in Tehran, where the Australian embassy kept imposing extra charges and had taken three months to give him a student visa though he had a scholarship. "They make problems for all people, not just for me." The main issue of discrimination in Australia is in the work force. He has been unable to obtain tutoring work at the university and feels he was passed over unfairly. Another advertised job he was well equipped to do was simply given to the incumbent. All other applications have failed. Several other Iranian friends have had the same experiences, some over much longer time periods: "I applied for casual work or part-time work but I couldn't find suitable work until now, during this one and a half years. There is too much discrimination between international and national students, or Australian and non-Australian residents."

The problem with obtaining work has made things significantly more difficult financially. But Aref is also conscious of a larger issue involved. "In this culture, in all Western countries, all things [are] based on economy and money. When you don't have any money, you don't live as a person."

Aref has no respect whatsoever for these social values. It is a marker of his sense of distance from Australia. At the core, the meaning of life is different.

Aref thinks that before coming to Australia, international students should be better informed about the systems, the relevant regulations, and their personal rights. He feels he has wasted much time searching the Internet for information. Despite this, Aref has learned what he needs and after only 18 months is on top of the issues involved in family living in Australia. He is fully confident in his capacity to interact and knows how the institutions and systems work. His well-developed network of Iranian friends provides a shared pool of information, emotional backup, and continuity of identity, which he is able to take for granted. Aref does not have a need to integrate more closely into Australian society. He is not planning to stay in Australia after graduation. For him, the possibility of staying does not arise.

LI-LIN FROM CHINA

"I don't want to speak English; it's too much."

Li-lin is in her early 30s and studying early education and primary teaching, which was her occupation in central China, at master's level. Unlike the other five students discussed here but like many of the East Asian students in the study, Li-lin is not comfortable using spoken and written English. She had worked for a long period at an international school, and her English proficiency was considerably better than that of many of the interviewees from China. But lack of communicative confidence—not knowing what to say, freezing at crucial moments, inability to ask the right questions or to nuance in negotiations—is a recurring theme throughout her account of the many problems she has faced in Australia. Li-lin has not always successfully dealt with those problems. She lacks institutional support and has few friends. It has been a difficult time for her. She has persisted and is in the final year of a three-year study program at two different universities.

On arrival she followed the advice on the university website and booked a room in the recommended city hotel. Later, she "realized they lied to me because there is cheaper accommodation." Turning to the private rental market, Li-lin moved into an apartment but found it was too far from university. Having signed a lease and paid a deposit for six months in advance, she found it very difficult to get the money back. Eventually she found shared accommodations through a Chinese newspaper. "I don't want to share with any other nationalities because I don't know them, but Chinese is familiar." She moved in with a younger woman, who handled all the bills and deceived Li-lin about the cost of the Internet, overcharging her repeatedly until Li-lin discovered it. The other woman also monopolized the phone so that Li-lin's family could not get through to her; the woman also brought her boyfriend to live in the apartment. They shared the living room; Li-lin was in the bedroom. "It was so inconvenient. He was always there. I cannot get out, I just stayed in my room. That's why I moved. I went to the house of my classmate's brother, from Beijing. There were so many people, mum and dad, his wife, him, the baby, and other students. One toilet. So I have to line up. Not convenient. Cooking is always a problem, so many people wanted to cook, so I have to line up and wait" (female, 33, education, China).

Li-lin moved several more times after that, but things are OK now. She is again sharing an apartment with another student from China and can use Putonghua at home. "Sometimes my roommate wants to practice English, so so much English. I said no, so I speak Chinese and she speaks English. She wants to practice. I don't want to speak English; it's too much."

She passed the International English Language Testing System test at home. But when she arrived in Australia she was "shocked, totally lost." She had a bad experience early; something simple was explained to her and she didn't get it, and then she asked about the same thing. She was made to feel stupid in front of others. She also struggled with the early assignments. "I didn't sleep for many nights . . . sometimes in order to write one sentence I have to think three hours or something. It's so difficult, so tiring." Her written English has improved. She has good basic conversational English. But the anxiety about communicating and negotiating seems to have become permanent. It is a problem of meaning as much as listening and speaking. She still has difficulty understanding when administrative processes are explained. In most of her classes there are few international students, and this makes it harder. In one program there are just three international students; the other two are from Korea and Indonesia. All three students are terrified when they are asked to give oral presentations, but no one has ever given them any coaching. The English support service is not very helpful. Each student has only a limited time. Normally Li-lin can work on only a few sentences before her appointment is over. The number of appointments per year is also rationed. She got into a lot of trouble one time at the English support service when, desperate for help with an essay, she used another student's name to get an extra appointment and was found out.

Teachers who are rude or unhelpful, or friendly to other international students but not to her; university information that lies to her; and campus services that do not help, leave her waiting, send her back and forth between different offices, or ignore her messages or questions—these are recurring themes throughout Li-lin's interview. Communication problems are usually at the bottom of these incidents. Often different expectations about politeness are also involved.

> If you go to the service people, because you don't understand the language properly, they take an advantage of you. They don't care . . . [detailed description follows of a problem Li-lin brought to one of the university services] . . . they speak so fast and I didn't understand. I ask them if they can speak slowly. She said: "I speak very slowly." I said "I don't understand." She said: "What do you understand? What don't you understand?" I said "sorry." She was so angry, so difficult. I was upset because I didn't understand. It's the same with my course coordinator. She is nice. But she was late and never said "sorry." Sometimes I didn't understand. I asked her. She said: "You're supposed to know. You are not a child. You are at master's level. Why do you still ask like a child?"

Spoken English also created a barrier when Li-lin dealt with customers in a restaurant where she worked. She did not know the names for the Western food.

Li-lin is lonely. She calls home three or four times a week. "Mostly my mum. I want to listen to her voice." She has no close friends. She has formed bonds with the two international students who share her anxieties in class but doesn't see them often:

Q. Do have close friends?
A. No.
Q. Just classmates?
A. Yes classmates, not friends. Just come to class and then "bye." So lonely. No one to play with. Nothing. I do have a friend, a Korean girl, but she failed already and was sent home. The Indonesian also

failed but she has PR, and she has a job. But she is always busy, she works full time at night, she works in a restaurant. I can see her very rarely, but we are good friends.

When asked if there are barriers to cross-cultural relationships, Li-lin says that "with the Asian students it's easier."

In this program we do have many Asian students, like Vietnam. Because we have trouble in understanding assignment sometimes, and we always ask each other. We don't ask Australian people, we ask each other. With the Australian students it's so difficult. Every time I say "hi, how are you?" they say "fine thank you" and no more. What else is there to talk about? One day my classmate was so friendly, he invited us to his house. He is married with many children. At the table, his wife asked me: "How are you? What are doing? Where do you come from?" That's it. No more conversation. We don't know what to say and they didn't want to talk to us anymore because it was boring.

"It's so difficult to meet people, it's so boring," says Li-lin. "And if you want to find a place to help you, there's no help." She has had no active friendships with local people. One nasty incident had put her more on her guard in the community.

I don't go outside at all. I want to make myself safe. But I did have trouble when I took the tram one day. I had a class in the city, I came home late, and there was a big man sitting in the back talking to an old woman and I turned around . . . I turned around, and he said, "What's your name?" I was so scared, I didn't want to say anything. He said, "You're so rude, you didn't talk to me." I didn't know what to do. He grabbed me by my shirt in my neck. The driver said: "Drop her, otherwise I will call the police." And he did, after the driver shouted at him. After he got out off the tram, he threw the bottle to me, the Pepsi bottle . . . he wasn't drunk. The driver said to me, "Why you came home so late?" And I said, I had a class, I had to. And the driver said, "Come home earlier, because the tram is not safe."

Li-lin's lack of ease in Australia is profound. "Everything is so shocking." It is compounded by her ongoing difficulty in figuring out the public transportation system, the fact that "the food is also different to back home" and "the weather also challenges me, it's so changeable." She has attended some student union meetings, but that does not help her connect better either. "It's too much for me. Too much English . . . [name of university] student union is run by Indian students. There are so so many Indians. So you cannot [participate effectively], you are Chinese. That's it . . . Every now and then they send us an email saying 'come to the postgraduate meeting.' I went there, and there are always all Indians, talking talking."

A student union official enrolled at the same university, who was from India, stated in his interview that it is difficult "for me to interact with the Chinese students. They don't understand English well and I speak too fast for them."

REFLECTIONS ON THE STUDENT STORIES

It is striking how the students vary in their orientations to home and host culture. The coupling of language and agency plays some part in the variations, affecting their capacity to integrate with locals. This is easiest for Cindi from Malaysia, Jade from Singapore, and Miguel from Spain, who step over most barriers with ease. But each student has also made choices, often different from the choices of the others. Of the five whose English language communication skills are very good, Cindi is deliberately moving away from the home culture as part of the process of integrating in Australia on her own terms—an option more readily available to a future doctor than most others. Nyasha from Zimbabwe and Aref from Iran will return home without question. They do not identify with the host country at all. Aref is always conscious of being an outsider in terms of values, and Nyasha has been Othered by a scarring incident. Miguel feels a mild tug in Australia but could live and work in many countries and does not have a strong national identity. He has moved far from his roots in the Basque country. Jade has options. At this stage he identifies as Singaporean Chinese and not as Australian Chinese.

The importance of proficiency in English stands out in these interviews. Most members of this group have been very successful in Australia and the same people have superior communication skills and good academic English. Two are native English speakers. Two others had become fully proficient in the education system at home. Another started with good English language skills by the same means. All five are also assisted by well-established intellectual confidence, good people skills, and in two cases, intensive life experience. Thus five of the six students combine their good to excellent English language proficiency with strong agency. They are clearly on top of their world. They have shaped the international education experience as they want, albeit within varying conditions, resources, and levels of constraint.

Cindi and Miguel are both global cosmopolitans with very strong academic achievements that have allowed them to cut loose from dependence on a home-country community. Jabe remains primarily Asia-focused in the Australian context, making his closest friends among other international students while moving in and out of local settings, mostly with ease. He comes closest to Berry's definition of "integration,"[5] connecting partially to the host society while retaining his presojourn group identity. Because Nyasha does not have an active home community in Australia and is fairly isolated in a small world, Berry might call her situation "marginalization," but it works for her as a temporary solution while she remains bonded to home. Aref is thoroughly networked and active within his diasporic national community inside Australia but has fewer connections with the host society than Nyasha has. He falls somewhere between "integration" and "separation" in Berry's sense. Neither wants more than he or she had received from Australia, except a greater measure of ease perhaps, and both look forward to regaining their real selves again.

The outlying case is Li-lin, who illustrates the point about communicative competence and agency in the negative. Her measurable language proficiency has reached the level of adequate, but she lacks communicative competence. Even where she understands the words, she has difficulty with concepts, processes, and contexts. This underlines the point the communicative sociability is relational (and imaginative), depending on much more than individual proficiency. For Li-lin, Australia is alien in many ways, but it is noticeable that communication difficulties and the accompanying social isolation are part of almost every problem she mentions. It is unclear whether the staring cause is a lack of agency and personal confidence or lack of communication skills. What is clear is that the two sets of problems are locked together, almost indistinguishable. They closely reinforce each other, and her lack of agency and lack of skills both contribute to the social isolation that has made it so much harder for her to learn the language and feel good about herself. Despite this she had enough tenacity to survive academically and emotionally into the final year of her program. Li-lin is closer to Berry's "separation" than "marginalization." She retains same-culture links within Australia and with her family back home. In Berry's sense she is not as obviously marginalized than Nyasha, but Berry's categories are less explanatory of emotional health and practical effectiveness than is the level and type of agency. Nyasha is on top of her life, emotionally stable, and has made a good fit for her degree. Li-lin hates Australia, struggles academically, and is unhappy. Nyasha's agency, well grounded in self-respect, is intact. Li-lin's is in jeopardy.

All six students report that on the whole their universities have accepted and supported them, though Aref and Jade both feel that their origins cost them when competitive selection decisions were made, and Li-lin has been more poorly serviced than the others in the classroom and the English language center. The doctoral students, Miguel and Aref, have had the best support. But the larger problems of cross-cultural relations have been outside, in the community. Both Li-lin and Nyasha have endured savage abuse using public transportation, and it is likely that this has contributed to their low level of local engagement. It has intimidated Li-lin sufficiently to keep her off the streets. While the dreadful incident did not subtract from Nyasha her graceful ease and fluent confidence with people, it has visited on her a sense of being an outsider in Australia because of her skin color—an alienation that by her own testimony she would not have otherwise felt.

CONCLUSION

Communications, cross-cultural encounters, and, above all, personal agency, together shape the international education experience. In conjunction these factors enable intercultural education and set limits on it, for internationals and locals.

This chapter has watched those issues play out in the lives of six different international students from six different countries. Though mostly successful in class and life, their experiences could have been better—and for some, much better. Moreover, their contributions to local institutions, students, and communities have been constrained by their conditions of existence. The country of education has been unable or unwilling to draw full benefit from the engagement.

Of course, six student stories are just that. We need to consider the larger body of evidence. Returning to the research literature, Chapters 5 and 6 work through the barriers, issues, problems, and cross-cultural potentials before international students in the English-speaking countries, in higher education institutions in general (Chapter 5) and in their classrooms (Chapter 6).

—————✦—————

CHAPTER 5

CROSS-CULTURAL RELATIONS IN HIGHER EDUCATION

INTRODUCTION: THE DIVIDE BETWEEN LOCAL AND FOREIGN

The problems of international students are not all language driven. Nor is cultural assymetry the always and essential cause. Being foreign also reduces the agency of international students. In turn this feeds back into cross-cultural relations.

For many international students, forming local friends, especially with fellow students, and partial immersion in the host country culture are primary goals of the sojourn. Without active relations with locals the cross-cultural experience is impoverished. Language acquisition is weakened. Local education systems also want engagement between internationals and locals. It offers the potential for genuinely mutual exchange and greater global awareness in the local student population. Strengthening relations between international and local students is a key objective for researchers of international education, education institutions, home and host country governments, and international students and their families. Numerous studies find that all students derive cognitive, social, and civic benefits from diverse interactions on a sustained basis.[1] But studies also find that in international education the quantity and intensity of cross-cultural contact are both disappointing.[2]

Engagement between international students and the larger local community in the country of education faces natural constraints. The students are temporary, and the locals have no intrinsic relation with them. One might expect matters to be more straightforward on campus where all students share the same life experiences, educational programs, and often the same places to eat and study. On the face of it, they should mix freely. This is far from being the case.

International students, especially those from China, Malaysia, Singapore, Indonesia, and India, often congregate with others from the same or similar background, with large numbers of same-culture fellows close at hand. It is often remarked that same-culture groups are obstacles to cultural mixing, though the research on the point is not clear cut. Less often remarked is the fact that local students also group and most hold themselves firmly separate from international students.[3] Otten remarks on the tendency of classroom students to spontaneously group along ethnocultural lines. "In contrast to the widespread reports of self-segregation among students of colour on U.S. campuses, this pattern is more typical of White students."[4] This is testified by international students whenever they are asked by researchers.[5] Research also shows that both of these broad groupings, locals and internationals, tend to see the other as homogenous.

In short, both local and international students are caught up in a process of difference making that points to the continuing salience of the foreign/local divide. This division seems deeply entrenched, manifest in both the weakness of local/international engagement and the tendency of both groups to stereotype the other in broad-brush terms. In cross-cultural relations in international education, the local/foreigner distinction is often the main element at play. All too often it then plays out as a distinction between white/nonwhite or between native speaker of English and English as a foreign language student and is the springboard for discrimination and abuse. Both groups homogenize the other. But discrimination is largely one-way. Both groups do *not* share equal responsibility for the cross-cultural divide, though both might be equally responsible for its solution.

Research suggests that international students are happy to have their specific identities acknowledged in a common relativist framework. But they do not want their nationality, culture, or foreignness and international student status to make a permanent and unbridgeable gulf between them and the local population

Local students are the key to change. They are presently in a strong position but at the expense of the internationals. Local students see no need to change themselves just because there are international students in their midst. The separation of the two groups reflects their own choice and preference. In the case of international students, studies repeatedly show that most of them want more local friendships and many would like to move seamlessly into local society for part of the time. They cannot. They are blocked of entry and initiative, and so robbed of agency.

This Chapter

The dynamics of this process of unequal difference-making are layered and complex. First, reifying distinctions are made by stereotyping. Group-defined differences can function as neutral ways of separating parts of the world, but host country stereotypes of international students often suggest a superior/inferior relation. Berry's distinction between separation and segregation will be used in this chapter.[6] Separation between groups means simply that there is little interpersonal contact between them. Segregation means that separation is imposed by one group regardless of, and possibly against, the will of the other. Both sets of dynamics are at play in international education, and often together.

Second, in segregation, discrimination, prejudicial encounters, and abuse and violence, difference-making plays out as exclusion, domination, and control.

This chapter discusses research on stereotyping, discrimination, and abuse, and traces how these social pathologies contribute to separation and segregation. It then explores the research on relations between local and international students.

DYNAMICS OF OTHERING

Cultural Stereotyping

We begin with the process of stereotyping, which is defined by Spencer-Rodgers as "cognitive structures that contain a perceiver's knowledge, beliefs, and expectancies about a social group." Spencer-Rodgers adds that stereotypes are conceptualized as "culturally shared beliefs about the attributes that characterize a group of people (consensual, cultural, or social stereotypes) and in terms of unique, personal beliefs about the attributes of a group (individual, personal, or idiosyncratic stereotypes)."[7] An important defining feature of cultural stereotypes is their consensual nature: there must be agreement among members of one group about the characteristics of another group before an attribute can be included as part of a social stereotype. Cultural stereotypes are defined by beliefs that are widely shared and include traits that are selected, endorsed, or generated most frequently when some class of individuals is described.[8]

Stereotyping typically rests on cultural essentialism. Cultural difference as defined by the stereotype is seen as determining of the characteristics of the persons being objectified in this manner. Stereotyping is a self-reproducing closure. It enables its perpetrators to avoid deep intercultural encounters while sustaining a self-defensive identity. Unlike some other pejorative relationships, such as discrimination or abuse, stereotyping does not require actual cross-cultural contact and flourishes best with minimal or no contact.[9] It involves not just difference making but distance making, depending on a low level of contact to sustain the pristine, reified stereotype. This underpins strategies of exclusion. Olson and Kroeger describe "an intentional creation of physical or social barriers."[10] They note that "the individual . . . seeks to create distance from others who are different from them so that they can remain comfortably in denial. Gated communities, ethnically distinct neighborhoods, and racially segregated cities serve as vivid images of such physical barriers. Ethnically selective clubs illustrate examples of social barriers. Intense nationalism is also frequently the result of this quest for separation from difference. Another implicit danger is the common tendency to relegate others who are different to a subhuman status. These 'others' from whom individuals in denial seek to keep their distance can become like objects or vermin in the individuals' minds."[11]

Clearly, stereotyping is more likely to be engaged in by local people than by international students. The latter need openness so as to engage in cultural learning and form practical relations with local people and institutions.

Spencer-Rodgers studied the "consensual stereotype of an extraordinarily heterogeneous social group, international students who are sojourning in the United States." The subject group was one hundred American college student host nationals.[12] Most previous studies of stereotyping had been in relation to groups with a high degree of overt homogeneity such as nationality or skin color. The question posed by international students is as follows: "Is it possible for people to hold a stereotype of a group that is extremely diverse in terms of race, ethnicity, and nationality, and religious, linguistic, political, and socioeconomic background?"[13] Spencer-Rodgers finds that in this case, yes. "The percentages of agreement among participants concerning the attributes of foreign students were substantial" in relation to both positive and negative qualities. In other words, "international students are regarded as a fairly homogenous outgroup by domestic students, notwithstanding the extreme heterogeneity of the foreign student population."[14]

The most common positive stereotypes in relation to international students, as expressed by local students, were intelligent (58 percent of local respondents), brave/adventurous (41 percent), hardworking (23 percent), determined (22 percent), learning about a new culture (21 percent), and friendly (20 percent). The main negative stereotypes were foreign/different (30 percent), "socially and culturally maladjusted" (29 percent), and do not speak English well (23 percent).[15] Smaller groups of 4 to 6 percent of respondents mentioned "lonely, anxious, and frightened," which were also negatively valenced. In addition 14 percent "described international students as naive and this characteristic was rated as the most negative attribute of the group. Related impressions included 'confused,' 'a little lost,' and 'clueless.'"[16] Among those with strong negative stereotypes, this was closely correlated to "prejudicial attitudes and social avoidance."[17]

Respondents did not focus much on "race, ethnicity, nationality, or specific cultural background of members of the group." Perhaps they saw international students as variable in these areas. But "an alternative explanation, or possibly a complementary explanation, is that international students, as a group, were merely conceptualized and categorized as a collection of individuals who are foreign."[18] As Spencer-Rodgers emphasizes, about one-third of respondents described the students as "foreign/different," and "it is noteworthy that this designation had a negative connotation for domestic students."[19] This finding confirms that the Othering of international students is vectored by their foreignness. The study also confirms that problems of communication and language barriers feed more generally into cross-cultural barriers. "The association of foreign students with difficult language and cultural barriers may also discourage host nationals from developing social relationships with members of the international community."[20]

This does not mean that problems of negative referencing of the Other can be overcome simply by higher levels of cross-cultural contact. In a study of artificially created cross-cultural partnerships Pritchard and Skinner conclude that "mere contact does not always lead to the mutual valuing of traditions."[21] Leong and Ward state, "It is generally accepted that intercultural contact can promote good will and understanding between members of two different cultures," but "some researchers have pointed out that intercultural contact may also result in negative experiences," especially when discriminatory behaviors are the norm.[22] Otten notes that contact can heighten tensions, and in some instances reinforce stereotyping, unless "the social experience of otherness" is "transformed into a personally relevant learning experience."[23] There is no universal rule about the benefits of cross-cultural contact. The type of contact, opportunities for mutuality, and the larger pattern of relations, such as prior status relationship between the two groups, are all in play.[24]

Nevertheless, over time contact is likely to break down the more simplified stereotypes.[25] In their study of cross-cultural workgroups Volet and Ang find that "negative stereotypes and ethnocentric views" severely inhibited the formation of culturally mixed groups. Both groups of students had stereotyped perceptions of each other.[26] Working in groups helped some students realize that they had stereotyped views and others had stereotyped views of them.[27]

Discrimination, Prejudice, and Abuse

Discrimination, prejudice, and abuse are difficult topics for research. First, direct observations are rarely possible. Second, it is difficult to establish operable definitions. *Discrimination* generally refers to negative evaluations and behaviors directed toward people due to their membership in a group, in this case international students. Discrimination robs people of agency by reducing freedoms, rights, privileges, and opportunities enjoyed by others. However, not every negative cross-cultural experience can be categorized as "discrimination."[28]

This is not to dispute the existence of discrimination, merely to note the difficulty of tracking it empirically and interpreting the findings. Discrimination is repeatedly reported in studies of international education and falls selectively on certain kinds of student. It is an extremely serious problem. Much research indicates that discrimination has negative impacts on students.[29] Leong and Ward note that "research has revealed a consistent relationship between discrimination and a range of maladaptive outcomes for both immigrants and sojourners."[30] In a study of graduate internationals at one university, Perrucci and Hu find "language skill, exposure/contact with Americans, and discrimination/negative attitudes have the strongest correlations with satisfaction."[31] Students satisfied with their academic program "felt that they were living in a social environment that did not discriminate against them and did not reveal negative attitudes toward their country." They "had more frequent social contact with U.S. students and felt good about themselves and their achievements."[32] They also reported better language development.

Studies by Lee and colleagues provide an extended empirical focus on problems of discrimination and racism affecting international students. Lee secured 501 returns from a survey of international students at a large U.S. public research university in the Southwest. The findings confirm that experiences vary according to national-cultural origin and physical appearance. Lee also provides data on "the negative effects of international students feeling treated unequally compared to domestic students."[33] She notes previous literature that indicates "international students do not all share similar experiences. Students from Asia and most other developing countries have reportedly encountered greater obstacles compared to students from Western Europe, Canada and Australia."[34] Lee finds that "students from developing countries experienced greater difficulty in social adjustment and felt they were treated less equally and fairly, compared to students from developed countries." Strikingly, when the basis of distinction was moved from developed/developing countries to predominantly white/predominantly nonwhite regions, the differences in student experience were sharper. In all areas, students from predominantly nonwhite regions reported less satisfaction and greater difficulties. The difference was particularly marked in relation to "difficulty in social adjustment," and to a lesser extent "treated equally and fairly." "Students from Latin America and Japan" were "subject to discrimination in ways more similar to students from Africa, the Middle East and other Asian countries than to students from Europe, Canada and Australasia."[35] Lee also finds that in determining whether the student would recommend the institution to others, the two strongest factors that affected the results were whether the student was from East Asia (China, Korea, and Japan) and the student's rating of being "treated equally and fairly." Students from East Asia were 0.43 times less likely to recommend the institution; students who felt they were not treated equally were 0.30 times less likely to recommend it.[36]

It appears that skin color remains determining of discrimination even among people who are nominally nonracist in outlook. Appearance serves as a trigger for cultural discrimination. Lee utilizes the concept of "neo-racism" to explain this process: "Neo-racism . . . is discrimination based on national order or culture." As defined by Spears, "neo-racism rationalizes the subordination of people of colour on the basis of culture," which is acquired through acculturation in an ethnic group, "while traditional racism rationalizes it fundamentally in terms of biology." Neo-racism maintains "racial hierarchies of oppression" and therefore remains a form of racism.[37] Neo-racism is about the preservation of power and maintenance of group identity and social coherence by mechanisms of cultural intolerance.[38] "Discrimination becomes, seemingly, justified by cultural difference or national origin rather than by physical characteristics alone and can thus disarm the fight against racism by appealing to 'natural' tendencies to preserve group cultural identity—in this case the dominant group. Underlying neo-racism are notions of cultural or national superiority and an increasing rationale for marginalizing or assimilating groups in a globalizing world."[39]

Lee and Rice conducted intensive interviews with 24 international students from 15 countries, focusing on difficulties ranging from a sense of unfair or hostile treatment to open cultural intolerance and confrontation.[40] They find that overall, statements of negative experiences related to "race, culture, or status as foreign residents" outweighed positive experiences by two to one. For white students the ratio was reversed. While students from Asia, India, Latin America, and the Middle East reported many instances of discrimination, those from Europe, Canada, and New Zealand reported no "direct negative experiences related to their race or culture." The problems arose in social interactions, dealings with faculty and administration, lack of equal access to funding or jobs, and "off-campus interactions such as housing and shopping."[41] Several students emphasized "feelings of inferiority" generated by either media stereotyping or direct insults in their interactions with local people such as negative remarks about their home countries, cultures, or lack of English proficiency.[42] For nonwhite students the "race issue" often arose early on, surprising those who never experienced it at home. "A woman from the Gulf region explained, 'The most difficult thing for me personally was the race issue. I wasn't that conscious of my race because of where I come from. Race issues do exist but it's more social class. American students would ask me why I spoke like a White person [and] I didn't get it. I had no clue what they were talking about.' She was often wrongly classified as Black."[43]

In Nasrin's study of non-European students in the Deep South of the United States, all participants reported discriminatory experiences in and out of class by lecturers, fellow students, and others. "To Tina," one study participant, "the issue was not being discriminated but how to minimize the effect of being discriminated." She had lived in the United States long enough to know "that discrimination would always prevail and she could not do anything about it."[44] Hanassah and Tidwell surveyed 640 international students at the University of California, Los Angeles. African students had the greatest "needs" in relation to stereotypes and discrimination. For Africans, discrimination ranked fifth of nine issues at 3.00 on a scale of 5. For Asians the issue was rated at 2.57, Southeast Asians 2.51, Middle Easterners 2.46, Europeans 2.10, Americans excluding Canada

1.95, Oceanians (principally Australia and New Zealand) 1.52.[45] In a further study drawing on the same data set Hanassah again finds discrimination varied by national origin. Appearance was often the trigger of discriminatory incidents. While discrimination occurred at the hands of students and staff, the problems were more severe outside campus than on campus. "The highest discrimination reported was by Middle Eastern students, as 46 percent felt that people in Los Angeles expressed prejudice toward people from their countries."[46] Students from Latin America (36 percent), Africa (33 percent), and Asia (29 percent) had greater concerns than those from Europe (19 percent) and Southeast Asia (16 percent). Europeans (8 percent) were less likely to have problems dealing with their classmates than students from the Middle East, Asia, the Americas, and Africa, who were all in the 20–22 percent range.[47]

In interviews with 12 students from Africa, Constantine and colleagues report that "participants generally indicated prejudicial or discriminatory treatment by others . . . interviewees typically noted that they were called names and racial slurs by White Americans."[48] Some also faced discrimination by Afro-Americans: "I think some [Black Americans] see themselves as better than Africans. You find a lot of [light-skinned] Black people, and I think they don't want to date us because they think we're too [dark-skinned]."[49] Constantine and colleagues add that "exposure to racial discrimination may increase these students' risk for developing or exacerbating mental health problems or concerns during the cultural adjustment process. In fact, there is a plethora of literature that documents the strong link between perceived racist events and negative health-related and psychological outcomes such as hypertension, cardiovascular reactivity, depression, general psychological distress, eating problems, and substance abuse."[50]

Solberg and colleagues remark that in the United States there can be a tendency to see "Asian" students as a "model minority" with less academic difficulties than students from Africa or Latin America, which conceals both the problems facing many Asian students and important variations within that large category.[51]

In New Zealand, McGrath and Hooker asked focus groups of international students the question "what acts as a barrier to effective intercultural interaction involving international students?" In response "a number of students mentioned rudeness, unfriendliness, and racist remarks."[52] Collins discusses media stereotyping of East Asian students in Auckland, New Zealand. Auckland houses the largest number of international students in any city in New Zealand.

Newspaper articles sought to show or imply that "Asians" could not drive, their presence was causing an increase in crime, they were putting undue pressure on public resources like health and education, and they were occupying and transforming key city spaces in ways unattractive and unacceptable to the local inhabitants.

> The media representations of these students have fixed a diverse group of individuals within a singular racial identity that is known by stereotypical economic, cultural, and social characteristics. These representations have further problematised the interaction between international students and the host population in Auckland while simultaneously implicating a cohort of young New Zealand citizens and permanent residents who are of similar descent within the same discourses. This process of Othering the Asian student, regardless of citizenship, has consequences not simply for the practice of exporting education in this city but also for the future of a multicultural Auckland and New Zealand.[53]

Also, "These representations are part of a process of racializing whose objective is to create a racial category, Asian, that can be known and controlled in the New Zealand context."[54]

These articles sought to create a social difference between a singular discursive Asian Other and an essential New Zealand self that by implication is white and speaks English as a first language. This fostered tensions based on identity category, which were then represented as a natural consequence of having international students in the city. Following concerns in China about the media targeting of Chinese students in New Zealand, the government of China withdrew support from New Zealand as an international destination for students. This caused a sharp decline in students traveling from China to New Zealand for education. This in turn led to an overall drop in the number of international students in New Zealand, from 66,093 in June 2004 to 37,231 in June 2007.

In Australia a survey by Schweitzer of 446 international students at one university finds that 9.9. percent of students reported difficulties in relation to discrimination.[55] Robertson and colleagues report a survey at one Australian university of 408 undergraduate internationals (79 percent of that total population) together with 121 staff members. One question asked "what, if any, racial discrimination have you experienced?" While this did not rank as a broadly distributed problem in relation to life inside the university, outside the university "racist remarks or actions" ranked third behind "difficulty making friends with locals" and "difficulty understanding slang, idioms, colloquial language."[56] Most incidents occurred in the street, when students were shopping or on public transportation. On campus, 46 racial incidents were mentioned by 20 students, including episodes when students' language use was laughed at in class by local students and "a perception that lecturers gave less attention to overseas students relative to native-Australian students."[57] The staff members did not acknowledge racism or discrimination as major issues, and no staff member "claimed firsthand experience of racial discrimination."[58]

In a survey of international students at the University of Melbourne, Rosenthal and colleagues asked the students if they had experienced physical or verbal abuse, sexual harassment, and exclusion in Australia. The problems most frequently reported were verbal abuse and exclusion, each reported by almost one-third of students.[59] Men were more often affected by verbal abuse, women by exclusion.

"Malaysian and Singaporean students report higher than expected rates of verbal abuse, while students from China report lower than expected rates." The researchers found the same in relation to exclusion, "though in this case students from UK/US/Canada and Europe also reported lower than expected rates of exclusion." Overall in relation to exclusion, Asian students had a higher than expected rate and others a lower rate than expected.[60] Students were also asked whether "people treat me differently because of my cultural background": 23.1 percent answered "very much" or "considerably," 40.9 percent "to some degree." On the statement "I feel uncomfortable in the Australian culture," 15.7 percent expressed strong agreement and 41.9 percent agreed to some degree.[61]

The 2006 Australian Education International survey, which covered both international students and local students, contains a number of findings that bear indirectly on questions of discrimination. There were 7,267 international education students in the study, including 3,585 in higher education. The survey asked both groups of students whether they felt they were treated with respect and courtesy by different groups within Australia. The largest gap between the groups derived from how the students treat each other (for more discussion, see the next subsection of this chapter). In addition, international students rated their level of respect and courtesy from all groups, except fellow international students, at a lower level than the corresponding ratings given by local students. International students also believed they were treated with more respect inside than outside campuses, consistent with other studies. There was a marked difference in the level of respect in the general community. International students rated this at 77 percent, local students at 89 percent.[62] The lowest levels of satisfaction were among students from East Asia (especially Japan and Korea) and Thailand, followed by other Southeast Asian countries. This again confirms that white students enjoy a happier experience than nonwhite students in relations with locals and that students from non-English-speaking countries in East Asia are especially conscious of limitations on the experience.

Communications and Discrimination

Spencer-Rodgers and McGovern examine the role of barriers to cross-cultural communication in shaping discrimination and prejudice among locals. They note that research has established that "effective intercultural communication" is critical to "favorable intergroup relations."[63] They use a sample of 154 local students of mixed background from two American universities to investigate attitudes to international students, focusing on "intercultural communication emotions (negative affect associated with perceived linguistic and cultural barriers)" as "determinants of prejudice," in association with four causal factors: negative stereotypes, intergroup anxiety, realistic threats, and symbolic/cultural threats. They find that overall, "intercultural communication emotions were strongly and uniquely related to prejudice toward . . . foreign students."[64] The research suggests "a broad range of adverse emotions, directly associated with communication between ethnolinguistic groups, can be a potent source of intergroup hostility."[65]

The participants' overall attitude toward foreign students was somewhat favorable but relatively unfavorable compared to the rating for American college students. "The mean score for intercultural communication emotions indicates that many American college students felt frustrated, impatient, and uncomfortable when encountering communication obstacles with the international student community." Some host nationals viewed international students as "illegitimate competitors."[66] The authors note "male graduate students reported significantly greater prejudice and less positive affect toward foreign students than did female graduate students."[67] Increased contact with host country nationals had mixed and contrary effects. At higher levels of contact, stereotypical beliefs and "general affective responses" became less potent predictors of prejudice. However, researchers found that "contrary to prediction, social contact did not moderate the relationship between intercultural communication emotions and global attitudes. That is, intercultural communication affect was strongly and uniquely related to prejudice for both low-contact and high-contact host nationals."[68]

Other research notes the communication factor. Wan's intensive study of two Chinese students in American universities is one of many in which the students testify that their appearance and spoken language can lead to being treated as different in an unfriendly manner.[69] Mori notes that foreign accents generate difficulties for international students as graduate teaching assistants. "Because of their non-American teaching methods and foreign accents, it is often difficult for them to gain acceptance, trust and respect from U.S. students even if the assistants are experts in their fields of study."[70] But like some other researchers, Mori also argues that international students' negative experiences are also conditioned by disappointed status and by "unrealistically high expectations about their abilities and the quality of their lives in the U.S."[71] Implicit in these arguments is that international students should accept less agency than they claim. Spencer-Rodgers also notes the difficulties faced by graduate teaching assistants.[72] There are two issues. One is that some nonnative speakers are difficult to understand. "Processing accented speech is cognitively and emotionally taxing."[73] The other is that the foreign accent triggers resentment and a process of Othering, regardless of communicability. "Non-native speakers of a language are rated less favorable than native speakers on a wide range of attributes, including competence and trustworthiness," note Spencer-Rodgers and McGovern.[74]

A review by Lee and Rice cites findings in a number of studies on the centrality of language and communication issues in discrimination and segregation.[75] In Nasrin's study of female graduate students from non-European countries who were enrolled in a U.S. university in the Deep South, "the term 'discrimination'" was introduced by the participants, not the researcher, and "came up while the participants were discussing about the language problem."[76] In a study of international graduate students at another American university, Perrucci and Hu find academic satisfaction is most strongly related to contact with U.S. students, language skills, and perceived discrimination, while social satisfaction is linked with martial status, language skills, perceived discrimination, and contact with U.S. students.[77] Their study also suggests that while language difficulties and differences figure as part of the problem of stereotyping and discrimination, communicative competence is part of the solution.

It is clear from these data that the [social] satisfaction of international graduate students with their experiences in the host environment is largely shaped by their language skills, self-esteem, and a feeling of positive involvement with their social environment. Contact with local (in this case American) graduate students is probably facilitated by language proficiency and strong feelings of self-worth and competence on the part of international students. When these individual and social resources of students are combined with a perception of the host environment as accepting and positive toward them and their country, the basis for satisfaction is established.[78]

The exercise of communicative language is associated with a sense of self-worth. Again it is apparent that communicative competence and active agency, linked in a triad with interaction with host nationals, bring a sense of belonging.

RELATIONS BETWEEN INTERNATIONAL AND LOCAL STUDENTS

Relations between local and international students are often researched.[79] It is universally agreed that cross-cultural student relations involving international students in English-speaking countries are both necessary and problematic.[80] As noted, it is also clear that international students want more and better cross-cultural relations, while the locals are much less committed.

Many studies find cross-cultural contact with locals is positively correlated to the psychological adjustment, social adjustment, educational achievement, and educational or life satisfaction of international students (and sometimes also local students), and that such contact can improve cross-cultural understanding immediately or on a lasting basis. Perrucci and Hu find that for international graduate students at one American university "contact with U.S. students" is primary in relation to academic satisfaction and also significant in relation to social satisfaction.[81] Li and Gasser find cross-cultural contact with host nationals is positively related to the sociocultural adjustment of Asian students and cross-cultural contact with host nationals is also positively related to student self-efficacy. "The effect of cross-cultural self-efficacy on sociocultural adjustment was partially mediated by contact with the hosts."[82] Again the picture emerges of an interactive triad of agency/communicative competence/cross-cultural relations, with positive feedback effects. But "cultural diversity and internationalization do not automatically lead to intercultural contacts and intercultural learning experiences," notes Otten.[83] Cultural differenced and prejudices get in the way.[84]

In the United Kingdom, Li and Kaye find in their study of international student problems at one institution that the most significant difficulties are financial problems and mixing with UK students. The latter problem substantially affects both students from developing countries and students from Western Europe. There is a strong association between problems with the English language and problems of mixing with UK students.[85] The UKCOSA survey provides data on cross-cultural mixing. It finds that 59 percent of the international students counted most of their friendships as with "conationals" or other international students, with just one-third (32 percent) citing a mixture of internationals and UK students, and 7 percent stating their friends were mainly UK students.[86] Yet just under a quarter of the students stated that "they preferred to mix with people from their own country and culture"[87] compared to the 59 percent who did so. The language factor was salient. Of native-English-speaking international students, two-thirds had UK friends, compared to 36 percent of the students from English as a second language backgrounds, and 29 percent of those from English as a foreign language backgrounds.[88] "Only 15 percent of Chinese students said they had any U. K. friends."[89] Many international students faced difficulties in forming cross-cultural relations with locals. Almost half (43 percent) stated UK students were hard to get to know, and just 60 percent stated UK students were friendly once one did get to know them.[90] Only 46 percent agreed that "the U. K. is a welcoming and tolerant society" and 19 percent disagreed, with the remaining 35 percent either ambivalent or failing to answer.[91]

Some international students also experience inhibitions in socializing with their hosts. Local students' values and leisure habits can be a barrier to ease of friendship and trust relations. Some research notes international student difficulties with the party lifestyle, the use and effects of alcohol and sometimes other drugs, and local practices of sex and romance. Lee and Rice discuss one student who "was frustrated with wanting to know more about the culture around him and wanting to 'mingle' but was surprised by the 'incredible' amount of partying and drinking involved in undergraduate life and was shocked with the open sexuality of American culture. He feels excluded from friendships and gaining the type of experience he hoped for because he doesn't partake in the usual activities of his peers."[92]

A strong finding of Bradley's UK study is that relations with local students rarely went past a "superficial level," partly due to local alcohol-based lifestyles. Local patterns of alcohol use were especially troublesome for female students from Southeast Asia.[93] The UKCOSA survey of international student experiences had similar findings.[94]

In their study within one university in Australia, Rosenthal and colleagues note that 67.4 percent of students perceived their social contacts within the university as of similar cultural background, while 76.7 percent of students stated this was so outside the university. "Social mixing outside the university is more culturally constrained than it is within the university":[95] 29.6 percent of respondents had no social contact with local citizens on campus; and 39.4 percent, a higher proportion, had no contact outside the university setting. Only about one-fifth of respondents had "very much" or "considerable" social contact with Australians in either setting. Students from Asian countries with large same-culture populations on campus had a greater incidence of interactions with people of similar cultural background and a lesser incidence of interactions with local students than students from other geographic regions.[96] Asian students' responses showed that "they tend to see mixing with people of similar cultural background as an alternative to mixing socially with Australians. The correlations between the two sets of items are significant but negative."[97] Those who spoke a language other than English (LOTE) off campus mixed more with those of similar cultural background than did non-LOTE-speaking students, and mixed less with Australians.[98] Students from English-speaking nations, South Asia, and Europe mixed the most with Australians. Students from Hong Kong, Latin America, China, and Indonesia did so the least. Off campus, the picture is similar. Students from the United Kingdom, United States, Canada, Europe, and India mixed the most with locals. Students from Hong Kong, Indonesia, and Malaysia did so the least.[99]

The Australian Education International survey of 2006, conducted by the federal government's education department, examined international student perceptions of cross-cultural relations. Across the higher education, vocational education and training (VET), and schools sectors only 70 percent of respondents "felt they were treated with respect and courtesy by Australian students." Perceived respect was greater in higher education (76 percent) than VET (65 percent) or secondary school (61 percent).[100] Across all sectors, respect was lowest for students from Korea (45 percent), Thailand (51 percent), Japan (59 percent), and China/Hong Kong (65 percent). In higher education there were complementary surveys of internationals and locals. International respondents were more likely to think that they were treated with respect and courtesy by other international students (93 percent of respondents said this) than by Australian students (76 percent). Conversely, Australian respondents were more likely to think that they were treated with respect and courtesy by other Australian students (91 percent said this) than by international students (80 percent), though the difference was less.

The two groups of students were asked whether they had close friends in Australia, among different groups of people. Of the internationals 39 percent had close friends in local community, cultural, or religious groups; among locals the figure was 74 percent.[101] Among international students, answers to the question about whether the respondent had Australian student "close friends" showed much higher incidences of such friendships among students from North America (the highest incidence at 84 percent) than Thailand, China/Hong Kong, and Korea, all at little more than 50 percent. The survey found that barriers to friendships with local students included a perceived lack of interest among locals in having international friends; the belief among some internationals, especially those from China and other East Asian nations, that their own lack of English language skills inhibited mixing; and the belief that Australian students should make the first move to initiate friendship.[102] Almost half the international students believed that "Australian students should take the first steps to make friends with international students"[103] but only 9 percent of the Australians agreed, pointing to an important cross-cultural difference in politeness regimes. No wonder many international students were disappointed by the outcomes.

The study also indicates differences between local and international students on their intentions for cross-cultural friendship. Whereas 81 percent of international students wanted more Australian friends, only 46 percent of Australians wanted more international friends. Among the internationals a high proportion from China wanted more local friends, though higher proportions of students from India and from North and Latin America were among the 67 percent of all internationals who tried actively to make friends. Almost half of the international students (48 percent) thought that Australians were *not* interested in having international friends, and only 24 percent disagreed with the statement.[104] Thus few internationals had turned their back on local friendship and for two-thirds it was an active priority—but less than a quarter felt Australian students wanted to be friends with them. Only 58 percent stated that Australian students were "friendly" toward international students, a low figure given that the threshold for being friendly is lower than for making friends.[105] Among local students there was pronounced ambivalence. Almost half (48 percent) were unsure about whether they wanted more international students as friends, although only 5 percent were opposed to it. Over half (51 percent) were unsure whether they had made an effort to have international student friends. Only 5 percent considered international students to be unfriendly, but over one-third were unsure about this. Half (50 percent) were unsure about whether international students should take the first steps in initiating friendship.[106]

A high proportion (89 percent) of international students had friends among students from their own country or among other international students, while 68 percent had Australian students as friends. Australian students showed the opposite pattern of friendships: 93 percent had Australian friends and 64 percent, international friends.[107] The survey also found 86 percent of internationals considered it important to develop an international perspective during the study program compared to 68 percent of local students,[108] further evidence of divergence between the perspectives and intentions of the two groups of students.

CONCLUSION

The research shows that most international students want stronger relations with local students and other local people, and they would like to sustain their identities and form themselves in the context of a richer set of relations with both same-culture and local groups. Most nonwhite students learn to drastically scale down their expectations. Sudden experiences of open discrimination and racism or an accumulation of rebuffs and poor encounters over a longer time force a change in strategy: a retreat from the ambition of open-ended holistic engagement and adoption of a more culture-bound existence, especially outside the classroom. For example, Hullett and Witte find that when "uncertainty control" processes are dominant, sojourners are more adaptive and feel more confident in interaction with local Americans. When "anxiety control" processes are dominant, individuals exhibit "greater tendencies towards isolation than adaptation" and are more likely to seek comfort "within the familiar settings of their own in-group" than risk cross-cultural interaction.[109]

The social processes of negative referencing, stereotyping, and segregation based on essentialist cultural categories—processes identified by Lee and collaborators as "neo-racism"—have their intellectual counterpart in the ethnocentric strand of cross-cultural psychology critiqued in Chapter 2. The adjustment and deficit paradigms imply that international students are the drivers of their own cross-cultural disappointment. They lack the language. They fail to initiate. They cling to their cultural heritage and their home language. They are inherently collectivist and group together too often, blocking each other from local engagement. In that literature there is no critical focus on local identities or local practices, and no modeling of mutual adjustment. But these steps are essential if intercultural relations are to be improved.

Though the importance of communicative competence is obvious, by itself it is insufficient to guarantee productive and creative relations between international students and local populations. There are other barriers to overcome. The social conditions must be right. While international students can work on their language skills and take the initiative rather than (as too many do) waiting for locals to approach them, they cannot determine the behavior of local people and the operations of local institutions. By and large, international students do not choose to separate from local populations, including local students—local populations do. Local populations refuse to engage with the foreign "Other" on equal terms. International students avoid the potential for frustration or humiliation and fall back on same-culture networks that provide support and stability. One side of the divide engages in segregation behavior; the other side engages in separation.

Stereotyping, discrimination, and local segregation must be addressed. These are primary factors in reducing the agency confidence of international students and slowing their language development— and by denying the very need for intercultural relations, eliminating the process of communicative exchange itself.

Unless relational cosmopolitanism is built on more than international student "adjustment," it will fail. Communications, and the need for openness and engagement, are factors that cut both ways. The communication difficulties and anxieties felt by local people, their own sense of inadequacy in the face of the unknown, feed into the destructive processes of stereotyping and occasional abuse. "Fear, she's the mother of violence."[110] Even international students with excellent language skills, like Cindi from Malaysia in Chapter 4, report that foreign voice tones and nonwhite appearance can trigger negative referencing.[111] Local people need to learn to speak to international students, as well as vice versa.

Chapter 6 takes the reader into research on the cross-cultural classroom and returns again to the difficult problem of relations between international and local students.

THE CROSS-CULTURAL CLASSROOM

INTRODUCTION: LANGUAGE AND LEARNING

For most international students, the academic program is the heart of the university experience. It is why they (or most of them) are in the foreign country, and it is often crucial in the evolution of their communications and vocational skills and their interpersonal confidence. For international students, academc success is vital. In higher education, students are coproducers of their own learning, or so conventional wisdom has it. But international student potentials are also shaped and limited by the cultural Other.

Church notes that a major determinant of successful "adjustment" appears to be academic success.[1] Other researchers find the opposite applies. Adjustment is a condition of academic success. Some note rather cynically that experiencing and overcoming stress is intrinsic to academic achievement. Boyer and Sedlacek find that one variable predictive of academic success among international students is "understanding and ability to deal with racism":[2] a line of argument that might be true but could also be used to rationalize or normalize the dark side of the cross-cultural experience.[3]

Cross-cultural academic practices vary from institution to institution, from program to program, and from teacher to teacher. A few teachers with a large number of international students in their charge take the opportunity to re-create the classroom as an intercultural learning program, stretching their own time and resources beyond the norm in order to do so. Others make an effort to adapt by varying their pedagogical methods and providing some students with extra help. Both groups of teachers might from time to time organize cross-cultural work groups to encourage interaction and mutual learning.

A third group of teachers make no adjustment for the presence of international students, regardless of their learning difficulties or their particular cultural and language backgrounds. These teachers argue that it is equitable to treat all students, local and international, in the same manner in curriculum design, teaching, assessment, and the allocation of help. International students must adjust to the program, not the program to them.

Many international students thus depend on language support at the edge of the academic program. But resources for support services are limited in large-scale commercial international education, of the type in the United Kingdom, Australia, and New Zealand, where the purpose is to maximize net revenue per student.

Many teachers and students overcome the limits created by these conditions. Others do not. Students from English as a foreign language (EFL) countries—including China, the world's largest source country for international students; Japan; Korea; Taiwan; Vietnam; Thailand; and Indonesia—face the main difficulties.

Research in Australia has suggested that some international students graduate with English language skills that are no better than the skills they had when they started.[4] If so this would be highly retrograde, for three reasons. It would limit students' academic development, stymie their capacity for cross-cultural relations, and undermine one of the primary objectives of the sojourn. For many international students, bettering their English language proficiency is a goal as important as gaining the university degree itself.

This Chapter

The chapter begins with a discussion of the research literature on language and international students. Only part of this large research literature can be discussed here. The chapter then looks at research on the cross-cultural classroom, including teaching, and combined workgroups involving local and international students. It becomes apparent that while language and cultural issues are intertwined, they are not identical. Researchers differ on which is more determining and in what manner.

ENGLISH LANGUAGE PROFICIENCY

There are two strands in research pertaining to English language proficiency and international students: work on communications in acculturation and cross-cultural relations (Chapter 2 and Chapter 5); and work on communications and academic learning, discussed in this chapter. Note that there are close interdependencies between language use inside and outside the classroom, but few researchers investigate this.

In the United States, Lee focused on graduate international students in their first and second semesters. The students were asked to identify aspects of classroom learning most problematic for them and named listening and oral communication, vocabulary, and writing. Cultural differences were seen as an obstacle. To help them develop oral communication skills, the students suggested that teachers should provide an atmosphere conducive to questions and give the students time to reflect. Teachers should avoid idiomatic language and slang and write key words on the blackboard to assist vocabulary development. They should provide models of the required written work and explain their expectations in simple language.[5] Lin and Yi, and Nasrin have similar findings.[6] Lin and Yi's international students had difficulties in understanding the various accents of instructors, in fully comprehending lectures, and in participating in class discussion. They needed more time than locals to read textbooks. Nasrin found that oral language was a principal concern, particularly understanding the American accent and when giving class presentations and spoken reports. Remedial programs had not been sufficient to overcome these problems.[7]

Trice notes that despite an increased number of international students studying in the United States, little is known about how academic faculty perceive their presence.[8] She conducted interviews in four departments in one institution: public health, architecture, mechanical engineering, and materials science. Teachers had varied perceptions of their international students in their units. Some teachers did not distinguish between international and domestic students. One stated: "Once they are here, they are all people we deal with."[9] Language difficulties, particularly oral communication—largely attributed to Asian students—were cited more than other problems. Students struggled in trying to comprehend lectures. One teacher noted that "the TOEFL (Test of English as a Foreign Language) scores do not seem to be indicative of whether the students can speak English or not."[10] The study also found that the teachers struggled for the resources to provide for the distinctive learning needs of international students.

Studies in the United States, Canada, and the United Kingdom have discussed issues and limitations in language support services. Cownie and Addison conducted a study of staff in charge of language support services for international students in British higher education institutions. A total of 94 institutions participated, and interviews were conducted with one respondent from each institution. Study participants said there was a need for better communication between lecturer-teachers and staff in language support. Teachers should allocate time to enable students to integrate their use of language services within their overall program. Language support services should be seen as just that—support—and not as responsible for language proficiency. Nor should language support services be seen as a last resort. Students should be introduced to the service early so their difficulties can be addressed.[11] Other studies point to the resource limits of support services and discuss the strengths and weaknesses of generic (metadisciplinary) approaches to language support. Because learning is shaped by disciplinary knowledge[12] and cultural factors, including prior learning, wholly generic foundation or support programs cannot solve all problems. In New Zealand, Li and colleagues interviewed 23 international students from a variety of country backgrounds and discipline areas.[13] The researchers noted that people from different linguistic and cultural backgrounds organize discourse differently and have varied classroom politeness regimes.[14] Language support services need to be nuanced so as to meet these varied learning needs.

Australian research suggests an interplay of factors that shape the academic success of students, including personal agency, cultural background, previous education, language proficiency, and teaching and support.[15] English proficiency per se is most often mentioned, especially by students.[16] Studies focus mostly on language-related learning difficulties perceived by students or academic teachers.[17] All research finds that EFL students often experience serious learning difficulties. Some but not all studies acknowledge that academic English requirements extend beyond testable language proficiency to include cultural and contextual factors. However, research has interpreted the role of cultural factors in diverse and often opposing ways. Some argue that the international students must be reprogrammed for Australian learning and its underlying culture. Others argue that Australian learning should be changed to accommodate the cultural specificities and educational histories of the students.

An early study by Samuelovicz[18] examines academic teachers' perceptions of the learning problems of international students in one institution. Teachers stated that these problems were compounded by differences in pedagogical traditions, especially students' undue emphasis on rote learning and reproduction rather than learning to apply knowledge, low level of class participation, "excessive regard for authority," and lack of capacity in critical thinking. In a widely cited study, Ballard and Clanchy agree, arguing that international students manifest "culturally shaped" approaches to learning that differ from local students' and are inappropriate in Australia.[19] Ryan emphasizes students should demonstrate creative, challenging, and questioning learning behavior.[20] There is a considerable literature along similar lines, premised on the notion of "Asian learners" who must be transformed. Asian learners are seen to rely more on memorization than understanding, to prefer surface approaches to learning and be textbook dependent, to be passive in relation to authority, to believe the correct answer is crucial, to focus on avoiding mistakes and so avoid risk, and to privilege harmony and cooperation.[21]

On the other hand, other researchers emphasize variations in learning approach between different groups of international students, and between individuals from the same background.[22] Some explicitly critique the arguments of Samuelowicz, Ballard and Clanchy, and others. These are seen as resting on ethnocentric stereotypes of the Hofstedian type, with doubtful foundations.[23] In teaching strategies that essentialize cultural difference, "Western pedagogic identity is constituted through . . . 'annihilation or emptying out' of the Asian other."[24] Doherty and Singh see this as the dominant pedagogical stance in English-speaking countries. Dunn and Wallace note that one view, commonly held though unsubstantiated in research, "is that students engage with a Western degree and want just that; the credential and an insight into Western outlook and practices, an unmediated Western Curriculum and pedagogy," jettisoning what they know.[25]

Hellstén and Prescott interviewed 48 international students, mostly from Asia, for one hour in semistructured format. Many of the students faced problems of oral communication and confidence. Language-related difficulties imposed extra time pressures: assignment preparation took longer, lectures were recorded and replayed, and the pace of conversation in English slowed when students translated in and out of their home language. On average it took them about 30–40 percent longer to master content compared to native English speakers.[26] But whereas some studies have suggested the need for lecturers to adjust their conversational style to the English proficiency of international students, those interviewed by Hellstén and Prescott argued the opposite. Delivering lectures in lower-level language registers was seen as unhelpful and a "gesture that further marginalizes them from the mainstream students."[27] Another paper by Prescott and Hellstén expands on these themes. The authors conclude that teachers' professional development should address the cultural and other assumptions routinely embedded in intercultural communication and that the reluctance of some students to approach persons in authority for assistance reflected values different from those of local students that needed to be taken into account.[28]

Singh interviewed international students from China in the final year of undergraduate degrees in Australia. American or British textbook English had not fully prepared the students for Australian spoken English, which they found difficult to understand.[29] The problem worsened when conversation involved unfamiliar topics. The students felt they needed to strengthen both language proficiency and their cultural understanding of Australian English. They also identified certain ways to overcome their sense of failure and develop independent self-confidence: forming friendships with student from other countries and taking part-time jobs that would enable English-language conversations with other workers. Language barriers tended to close off both possibilities.[30] Singh's study confirms that students' academic difficulties are partly driven by classroom practices in Australia differing from those in China. Chinese pedagogies were more teacher centered than student centered. In Australia students had to say more. Critical thinking was valued.

Tran criticizes much of the English-language research on academic writing by students from China and Vietnam, pointing to the widespread tendency to "essentialize cultural rhetorical patterns." Her study shows that students from China and Vietnam might appear to share some features of a common approach that has been called "collectivist," but this insight is only one relatively superficial element in understanding the various individual strategies in second language learning and expression that the students employ. "Their ways of constructing knowledge in the light of this norm appear to be complex and different."[31] Once again, as with the cultural fit hypothesis, an analysis grounded in cultural essentialism is unable to explain what empirical observation has to tell.

In their study, Mulligan and Kirkpatrick report that few international students had a strong understanding of lectures. "Many lecturers are still failing to accommodate the cultural and linguistic diversity of the classes they teach."[32] To Borland and Pearce "a major shortcoming of the modern multicultural university" is its "failure to adequately understand the implications of diversity" in relation to "language, literacy and cultural understanding." Universities have failed to sufficiently develop educational strategies enabling "the university to be inclusive of all its students," rather than just those "considered to constitute the majority group."[33] Like other researchers, they find the cross-cultural competence of international students is closely allied to their English language proficiency.[34]

Other research avoids the "Asian learner" stereotype and the debate about it. Most students who enter Australia take an International English Language Testing System (IELTS) test in speaking, listening, reading, and writing. However, both Pantelides and Carroll identify students who met the IELTS entry requirement but have poor academic English proficiency.[35] Some studies find no statistically significant relationship between IELTS and academic performance, or a negative correlation.[36] Further, internationals starting with low proficiency may succeed if the learning setting is conducive enough.[37] This raises doubts about whether IELTS should be used to determine educability. On the other hand, a number of other studies find IELTS does constitute an effective predictor of performance.[38] Poyrazli and colleagues identify a positive relationship between student scores in the reading and writing subtest, academic achievement, and also student adjustment.[39] Studies by Kerstjens and Nery, and Bayliss and Raymond, find the reading subtest predicts academic performance.[40] In summarizing the debate in Australia, and the similar discussion in the United States, Rochecouste and colleagues state that "overall IELTS text scores have not been found to be definitely or strongly correlated to academic success."[41]

While these results together are inconclusive, a key problem generated by the centrality of IELTS in Australia is that efforts to improve quality are often focused on raising IELTS intake standards, constituting an ethnocentric reflexivity, not on improving cross-cultural teaching where deeper gains are to be made.

Pantelides used both written questionnaires and interviews to study 12 non-English-speaking-background (NESB) students from several ethnic groups who were enrolled in first-year undergraduate engineering in one institution. Four academic teachers were interviewed separately. The study is small but insightful.[42] Academic staff stated that although students achieved the minimum standard of English required at entry, their language proficiency was inadequate to academic English requirements, especially in writing. Some teachers were unaware of students' cultural and educational backgrounds and the nature of their learning difficulties. They were also unsure of what constituted effective English language skills and how these skills could be developed. Teachers also remarked that extra efforts in support of NESB students were not recognized or rewarded by the university, and there were resource constraints. When asked whether they had adapted the format of lectures to make them more accessible, the teachers said no; they did not have enough feedback to know which adaptations would assist. The students said they needed more time for reading texts and found it difficult to follow lectures. One stated that the only way he could understand the theory in his course was by committing himself to three to four hours of preparatory and revision reading each evening.[43] Some stated that expectations about written work were unclear. The students felt that their academic teachers ignored their learning needs and simply expected them to do everything required, triggering students' frustration.

In the study by Robertson and colleagues, again at just one institution, teachers and students emphasized similar problems. The majority of students, particularly those from Malaysia, had incomplete understanding of lecturers' spoken English and felt unhappy with their own oral performances in class. Additionally, the students reported that their lack of confidence with English hindered their ability to speak in front of the class. Other issues included student problems with colloquial language, writing essays, and interpreting questions. Both students and teachers agreed that the speed of lecturers' spoken English exacerbated problems of understanding. Teachers' responses were generally similar to those of the students but with different emphasis. While students reported that lack of proficiency and confidence in English hindered their ability to speak in class, teachers often saw the lack of classroom participation as driven by cultural differences in the approach to learning. Students saw communication as coupled with agency, while teachers saw communication as coupled with culture. This suggests the "Asian learners" argument might have noncultural roots. It also suggests that students' lack of agency—for example silence in class and even deference to authority—is not so much culture bound as a product of the learning environment.

CROSS-CULTURAL RELATIONS IN THE CLASSROOM

There are two aspects of cross-cultural relations in the classroom that involve international students: relations between teachers and their international students and relations between local and international students.

Teachers

Fallon and Brown note little is known about how the presence of international students in UK higher education affects teachers and teaching.[44] They used a small-scale postal questionnaire survey and follow-up telephone interviews with academic staff working with non-UK postgraduate students[45] in four institutions. Many teachers agreed that international students triggered the need for alternative teaching methods. Many expressed confusion about assessment standards for non-UK students. In the U.S. study by Trice, all teachers agreed international students provided an international perspective, broadened the dynamics of classroom discussion, and added to domestic students' overall learning.[46]

In a subsequent study, Trice reports on the strategies used by teachers and academic units in response to international students.[47] The disciplines of architecture and public health introduced more adaptations to address the specific needs of international students than did engineering. In the classroom, teachers used more teaching aids, spoke more slowly, and avoided colloquialism. In these disciplines technical knowledge was context bound and best understood in the society where it was used. It was therefore essential to create a learning environment reflecting the cultural diversity of the student body, so contextualizing future graduates' practice. This helped students to learn from each other as well as from their teachers. In engineering, knowledge was seen as universal so that cultural background and context of graduate practice were less relevant to the learning process. Another factor was that in engineering, many international students stayed on to work in the United States after completing their studies. Trice remarks that certain factors shaped individual academic responses: not just discipline but also age and whether the academic had overseas experience. Staff without overseas experience believed it was not important to make special accommodations for international students. Senior academic faculty were more attentive to student needs than those aged less than 40 years.

In the study by Trice and Yoo, research students identify the cultural sensitivity of doctoral advisers. Those from the physical sciences and engineering exhibited the lowest cultural sensitivity.[48] Several researchers find teachers from non-Anglo-American backgrounds exhibit greater empathy with students from Asia and Africa. Olson and Kroeger state second language proficiency and "substantive experience abroad" make a difference.[49] Schuerholz-Lehr comments that while there have been many studies of teachers' global awareness and cross-cultural sensitivity and knowledge, "less conclusive evidence is available as to whether and how such traits in faculty translate into actual classroom practices."[50]

Most teachers dealing with large numbers of international students recognize cultural differences. Many also see local identity as fixed and essentialize the differences, failing to understand identity and culture are open and fluid and in continuous negotiation by students and teachers.[51] Many teachers in international education want cultural inclusivity in curriculum and pedagogy[52] if only to transmit the curriculum more effectively. However, research suggests academic teachers who understand the learning difficulties of international students, and more so those who glimpse the potential benefits of intercultural learning, are not always in a position to respond. The commercial purpose of international education in the United Kingdom, Australia, and New Zealand mitigates "thick" teaching strategies tailored to the different backgrounds and needs of each learner, or provision of English as a second language specialist teachers alongside subject teachers. Bartram notes that in a study of one program conducted across institutions in the United Kingdom and the Netherlands, staff from both institutions endorsed "sociocultural needs" but placed limits on them. "Their overriding perception was that student support needs were growing and extending in some cases beyond what they considered appropriate."[53] Teachers perceived undue student dependency. Some attributed this to consumer culture and wanted students to take more responsibility for their own work.[54] Student agency is invoked but as a means of reducing cross-cultural support.

Local and International Students

The different educational traditions of local and international students can be an obstacle to the ease of classroom relations. Tatar compares the attitudes of Turkish and American students to classroom discussion. At issue was not merely communicative competence, but values and protocols. The Turkish students "did not feel comfortable expressing their ideas without doing careful thinking and preparation to assess their content value in advance . . . The students perceived it as inappropriate to contribute through their personal experiences unless they thought that they would be useful to others. Likewise, they expected other contributors to present information valuable and relevant to every member of the class that would lead to new learning. These perceptions were reflected in the silence of the study students when their ideas did not meet their criteria."[55]

Turkish students did not find aural participation a major assistance in their development, though it had marginal benefits such as confidence building.[56] They were critical of local American students "they perceived as talkative . . . who spoke frequently and often expressed their personal opinions." These students were seen as "dominating discussions or patronizing others in groups by using their language advantage," resulting in "intimidation and a sense of exclusion" and "wasting class time with excessive talking and by taking discussions into irrelevant directions."[57]

National variations in teacher-student relations are a long-standing topic in educational research. Zhang compares Chinese students in China and American college students in the United States, in their expectations and experiences of out-of-class relations with teachers, such as visits to staff members' offices and communications. In comparison with the American students, Chinese students and their teachers engaged in less in-class interaction. Student questioning could be seen as "disruptive and disrespectful."[58] But "the pastoral role of Chinese teachers requires an on-going, extracurricular involvement with students" with more out-of-class communication than in the United States. Most students are in campus residences. "Chinese teachers assume the multiple roles of being an instructor, authority, parent, and model, which requires them to care about students' overall development, including their study, life, and problems."[59] In the United States more class contact is through e-mail than it is in China. Student satisfaction with the out-of-class contact is higher in the United States, probably because expectations are less.

In the United Kingdom, Pritchard and Skinner reported on outcomes of cross-cultural partnerships in student learning. Results were mixed. As a result of the experience certain international students grew more uncertain about whether they enjoyed interacting with people from different cultures, displaying "a tendency to become discouraged, sometimes avoiding contact." Overall there was growth in the proportion that enjoyed contact, but some local students also became uneasy about cross-cultural contact. There were mixed results in relation to cultural openness. "Mere contact does not always lead to the mutual valuing of traditions."[60] On balance the negatives were outweighed by the positives. "The project resulted in the formation of some durable friendships and increased enjoyment of cross-cultural interaction on the part of the internationals, as well as a greater confidence in their ability to engage in it successfully."[61] Carroll notes research showing that international students preferred working in a multicultural group to working in a same-culture group because it was their only chance to interact with local students.[62] Ippolito finds some international students were indifferent to the potential benefits of working in a cross-cultural group, in part because of communication barriers.[63]

In Australia a report prepared for the Australian Learning and Teaching Council in 2008–2010 summarized the benefits of international/local student interaction as follows: "Increased awareness and understanding of different perspectives; better preparation for the workplace; improved English language skills of international students, and a greater feeling of belonging." At the same time, the report identified obstacles, including lack of teaching time in which to foster interactions as a result of large class sizes and content-heavy curricula, differing levels of English language proficiency, lack of local student time on campus due to paid work commitments, and the absence of sufficient common ground in prior education, culture and language, and academic aspirations.[64]

Some Australian studies, like Tatar, suggest the two groups of students harbor different values and objectives. Volet and Ang note Hong Kong and Singapore students may be "more achievement oriented" than Western students and thus reluctant to join mixed work groups. Cooperation is also inhibited by differences between the collaborative methods used by many internationals and the more individualist styles of locals.[65] Volet and Renshaw compare matched groups of international students from Southeast Asia with local Australian students. "Cultural/educational differences" in the goals they held at the beginning of university study disappeared after one semester.[66] International students lowered their academic expectations, thereby converging with the expectations of local students. Certain differences remained. One was a greater use of collective learning methods among many Asian students.

Ramburuth and McCormick compare the learning styles and preferences of newly arrived Asian students with those of locals. "Asian international students demonstrated significantly higher use of deep motivation, surface strategies, and achieving strategies, whilst Australian students demonstrated higher use of deep strategies and surface motivation." The Asian students were "more 'collaborative' in their learning styles."[67] The researchers conclude that "significant differences between the Australian and international students on several learning constructs investigated in the study, serve to draw attention to the nature of learning diversity present in Australian tertiary classrooms . . . For Asian international students, these could include prior learning experiences in home countries, fewer distractions while studying away from home, family pressure and expectations, and the costs and short time-spans for studying abroad."[68]

Like Pritchard and Skinner in the United Kingdom, Volet and Ang focus on mixed work groups. They investigate the problem of lack of interaction between international and local students. Students in both categories exhibited separation behaviors. For both groups, working with those of similar linguistic background maximized empathy and ease of communications. Language is one factor at work: "Language issues explain why many international students keep quiet in class at the beginning of their study in Australia as well as prefer to stay with people who speak their native language . . . it also explains why international students are not more proactive in seeking the company of Australian students to complete group assignments."[69]

Some local students also report that lack of English proficiency among international students inhibits relationships. Here Volet and Ang separate communications issues from "cultural-emotional connectedness."[70] Cultural factors may outweigh language factors.[71] "A major question is the extent to which communication problems are real or whether they are impeded by a lack of goodwill—from either side—to make an effort to understand each other and to tolerate a degree of broken English."[72] While the sense of belonging and bonding in conational peer groups is enhanced by common language, language is not always essential to cultural empathy. "Otherwise, why would Singaporean students—for the majority of whom English is the first language"—mix with Indonesian students rather than Australian students?[73]

The last point suggests that the foreign/nonforeign distinction may be decisive. Volet and Ang are not convinced of this. "It could be argued that the common condition of being new in a foreign country is what brings students together." But anecdotal evidence of difficult inter-cultural relations between Southeast Asian internationals and American exchange students undermines this explanation.[74] Going beyond the argument of the authors, it can be suggested that foreignness, cultural commonality, and linguistic commonality are all at play—and one or another may be determining—depending on the context and the cultures. The cultural and linguistic differences between Southeast Asians and Americans are too great for an empathy based on shared foreignness; or perhaps the local context Others them in different ways along the Western/non-Western divide, and this differentiates their common foreignness. But in the Australian setting, the Othering of Singaporean and Indonesian students is similar and brings them into a common position in relation to the dominant culture. This reinforces their shared experience as foreign students, despite linguistic and religious differences.

As students progress through the later years of the program, they evidence more negative attitudes to working in culturally mixed groups.[75] Both Australian and international students appeared to prefer working on assignments "with their 'own people.' According to the authors, four types of reasons are identified: cultural-emotional connectedness; language; pragmatism; and negative stereotypes." Both groups of students mentioned all four reasons, but international students gave much more importance than local students to cultural-emotional connectedness.[76] This refers to "the students' perceptions of feeling more comfortable, thinking along the same wave-length, and sharing a similar communication style and sense of humour when interacting with peers from the same cultural background."[77] Many of the international students indicated that connecting to students from the same nation and "ethnic background" helped them "to maintain a sense of identity in a foreign country." Further, when peers of the same nation and ethnic background are absent, "cultural-emotional connectedness" tends to be extended to students from "the next closest culture." The authors note that "the fact that many Asian students would prefer to team with other Asian students rather than with Australian students may be a way of minimizing cultural distance."[78]

The priority placed on cultural-emotional connectedness therefore creates "major stumbling blocks in the formation of culturally mixed groups."[79] Some international students also indicated that in their view, Asian students work together more and better than local students do. Few Asian students indicated that cultural mixing during study was important to them. Volet and Ang are concerned that most students will not risk "moving outside their comfort zone" to work with people from a different culture. Negative stereotypes and difficulties with communication were other obstacles. The experience of working in the cross-cultural groups often helped to correct misperceptions and stereotypes. However, "it may be naive to think that one successful cross-cultural experience will naturally lead to students' pro-active involvement in cross-cultural encounters later on. This was sadly clear in the interviews with the six culturally mixed groups which revealed no evidence that any of the students would deliberately form or seek to join culturally mixed groups in the future."[80]

The experience of combined work groups showed that the cultural factor could be diminished. Some students came to realize that cultural differences may be less important than similar goals and "mutual commitment to invest time and energy in the task."[81] But internationalization of university education is unlikely to be achieved unless the students, especially the local Australian students, become "fully committed to developing inter-cultural awareness and an understanding and acceptance of each other."[82] Both parties share "some responsibility" for the lack of cultural mixing, and both must be prepared to make intercultural education work. To create and maintain mixed-culture work groups, firm intervention is needed.[83]

A study by Summers and Volet worked with a sample of 233 business studies students in one Australian university, one-third international. The researchers investigated attitudes held by students in different years of study, the relation of these attitudes to the students' prior experience with multiple languages, "whether attitudes are related to observed behaviour, and how attitudes change" when participating in "diverse or non-diverse" groups.[84] They remark that group projects should be long enough in duration "to allow culturally mixed groups to surmount initial difficulties and reap the longer term advantages of cultural diversity."[85]

Attitudes to self-selecting mixed group work did not significantly alter between first and third year and were more positive among the 92 percent of internationals and one-third of local students who were multilingual. The two multilingual groups did not differ significantly on the point.[86] Prior "intercultural experience" provided the necessary skills for culturally mixed groups.[87] At the beginning of group tasks, local students were more likely to have negative attitudes to mixed-group work, especially local students who self-selected into same-culture groups.[88] However, there was no difference of attitude between international students who selected into same-culture groups and those who selected into mixed groups. "Members of non-mixed international groups reported significantly more positive pre-task attitudes than students who formed local-only groups. This lends itself to the interpretation that it was primarily the more negative attitudes of local students who favoured non-mixed group work that posed a barrier to international students joining mixed groups. Whether or not international students find their way into mixed groups appears to have little to do with their own attitudes."[89]

Worryingly, the participants as a whole had "significantly less favourable attitudes" to mixed cultural group work "at post-task than at pre-task."[90] This was true of both the monolingual and multilingual students.[91] But there were no statistically significant decline in support among students who were members of mixed cultural work groups, and no significant difference for monolingual members of non-mixed groups. Multilingual members of nonmixed groups became less favorably inclined to mixed-group work, presumably because the same-culture group work was satisfactory to them.[92] That result suggests that cultural separations can become more entrenched over time. The most positive outcome from both this study and Volet and Ang's study is "that students who have an experience of mixed group work perceive that it was not problematic for them."[93] But overall, Summers and Volet conclude that "students' experiences of group work at university are not serving the educational and social goals of internationalization."[94]

> A strong possibility here is that students' self-selection into mixed or non-mixed work groups throughout their studies has meant that the students most likely to have developed more positive attitudes as a result of regular mixed group work experiences . . . [have] managed to avoid these experiences. This again suggests the need to enforce "culturally mixed group work (either self-selected or tutor-allocated)" to generate a "positive attitudinal shift." . . . Our results thus provide further support for the view that interventions aimed at increasing local students' willingness to work on group assignments with international students are required to enhance students' intercultural competence via intercultural work experience, and to provide international students who aim to maximise their intercultural experiences at university with more opportunities to fulfil their goal.[95]

CONCLUSION

Language proficiency by itself does not ensure effective student agency, active cross-cultural relations, academic progress, and student freedom. But it helps. Likewise, active cross-cultural engagement, free of deficit-making and cross-cultural tensions, can help to build communicative agency. Cross-cultural contact per se does not deliver all these outcomes. Not all cross-cultural contact is productive or even breaks down stereotypes. Nevertheless, the right kind of cross-cultural contact is likely to make a significant difference. This can be created in the classroom. Often it is not.

To summarize the main argument, the essential elements of generative intercultural relations in international education are active student agency, communicative competence, and cross-cultural engagement, in local conditions that favour relational cosmopolitanism. The interplay is complex, but the point that must be emphasized is the need for favorable local conditions. There must be sufficient common ground between the parties in the form of a common language (in this case English), enough shared cultural knowledge, mutual openness and flexibility, and a common motivation to engage. Given that by and large international students are prepared to be more open and flexible, the key variable at play is the position of locals.

Intercultural education requires cosmopolitan perspectives and learning ambitions in the local student body. This is the most difficult element to achieve. What matters above all is the *motivation* of local students. Volet and Ang, and Volet and Summers suggest that adequate quality and quantity of motivation will not emerge spontaneously. It needs to be prestructured by teaching strategies.

Chapter 7 provides an integrated cultural theorization of international education as an alternative to the ethnocentric vision critiqued in Chapter 2. Chapter 8 takes up the practical educational challenge posed in the conclusion of the present chapter.

CHAPTER 7

---◦✦◦---

CONCLUSION 1

INTERNATIONAL EDUCATION AS SELF-FORMATION

INTRODUCTION: "I HAVE MY LIFE"

This chapter is the first of two concluding the argument of this book. It summarizes what we have found about international students in cross-cultural settings. It provides a cultural theory of mobile students as human agents and what happens to their identities, their sense of themselves, in the country of education.

The key idea is that the border-crossing form of international education (and perhaps all higher education) is best understood as a process of *self-formation*.

The idea of higher education as self-formation is simple and far reaching. It puts the student in the center of the frame. It also acknowledges that her or his setting and conditions are often challenging and transformative. Even so, the student has chosen to experience that transformation. The point is that international students *change themselves* in the country of education. They place themselves in the path of change. Some let it happen. Others run to meet it. Often, though not always, they have an end in sight. There is a kind of person they want to become, though no human identity ever becomes completely fixed and final.

Self-formation means working on oneself. All people do it, but some do it more persistently and deliberately than others. In self-formation people consciously fashion themselves as they go, working critically and using feedback from themselves (and others). They have difficulty making themselves what they want to be. Mostly, things work out differently from the way that was imagined in advance. But people persist, reshaping their intentions as they go. They oscillate between pushing against what they see as their own inadequacies, temporarily accepting those limitations, and then thrusting forward again. For international students, changing themselves is the whole point of international education. They take on this great challenge because they want to acquire certain educated and personal attributes. Most of them want to better their English language proficiency. Many want to broaden their understanding of the world and their future geographic mobility. Many want to augment their careers and future earnings, piloting a successful course through life with the help of a foreign education. Many want to live and develop themselves away from home, and this often becomes increasingly attractive.

For some, just gaining the scope to engage in free self-formation is a great benefit of international education. As one 19-year-old female art student from India said during the research interviews conducted with two hundred students in Australia:

> I love it here, I'm comfortable. You see the thing is, I fit in over here. I don't fit in, in India, I'm a feminist, OK, I'm a strong minded woman and in the Indian sub-continent it is very difficult. [Here] I have the freedom to lead my own life and I am not expected to come home and . . . I don't have all the social pressures to deal with. I have my life.
> Q. How does living in Australia compare with living back home? What are the main differences?
> A. The way I am treated. I'm treated like a human being over here. In my home city, it is impossible for me to go out, even to buy a packet of biscuits. Men trying to touch me and so forth. You have a big proletarian mass in Mumbai and as a result, a woman can't go out very easily. Here I can walk on the roads, and when I come to uni, I don't have to disturb the boys. There are people opening the doors for me, there are people looking out for me. That's a whole new experience. That is the biggest difference. And privacy, being a woman . . . you're respected.

International students become a mixture of two different people: the person they were when they arrived in the country of education and the person they are becoming. It is not easy. Studying and living in a new country brings struggles, doubts, and tensions with it. Like all students undergoing tertiary studies—but more than most—many of the changes that happen to them are unexpected, outside the plan. International students change in unforseen ways and acquire unexpected new ideas of themselves. Nevertheless, they find themselves self-managing those changes too. Even when changing identity "just happens" during the course of the sojourn—the product of their cognitive, affective, and social experiences—the students monitor that change, processing it and reshaping it over time.

International students are not always in charge of their own destiny, but they are in charge of their own identity. The idea of international education as a process of self-formation means that instead of seeing the international student as a weak, deficient, or inherently divided human agent—as some of the research in psychological counseling would suggest—the international student is seen as a strong agent shaping the course of her or his life. At the same time, this does not mean that *anything* is possible—that the student can be whatever she or he wants. International students form themselves under conditions that they do not control. Those conditions are not the same for each international student. Some have a richer set of options, or personal attributes that help them to blend in within the country of education. Others do not. For many the learning curves are long and steep. There are problems, doubts, and confusions. It is can be a struggle to survive, materially and mentally. Students must grapple with unfamiliar cultures in their educational institution and the society. Communication is often a problem. Students can find themselves personally isolated. The attitudes of local people, and the interactions of students with them, set boundaries. If the international student experiences stereotyping, abuse, or discrimination, then her or his engagement with and learning from people in the country of education is more restricted than it might otherwise have been. These conditions place limits on the capacity for experience and exploration. The blocks and barriers they experience send self-forming international students down some pathways and not others.

Education as self-formation is both a normative ideal and a living, breathing reality. It already exists. It can be observed empirically, in students' daily worlds and in their classrooms. It is also an ideal that shapes the approach taken to international education. All people should be self-determining of their own lives. The idea of international education as self-formation encourages institutions and teachers to build strong, conscious student agency and work with it rather than suborning or coercing the student. Here reflexive self-formation in education is like the larger project of democracy (of which it is one part). Actual democratic practices exist. They are not an empty utopia, but there could be more and better democratic practices. Likewise, the conditions of freedom experienced by international students should be expanded, and the capacity of these students (and all students) for self-formation in the country of education should grow.

International students should be respected as self-determining humans—no more and no less than the citizens of the countries in which their education takes place respect each other. These ideas of independent agency, self-formation, and equal respect in turn provide the basis for healthier intercultural relations in the country of education—for the relational cosmopolitanism discussed in Chapter 3.

This Chapter

The chapter develops the notion of human agents as historically located, open, and self-determining and the implications of this for self-formation in international education. This idea of human agency in *Ideas for Intercultural Education* is contrasted with the educational subject in much of cross-cultural psychology as was originally discussed in Chapter 2. Yet psychology also provides much of the evidence for self-formation considered in this chapter. The problem with cross-cultural psychology is less with the empirical work, which is often sharp, than with the theorizations and interpretations. The chapter discusses different strategies used by international students in shaping and managing their self-formation. In doing so it reinterprets certain evidence gathered by psychology, in cultural terms.

LEARNING AND AGENCY

Transformative Learning

People learn in two ways: incremental learning and transformative learning. The latter plays a large role in international education In incremental learning people add to their knowledge bit by bit, on the basis of what they already know. Most learning is of this kind. People do it continually. But transformative learning, which plays a large role in international education, happens less often. It is qualitatively different. Transformative learning involves an imaginative leap into a new appropriation of the world, a new way of looking at things, or a new synthesis of what is observed. In transformative learning, people learn by creating something new in themselves.

Nothing is ever completely new. What is transformative for one person, such as a student, might be already known to another, such as the teacher. And even in major creative activity in the sciences or the arts, when people think of something new they always draw on material already known to them in the past.[1] But there is always an element of newness in creation, whether a new thing is born or there is an interpretation different from what came before.[2] In major creative activity the newness is new to everyone. In transformational learning of all kinds it is new to the person who does the learning. Transformational learning is like "punctuated equilibrium" in evolutionary theory.[3] Evolution is characterized by long periods in which little change occurs, punctuated by periods in which accelerated innovations and transformations are compressed into a short space. Likewise, for most of the time people go on much as they did before, in path-dependent fashion, learning bit by bit. But every so often they undergo a new experience, perhaps a personal crisis of some kind, that creates the need to rethink things fundamentally or grapple with a major new problem. Or they move to another country and must take on board a new culture with effects across the different parts of their lives. This propels them into a sudden, new level of knowledge and understanding.

Learning a new language often entails transformative learning. Language learning is especially relevant to intercultural education because it is often part of the process and involves elements of both incremental learning and transformational learning. People prefer to learn a new language that is close in form and content to their native language, a neighboring language. It is easier for speakers of the Malaysian national language to learn Tagalog, the foundation for the national language of the Philippines (which is a related language), than to learn German. It is easier for an English speaker to learn French, where there is much in common, than Putonghua, the national language of China. When acquiring a neighboring language, the learner can build knowledge of the new language on the basis of elements of common vocabulary and grammatical structures. This is incremental learning. When learning a language that is very different in form and content, it is harder to make incremental learning work, except through continuous translation in both directions, which is slow and difficult. But as the learner works at it, every so often there comes a breakthrough when whole slabs of the new language start to fall into place. Having been exposed to the new language over time and stored it away in memory without learning to reproduce it, the learner finds that it suddenly gels in the conscious mind. This process of sudden gelling is transformational learning. It happens from time to time in all language learning and becomes more crucial in the case of languages wholly different from those the learner already knows.

Different fields of knowledge make varied demands on our incremental and transformational learning. Much of mathematical learning involves incremental learning. One mathematical formula and application leads to another. But the process is also punctuated by imaginative leaps: think of the transition from arithmetic to simple algebra to quadratic equations. One of the arguments for liberal education in the humanities is that it directly fosters this capacity for imaginative reappropriation, this reenvisioning of the world.

Some learners seem to be better at one of these two kinds of learning rather than the other. But it is likely that in much learning, and in all complex learning in higher education, *both* forms of learning are in play. Students in higher education form themselves by using both incremental and transformative learning. Here transformational learning has the deeper implications for self-formation. In transformative learning, people change. They have reimagined the world in some way and so reimagined themselves within it. The world never quite goes back to what it was. The person's identity, or sense of self, also changes.

International education is very fertile in its transformative educational experiences: learning a new language more fully, learning a different set of rules, learning to behave in new ways in every situation, learning how to learn in new ways. Educational transitions are always associated with a measure of identity change. The transition from elementary to secondary education, the transition from secondary education to higher education within one country, and later the transition from higher education to work and profession all trigger transformational learning. Arguably, there is no educational transition more profound than that involved in international education. For many international students, especially those moving from one language of use to another, the transition from home-country education system to the foreign-country education system is wider in terms of cultural difference and more prolonged in duration than local students' transition from school to higher education. At the same time the changes are also intense, especially early in the student's stay, because all of the changes are compressed at once into the same few years. International education demands more of the imagination than does domestic education. Periods of punctuated equilibrium, sudden bursts of rapid and concentrated change, are essential if the student is to survive and prosper. International students do not all transform themselves dramatically, but many do. On average they undergo a greater change in identity than do most local students, all else being equal. Interview data suggests that many students will themselves to achieve profound learning and change. They are disappointed if they do not change as they hope; for example, those unsuccessful in immersing themselves in English or forming a range of close local friends.

This notion of transformative learning offers a potential solution to one of the mysteries in the research in cross-cultural psychology on international education. As noted in Chapter 2, some researchers assume that the greater the cultural distance between the home country and the host country, the more difficult it is for the student to adjust successfully in the host country and to be proactive on her or his own behalf. The clear implication of the "cultural fit" argument is that international students coming with backgrounds very different from those of Western and English language and culture are in *deficit* when compared to other students. But as was also noted in Chapter 2, empirical data fail to confirm the cultural fit argument. Students from, say, East Asian background are not less likely to adjust in the new country or act as effective agents when there. The cultural fit argument assumes that students learn by extrapolating on the basis of similarities. The potential for qualitative transformation is ignored. But what seems to happen with many students is that where the cultural difference is substantial, and there are reduced opportunities for incremental learning, the facility for transformational learning kicks in. Some culturally distant students find ways to engage imaginatively with their cultural others in the country of education, without ceasing to be culturally distant. Others devise new identities, which combine themselves and the other. As will be explored further later in this chapter, the students develop a range of identity strategies.

Agency Freedom

If *identity* is what a person understands themselves or others to be, *agency* is the sum of a person's capacity to act. The Nobel Laureate Amartya Sen places a central emphasis on freedom as self-determination. He defines an *agent* as "someone who acts and brings about change, and whose achievements can be judged in terms of her own values and objectives, whether or not we assess them in terms of some external criteria as well."[4] "Responsible adults must be in charge of their own well-being; it is for them to decide how to use their capabilities. But the capabilities that a person does actually have (and not merely theoretically enjoys) depend on the nature of the social arrangements, which can be crucial for individual freedoms. And there the state and society cannot escape responsibility."[5]

A person's "capability" refers to the things that the person may choose to do or to be. It extends beyond a person's role in the productive economy to include civil and family life. "Capability" includes not only a person's abilities, native and acquired, and her or his material resources but also the conditions in which agency is exercised, including opportunities and constraints in the "social arrangements" around that person. The freedoms available to human agents are crucially important.

According to Sen, free human agency embodies three elements. First, an active human will and centered conscious identity, which is the seat of self-directed activity. Sen calls this "agency freedom." The second is freedom from external threat or constraint. He calls this "control freedom"; other scholars term it "negative freedom." The third element is freedom as the capacity to act, which Sen calls "effective freedom" or "freedom as power." Some call it "positive freedom."[6] Effective freedom depends on the material means and social arrangements that enable people to act, to put their choices into practice. Simply put, control freedom and effective freedom can be understood as the defensive and proactive moments of human agency.

In this constellation of freedoms, agency freedom is especially important. It is here that reflexive self-formation is guided and challenging transformations of identity are negotiated with the self and implemented. Sen remarks that the perspectives of "well-being" and "agency" each yield distinct notions of freedom.[7] The notion of well-being suggests a choice-making individual, but it does not necessarily imply an active or interactive individual. The notion of agency suggests an intrinsically active and proactive human will. In the well-being perspective, the person is seen as a beneficiary whose interests and advantages are foremost. In the agency perspective, a person is seen more as a doer and judge. The two different notions of freedom also have different implications for human goals and valuations. As Sen puts it, "the well-being aspect of a person is important in assessing a person's *advantage*, whereas the agency aspect is important in assessing what a person can do in line with his or her conception of *the good*. The ability to do more good need not be to the person's advantage."[8] The example he gives is that of the person who chooses to save the life of another despite an inconvenience to herself or himself. Sen notes that in recent debates the perspective of well-being has occupied more attention than that of agency, signifying the impact of utilitarianism and of neoclassical economics. But well-being alone is insufficient to serve as the foundation of identity. Agency is at the core of self.

Notions of "autonomy" and "personal liberty" relate to this special role of agency freedom in personal life, which extends well beyond considerations of economic well-being. People are not motivated solely by money. Money and the capacity to earn it are important drivers of behavior but not the only drivers. Dignity, happiness, family friends, satisfying work, the scope to create, and much else are also important. Self-forming human agents choose their own dreams and agendas from the menu of the available and possible, and sometimes a little more.

SELF-FORMATION

The notion of education as self-formation is a humanist conception of education. In this conception, people, their freedoms, and their self-formation in education according to their own desires—albeit a self-formation pursued in conditions that they mostly do not control—are seen as ends in themselves. The humanist idea of people as ends in themselves is consistent with the essential nature of learning, which is about the growth of individual capabilities and sociability. In that respect education has more in common with child rearing and parenting than it has with, say, the manufacture of inanimate goods, such as semiconductors or bathtubs.

Sen also makes an argument that the enhancement of individual freedoms in the form of human capability provides the optimum conditions for economic and social development. For example, improvements in the education of women in the developing world are consistently associated with reduced birth rates, reduced infant mortality, and better child health. This is because education augments human agency. It enables women to assert themselves and make better decisions: "There are in fact many different ways in which school education may enhance a young woman's decisional power within the family: through its effect on her social standing, her ability to be independent, her power to articulate, her knowledge of the outside world, her skill in influencing group decisions and so on."[9]

By the same token, education unquestionably enhances the productive conditions for economic growth. But this is not the ultimate value of education. Economic growth is only a means to an end, which is the enhancement of humans. "The acknowledgement of the role of human qualities in promoting and sustaining economic growth—momentous as it is—tells us nothing about *why* economic growth is sought in the first place. If, instead, the focus is ultimately on the expansion of human freedom to live the kind of lives that people have wisdom to value, then the role of economic growth in expanding these opportunities has to be integrated into that more foundational understanding of the process of development as the expansion of human capability to lead more worthwhile and more free lives."[10]

International education as self-formation is an inclusive idea. It takes in all the outcomes for students usually associated with higher education: the notion of education as an investment in future earnings (human capital), the notion that students acquire knowledge and personal sensibilities (liberal education or cultural capital), the notion that students change and augment their relational networks during the process of study, the notion that they acquire new values and beliefs, the notion that they become freer people; and the notion—in the case of international and sometimes local students—that they become more cosmopolitan.

As part of the ongoing process of self-change, students may draw on any or all of these elements. They take in their own mix of effects of higher education in the way they live their lives during and after the period of study. These different roles or effects of higher education are often seen as in tension with each other. For example, education for investment in human capital is often counterposed to liberal education, as if the two cannot coexist. Certainly, in J. H. Newman's *Idea of a University* it was famously argued that liberal education and vocational education had different purposes,[11] and in the academic mission or marketing the two can be in tension. But there is no necessary tension within the process of self-formation. Students can immerse themselves in a field of knowledge, which is a succession of transformative experiences, and still have ultimate career ends in mind. For example, the two objectives coincide in certain kinds of elite liberal formation that create in students cultural capital in the sense of Pierre Bourdieu.[12] Alternatively, students may follow a liberal program with a vocational program or do them side-by-side. Both kinds of education can contribute to the process of reflexive self-formation.

International Education as Self-Formation

While all higher education students (and all human subjects) are engaged in a continuous process of self-formation, international students provide a particularly clear-cut example of self-formation in action. Most live away from their families. They have a high level of practical autonomy and openness to change. They often undergo dynamic and far-reaching self-transformation. These transformations should not be romanticized. For many students self-change is more a matter of necessity, of survival and coping, than a voluntary adventure. Often agency never achieves full confidence. Though the outcomes can be rich, the journey is often difficult. Fazal Rizvi says of a cosmo-politanism driven by global markets that its promised transformation is "inherently contradictory," pulling people between "cultural flex-ibility" and "cultural uncertainty and confusion."[13] Something of this happens to many international students, in their individual transfor-mations that are vectored by the global student market.

International students epitomize, more than most university stu-dents, a mature process of conscious self-making. But the self-forming effects of international education need not be confined to interna-tional students. If those students take part in genuinely intercultural experiences inside and outside the classroom, in which people from different cultures meet on more or less equal terms and begin to learn from each other, the possible kind of self-formation broadens accord-ingly. Then international education can contribute markedly to the self-formation of many *local* students as well. One of the problems of existing international education programs in the English-speaking countries is that they contribute little to the self-formation of most local students. These programs do not motivate local students to become someone different. Their self-formation takes place elsewhere.

In summary, international education as self-formation is agency centered, complex, reflexive, open, historically grounded, and subject to relations of power.

Self-formation is *complex* because it is comprehensive of a broad range of roles of education and life projects, and it cannot be compre-hended by a single set of standard indicators or numerical measures. To understand the self-formation of a single international student holistically, it is necessary to synthesize all the different elements at play. This can only be done through complex judgment. But individu-als do make such judgments about themselves, on a continuing basis.

Self-formation is *reflexive* in the sense it is practiced by human agents who are self-conscious and aware of their own changeable per-spective. In a cross-cultural setting, in the words of Rizvi, persons are aware how their perspective "is subject to transformation as a result of its engagement with other cultural trajectories." Reflexive agents can identify and challenge their own assumptions.[14] The process of continuing self-change involves acts of imagination, in which the agent considers being different and how that might be, self-criticism of the agent's existing practices, and changes to those practices. Not all such imagining and self-criticism plays a role in the alteration of a person's identity.

Self-formation is *open* in the sense that a person's identity, or sense of self, is always changing. This identity is continually being affected by social conditions and encounters in a relational setting and by the agent's continuing reflections and self-criticisms, in a running dialogue between self and circumstance. The self is also open in the sense that it will be affected by contingencies that cannot be exhaustively forecast and that under new conditions people may do different things. The point here is not simply that people do not know and cannot control their futures. Self-formation is about potential. It cannot be exhaustively observed in what a person has already done. It has limits, but these cannot be fully tested.

Self-formation is *historically grounded* in the sense that it takes place in particular times and places and is always affected by its locations: the self may be active in more than one place simultaneously, linked to home by communications and media systems while living in the country of education. Self-formation is shaped in institutions, professional environments, and informal settings. The notion of higher education as self-formation brings the formal higher education system and informal networks and experiences closer together. For example, in international education it means that the cross-cultural in the outside community as well as inside the classroom shapes the student. Self-formation is affected by material economic systems, which impact the student directly, for example the cost of tuition; and indirectly, for example the availability of paid work and the funding of higher education institutions. It is also affected by systems of policy and regulation. Self-formation is subject to relations of power, which are typically uneven. Most international students experience an asymmetrical environment. Not only must they fit with local authority well enough to survive—and not only do local students have a stronger knowledge base and ease in social communication—at times international students are subordinated by hostile discriminatory acts that set limits on the potential for self-formation, for example, by discouraging or blocking a closer integration with the host culture.

When higher education is seen as a process of self-formation, rather than other-formation by institutions and teachers, this alters what might be expected of institutional education and teaching/learning. Education as self-formation gives substance to the idea of "student-centered learning." But it goes beyond the notion of the student as a consumer in the marketplace motivated by solely economic ends with monetary value, though the notion of investment in one's economic future remains part of it. It also pinpoints the role of the teacher in international education. In defining international education (and all higher education) as a process of self-formation, the point being made here is not that the student must do the actual learning nor that learning is a "coproduction" of teacher and taught, though both these points are true. Nor is it being argued that teaching is unimportant. On the contrary, in this more mature model of education the teacher is a crucial agent of change. Rather, the point is that international students are autonomous persons who make choices about who they are and who they want to become. *They* decide how they will use education to further the personal project of their life trajectory and identity. Like all humans, international students are an end in themselves. This is more important than their contribution to the revenues of the English-speaking university, or their future contribution to economic and social enrichment in one or another country. Teaching, student services, and institutional organization should respect international students as self-forming persons.

STUDENT STRATEGIES OF SELF-FORMATION

In sum, international students change their circumstances in order to change themselves and their own potentials—whether their life project is understood as psychological, relational, driven by status acquisition and desire for upward social mobility and relative advantage, career building or wealth creating, intellectual, or cultural. Their self-formation is continuous. It happens in observation, experience, thought, memory, and learned habits, as well as (and often prior to) the conscious fashioning of the self as one's own project that is typical of the educated life.[15] International students open themselves at least in part to the host country culture, if only to integrate enough to survive. Their self-formation nearly always entails a change in identity.

An emphasis on active agency points to different kinds of observations and findings than those that are derived by positioning sojourning students in a stress and coping framework (often with focus on negative factors), as in the case of much of the literature in counseling psychology.[16] Compared to most people, international students have relatively open possibilities within their worlds, and lives that change quickly. They also exercise a high degree of selection control over their associates. International education is often difficult, but as well as barriers and problems, it presents opportunities for growth and self-formation.

International students have some control over their immediate environment and can also mix and match cultures. They choose what to bring with them and what to leave behind. In the study of two hundred international students in Australia, a 27-year-old male business student remarked: "There's hell a lot of differences between living there and living here. The advantage of living out here is it teaches you how to be independent, the survival of the fittest. How to do things, manage your entire life. Back home, you have your parents to support you, [there is] back up. Out here, there is no back up; you're on your own. There are crucial decisions, and the decisions have to be taken by you, not by your parents. You learn a lot."

Many factors affect each international student as an agent: the dynamics of groups and networks, culture and language, gender and class, institution and place. The degree of cultural determination is itself variable, and this variation is only partly under the student's own control. Unless that larger relational picture is understood, it is easy to make the mistake of focusing too much on the agency side of the structure/agency dyad. In the process of self-formation in the country of education (the host country), the sojourning student fashions herself or himself using not only the identity resources she or he brings to the country of education but also those identity resources in the conditions that she or he finds there.

Self-formation is lifelong and can take many different forms, but there are common elements and main lines of strategy in such projects. For those international students who cross cultural boundaries as well as geographic borders, the most important common element is *cultural plurality*. The project of self-formation is a work of the imagination in which the identity possibilities are configured by coordinating more than one identity or cultural set. Here self-formation is configured in one of two different ways—and in the case of most individuals, to at some degree in both ways. These two methods or strategies in managing personal identity are frequently alluded to in the academic literature, especially that in psychology, though various terms are used to refer to each of them. In this book they are referred to as *multiplicity* and *hybridity*.

It is significant that although mainstream psychology has difficulty in fully acknowledging self-formation, it generates much research evidence that points to self-formation in action, using strategies of multiplicity and hybridity. In the section that follows, evidence that was originally gathered largely in cross-cultural psychology is reinterpreted in the terms of socio-cultural analysis.

Multiplicity

The first strategy of self-formation is multiplicity. The temporarily sojourning student is more than one person and lives more than one kind of life. Often the result is a bicultural self, as is suggested by

Berry[17] and Pedersen[18] in psychology. Berry emphasizes that two different identities/cultures can coexist in sojourner identity with varying emphases on one or the other. In reality, with some international students mixing with fellows from other backgrounds, the multiplicity can go further than two sets of culture/identity to involve three or more.

In the case of a bicultural strategy, frequently the fault line between the two different selves is language. The student operates as one person in the home-country language and with same-culture peers and as another somewhat different person in the host-country settings using the host-country language. Oddly, research in cross-cultural psychology places more emphasis on the fault line of place. Running through Berry's influential formulation is the bicultural vision of an identity that oscillates between a heritage foundation and a newer experience of acculturation in the host country. In their summaries of the literature on international students' adjustment, Church and Pedersen find this kind of multiplicity is commonly practiced.[19] They suggest that identity takes the form of an upper and lower layering, akin to the findings of an archaeological dig. The student maintains a set of apparently "fundamental" home-country beliefs and practices in areas seen as central to the personal story, such as family and marriage relations, religion, and, often but not always, national patriotism. At the same time, the student layers over the top of this a new set of daily practices that facilitate association with locals and international students from other cultural backgrounds in the country of study. The new practices may include new eating habits, interests in local sports, greater openness to making friends, and new associations across cultural and gender boundaries. Along with them the student develops a heightened sense of cultural relativism[20] and, as Church notes,[21] reflexivity, a more conscious, even deliberative approach to personal choices and identity formation. Students who are bicultural by birth tend to have a more constructive practice of cultural mixing; the same is true of those who migrate.[22] It is true also of those who acquire a measure of biculturalism in intercultural relations.

The research evidence suggests that these effects can vary by origin. Hanassah and Tidwell's study of 640 international students at one United States university finds that the Southeast Asian students scored the highest on awareness of differences in philosophies and cultures, awareness of one's own values, understanding of self, and understanding of others. On average they had also undergone greater changes in these areas than students from other groups.[23] To again quote from the study of two hundred students in Australia, here is an excerpt of an interview with an 18-year-old engineering student from Indonesia:

> Q. Are there risks and problems you did not know about, or under-estimated, before you came?
> A. Maybe the principle of life. Because in Indonesia freedom is not really encouraged. What is right, what is wrong, [that is what] is really respected. But here I learn that freedom is really appreciated. As I experience it, I change a little bit of my values into Australian. My parents, they are pretty shocked actually. But it's hard for me, because I can't jump to Australian culture, and I can't really be Indonesian anymore . . . I have become more individualistic. It's normal here, but I can't be that, you know, because I am still Indo-nesian . . . Home sweet home . . . still, I like Indonesia. Melbourne is a good place to study, [there's] no pollution at all, the system is really beautiful; in Indonesia we don't have that. Still, Indonesia has all the cultural friendliness, the warmth of the family. I still can't get it here.

Yet the Berry formulation of multiplicity has its limits. It assumes identity is a linear narrative, a biography neatly presented in sequence, as if memory and experience do not coexist in the present. The impli-cation is that memory and experience are irretrievably divided from each other. But memories, like the present, are continually reinter-preted. It is also a mistake (Berry does not make this mistake, but some of those working with his concepts do) to assume that interna-tional students never change fundamentals like family, religion, and life ambition. Some do change their core beliefs. There are many possible configurations of bicultural and multicultural identity.[24] Rather than privileging either the old or new culture, Lee and Koro-Ljungberg point to the contested nature of the terrain. "Cultural maintenance and adaptation do not represent opposing forces that influence cul-tural identities; rather, they construct a bi-cultural position which can be labeled as acculturation." They note that "this process is tradi-tionally viewed as mutual and democratic, ignoring the oppression and dominance inherent in the position of the dominant culture."[25] As Chapter 4 made clear, international students' encounter with host country culture is rarely benign.

Hybridity

The second strategy of self-formation is hybridity. Here the sojourn-ing student synthesizes different cultural and relational elements into a new self-formed hybrid self. Hybridity means that the student is likely to take a transformed self back home at the end of the sojourn, if it does end. Rizvi talks of

> The idea of hybridity, with its connotations of mixture and fusion . . . as a space in which we must learn to manage cultural uncertainties, as we imagine and project both the nation and the global condition. If hybridity is a basic characteristic of cultural globalization then we cannot know cultures in their pristine and authentic form. Instead our focus must shift to the ways in which cultural forms become separated from existing practices and recombine with new forms, in new practices in their local contexts against global forces. In a world in which flows of information, media symbols and images and political and cultural ideas are constant and relentless, new cultural formations are deeply affected by hybridization. In a world increasingly constituted by flows of finance, technology and people, through tourism, education and migration, hybridization has become a condition of social existence, can no longer be regarded as something exceptional.[26]

Anderson suggests that the notion of integration with the host society is "problematic." International student identities exhibit "ongoing movement, complexity and tension rather than endpoints and neat resolutions." The notion of hybridity encompasses this. Hybridity imagines difference in identity, nut instead of closed identities in confrontation with an Other, "Otherness is a potential resource within hybridity and openness to others is an important objective for all students."[27] The notion of synthesis or integration of different elements in the self-formation of identity, which like multiplicity is associated with a heightened reflexivity and sense of cultural relativism, recurs in studies of intercultural relations. Goldbart and colleagues describe higher education as a "contact zone" in which different cultures "wrestle with each other" in conditions of unequal power relations.[28] Rizvi cautions nevertheless that while hybridity is "a useful antidote to cultural essentialism," it alone does not explain cultural relations. It remains necessary to explain "how hybridity takes place, the form it takes in particular contexts, the consequences it has for particular sections of the community and when and how are particular hybrid formations progressive or regressive."[29]

Mostly the hybrid self plays out a little differently according to the context and the person. There is often multiplicity as well as synthesis. Likewise, the student with multiple identities, or roles, carries common elements from role to role. A partial integration takes place. Without some element of hybridity, multiple identity is likely to be experienced as fragmentation and/or contradiction.[30] Partial hybridity emerges as part of the process of managing multiplicity. In other words, the distinction between these two principal strategies is never an absolute one, and there are more or less continuous interactions between them in practice. Arguably Berry's notion of "integration," replicated in policy as multiculturalism, involves elements of both. Berry's notion of "separation" emphasizes multiplicity in that it maintains distinctions between cultural sets. Berry's "assimilation" emphasizes the process of hybridization (identity combination), although on asymmetrical terms so home-country identity eventually becomes dissolved into that of the host country.

Each of these strategies of self-formation can be described with a distinct metaphor. Such metaphors have their limits, but it can be said that multiplicity is associated with a process of dividing or differentiating. Hybridity is associated with a process of integrating, suturing, combining, or recombining. In other words both strategies are additive but in different ways. It is interesting that some scholars prefer to imagine one and some scholars the other. For example, Church seems more comfortable with hybridity than multiplicity. Pedersen emphasizes the bicultural.

Nevertheless, splitting and recombining can be understood as two sides of the identity formation coin. It is important to recognize that neither multiplicity nor hybridity involves giving up or displacing elements of prior identity in any absolute sense. Identity displacement is a third strategy for identity formation. But mostly that strategy is not one of self-formation; rather, it is imposed on students from outside. Some pedagogical methods seem premised on identity displacement, at least in terms of the student as learning or educational subject. Doherty and Singh describe a process of identity displacement in the foundation courses provided to international students in Australia. This strategy is secured by essentializing cultural differences and imposing on students a "pure" Anglo-Australian curriculum[31] that cuts off any possibility of multiple pedagogical affiliation and hybridity.

Conditions for Strategy Making

For cross-border international students, each strategy of self-formation, multiplicity, and hybridity rests on the three conditions first mentioned in Chapter 1: cross-cultural experience, communicative competence, and individual agency.

The first condition is interaction with people and institutions in the host country. This is essential to building an identity that draws on elements from that country. When there is a substantial zone of interaction between international student and the host country nationals, this maximizes opportunities for creative identity making. On the other hand, separation, segregation, stereotyping, discrimination, and racist abuse limit the scope for identity formation because they reduce productive encounters. Discrimination can foster identity splitting and conflict,[32] instead of identity suturing in the form of hybridity or multiplicity.

The second condition is the skills of cross-cultural communicative association and relationship building. As noted in Chapter 2, these are much discussed in the research literature: openness and directness in communication,[33] empathy, capacity to initiate and capacity to respond, capacity to learn quickly, capacity to enter the zone of the other's imagination. Above all, there is practical capacity to communicate. Many researchers also instance the capacity to imagine and relate to diverse culture/identity sets. Allan nominates the capacity to relate to people whatever their cultural background and, "as a result of encountering cultural diversity," enhancing one's own cultural identity.[34] Cannon's study of Indonesian sojourners finds that they learn to become more tolerant and to understand divergent points of view.[35] "In psychological terms, they have become more complex. Complexity is the result of two broad processes: differentiation and integration." They move to a "third place" they share with other experienced sojourners, "the unbounded point of intersection where interactants from different cultural and linguistic backgrounds meet and communicate successfully."[36] Matsumoto and colleagues, and Savicki and colleagues identify emotional regulation, openness, flexibility, and critical thinking.[37] Leong and Ward discuss tolerance of ambiguity and attributional complexity.[38] Ying and Han analyze "accommodating style." Redmond mentions "social decentring," the capacity to take in another person's thoughts and feelings across cultural lines.[39] Kashima and Loh highlight variations in the need for cognitive closure and show that students with a greater tolerance for cultural ambiguity and complexity exhibit higher levels of psychological and sociocultural adjustment. Ying and Han note gender factors. "A growing literature suggests that young Asian women exposed to Western culture may acculturate faster than their male counterparts."[40] In their work on intercultural communication barriers among local students in the United States, Spencer-Rodgers and McGovern find "male graduate students reported significantly greater prejudice and less positive affect toward foreign students than did female graduate students."[41]

The third condition, common to each of these two strategies of identity management, is an active, shaping, centralizing, coordinating *self-will* that is robust enough to sustain identity while managing cultural plurality. This coordinating self navigates plural identities, managing the tensions and conflicts between roles, between different groups, and between sites. It makes choices and propels the agent into active social relations. In its most reflexive form, the centralizing self deliberately sets out to remake personal identity and life trajectory, a difficult task that is not always fully successful. This centralizing, coordinating aspect of the person, and the manner in which it works, is now considered more closely.

The Centralizing Self

As noted, some students handle ambiguity and "uncertainty management" better than others. Bradley suggests that some students, those who adapt particularly quickly and readily, are able to "carry their worlds with them in their known set of behaviours and perceptions of self."[42] This implies not only that agency rests on powers of perception and responsiveness but that facility in these domains is particularly beneficial for mobile agents, and that they draw a part of their identity from mobility itself. (At worst this collapses into addictive sojourning, the will to travel without terminus.) Pyvis and Chapman suggest that identity can be variously understood in terms of the labels and memberships applied to selves and others, as multiple affiliations, as a "learning trajectory" (that is, a process of self-formation that encompasses a journey from the old self to the new self), and also "a nexus of multi-membership where we define who we are by the ways we reconcile our various forms of identity into one identity."[43] The centered self-will is a centering self. This is not the notion of a singular, bounded individual, or identity with a capital "I." The centered/centering self is only one of the elements of personal identity at play.

Kettle provides an intensive study of a single Thai student who is "working as an agent of his own change."[44] Kettle argues that "the self is the site of multiple subjectivities," and agency is the process of producing the self.[45] The process is linked to duration. The Thai student feels that he has no agency until he can interact effectively with those around him in the country of education, and as that communicative capacity grows so to does the sense of proactive agency.[46] Singh models international students as agents of their own formation process, while also constituting "media of transnational global/national/local connections."[47] The focus on the agency aspect of international student identity in Singh's study is more explicit than in other research.[48] Asmar makes the point that most of the literature on international students and intercultural relations downplays the active, self-determining agency of students,[49] imagining them as relatively passive and in deficit and neglecting their own conceptions of the self-forming sojourner project.

Nevertheless, a notable feature of much of the empirical research, including that in psychology, is that it identifies the will to self-determination, by one or another name, as a key piece of the puzzle. There is the "approach coping style" discussed by Ward and colleagues.[50] Yoo and colleagues identify the roles of "emotion recognition" and "emotion regulation," finding that recognition of anger assists the process of adjustment. However, recognition of fear and sadness do not. Anger is more readily harnessed to personal strategies of agency formation.[51] Chirkov and colleagues focus directly on self-determination.[52] Savicki and colleagues emphasize positive, agency-building factors in determining successful intercultural adjustment rather than defining adjustment in terms of the minimization of psychological stressors.[53] Ward and colleagues find that "cross-cultural research has demonstrated a stable association between an internal locus of control and psychological well-being and satisfaction, independent of the origins and destinations of sojourners, immigrants, and refugees."[54]

Other notions combine communicability with the centered/centering will: Li and Gasser on cross-cultural self-efficacy, Hullett and Witte on uncertainty control, the work of Matsumoto and colleagues, and notions of self-construals and self-ways used by Yang and colleagues. Ward and colleagues focus on extraversion, which suggests both communicability and agency. Communicative capacity by itself is not enough to ensure strong agency, but it helps. Perrucci and Hu remark that a sense of self-worth helps students to communicate in the host environment.[55] Strong agency helps sojourners to acquire and execute communicative skills. The vice versa also applies. Communicative capacity helps to sustain and build agency and self-worth, amid the downward pressures on status and the continued self-questioning of one's own day-to-day competence. Even so, sojourning students without a fully adequate communicative capacity must have strong personal drive.

The research does suggest that compared to local students, international students, especially those from cultural backgrounds different to the host country, stand out in the exercise of autonomous volition. Exceptional personal drive is instrumental to their success. Rather than seeing the typical sojourning student as a fragile, undermined person in the throes of cultural conflict, it is more useful to recognize that the stresses of an intercultural sojourn—which no doubt taxes the life energies and imaginative capacity of those that undertake it—calls up a robust personality. Weak personalities are less likely to try it or to survive it. It needs a strong sense of identity to self-engineer strategies of multiplicity and hybridity. Even while international students are being subordinated by professional practices that place them in deficit, their sense of self is robust enough to adapt to those practices while managing their own emotional reactions to being stripped of status.

THE COUNTER NOTION: STUDENTS AS "OTHER-FORMED"

This notion of international education (and all higher education) as a process of self-formation can be contrasted with the dominant notions of international students that figure in mainstream psychology in the English language countries, especially cross-cultural psychology. Knowledge matters, especially when it becomes manifest in the behavior of professionals and their systems of administration. Mainstream psychology has been influential in shaping education policy, institutional administration, much of teaching, student counseling and welfare, and marketing. All of these activities are normative in intent. They model humans and human action and prescribe changes to human agents and their conditions that would bring human action closer to the imagined model. Psychology is also quantitative in temper, in that its methodological objective is to mathematize human behavior and social relations for analytical and prescriptive purposes and to supply data for the organizing of systems and the managing of people. It tends to exclude those elements of education, people, and cross-cultural relations that cannot be so reduced to mathematical form.

The systems and practices informed by mainstream psychology secure enough purchase to affect behaviors. But in our judgment, the cross-cultural psychology outlined in Chapter 2 is less explanatory of international education and of human agency than the cultural notion of higher education as self-formation. Often psychology's grasp of the empirical evidence is strong; the problem lies in the theorizations and assumptions used to interpret the evidence. Mainstream psychology (like its reductionist social science twin, neoclassical economics)[56] models human behavior in relatively narrow terms. It focuses on some elements but excludes others. Arguably, the notion of self-formation contains the insights of psychology but is broader in its reach across human action, though it does not lend itself to a mathematical model of agency. Arguably, higher education as self-formation is more inclusive of the range of student objectives and institutional functions of education. Most importantly, it understands that there can be more than one culture and more than one possible identity and identity is in a continuous process of change. In contrast, orthodox cross-cultural psychology, when applied to international education, too often falls into an ethnocentrism that is highly prejudicial to international students. In its normative mode psychology often tends to pathologize difference. When the norm is defined in cultural terms, as in the psychology of foreign student adjustment in English-speaking countries, non-Western identity becomes seen as a deficit.

Why is it so? The dominant strand of the social sciences that developed in the twentieth century was focused on social order. The purpose was the shaping and managing of populations according to the programs of the state. Mainstream psychology, economics, sociology, and political science all came to model identity as fixed and closed rather than open, and to work with equilibrium models of the individual and social relations. The individual in psychology has a fixed identity, the individual in economics has a pregiven set of utility preferences, and so on. But these models have always been unrealistic. For example, international students live in a world in which change is continuous, far reaching, open ended, and unpredictable. There is no point of rest for their human identity (or for the identity of any other person).

With their predilection for managing and normalizing people, the mainstream social sciences also tend to see human behavior as *other-determined*, whether by the environment, the institutional arrangements, the forces of the market, or professional or institutional authority. Thus they tend to downplay the potential for self-determination or work with an attenuated concept of agency focused on negative freedom, as in orthodox economics. There are exceptions to this generalization, of course. Social science contains a plurality of approaches. Sen, who won his Nobel Prize in economics, introduces a philosophical argument about self-determining agency and capability into development economics, where it subverts conventional economic assumptions about scarcity (human capability is not subject to necessary scarcity) and freedom as negative but not positive freedom. And as discussed in Chapter 2, one strand of cross-cultural psychology works with notions of strong human agency and has attempted to get to grip with both plural identity and identity change. That work, which was discussed earlier in the chapter, as it offers one important way forward for intercultural studies in international education.

Psychology offers much to our understanding of cross-cultural relations, but also not enough. Psychology does not have the empirical tools to model the whole of the mind in the manner the human genome project is mapping the genetic code. Using sharp observational tools and analytical precision, psychology secures brilliant insights into particular facets of human behavior. Potentially, these insights add to the knowledge of self-formation. Problems arise when particular insights are extrapolated into something bigger than they are, or the gaps are filled using ungrounded normative assumptions of human behavior and social relations. Psychology claims to be a universal framework for explaining human behavior, but without a relational sociology or notion of historically located human agency, it fills the gap at the level of the social with abstract simplifications that exclude much of the human agency they purport to describe.

For example, mainstream psychology has evolved the "Big Five" personality descriptors that are widely used in empirical design and data interpretation: openness, conscientiousness, extraversion, agreeableness, and neuroticism. Overlapping at the edges, if not downright ambiguous in relation to each other, the Big Five personality descriptors function as broad-based metaphors or containers for often heterogeneous insights. What they include is definition driven; what they leave out or pathologize is what becomes ignored or disliked in psychological research. But they can be operationalized mathematically (notwithstanding eclectic variations between different studies in their use). Together they sustain the illusion that psychology has a comprehensive theory of human personality in which identity is single and holistic, and normally invariant. But psychology struggles with central aspects of human identity—aspects that cultural analysis can encompass more effectively, for example, in the notion of education as self-formation.

Gaps in Psychology

In sum, the theorization of international education as self-formation exceeds the reach of cross-cultural psychology (especially its mainstream variant) in a number of ways.

The first aspect of identity that psychology fails to encompass is the *open and fluid* character of identity with its capacity for change over time, including *agent-driven* change. As was shown in the review of the literature in Chapter 2, when psychology studies identity change, it models identity as moving between rigid categories and mathematizes identity in terms of the proportionality between these categories. Fluidity is lost. But identity change is not always linear and incremental, no more than learning is always linear. Identity change has its transformational moments, its qualitative leaps. Further, in much cross-cultural psychology the potential for free self-determination tends to be obscured by the identity categories that are used. In research studies, these categories impose psychological definitions of what is possible onto the empirical terrain in research. Worse, working with fixed categories of identity as it does, psychology often also privileges a reified ideal Anglo-American or Western identity over other identities. At that point the tools of analysis become ethnocentric means of cultural domination with the intent of controlling and remaking Other identity.

Second, there is the common tendency of human identity to take in *plurality*, through multiple and hybrid forms, as was discussed the previous section of this chapter. Again, psychology models multiplicity in terms of combinations of fixed categories that together form a mathematized unitary set, as if identities are equivalent in relation to each other. Where cross-cultural psychology does acknowledge that plurality in agency and identity are possible, it often becomes fixated on binary thinking, developing simplified half-truths such as Hofstede's individualist/collectivist distinction. Studies using such binary conceptions can produce insights, but binaries are inflexible and tend to conceal as much as they reveal.

Third, there is central role played by the *imagination and creativity* in the self-evolution of identity. Reflexivity, creativity, and the imagination are too difficult to observe and too complex in form to be apprehended convincingly in the regression equations used in psychology for relational modeling. These qualities can only be apprehended holistically using synthetic judgments[57] that acknowledge historical context. These intellectual functions fall outside psychology as it has defined itself. Psychology touches on elements of the imagination but cannot take it further.

Fourth, as this suggests, there is the location of individual identity in *historical conditions and a relational social environment*. Both of these factors affect the potentials of agency, without exhaustively determining what individuals think and do. But psychology begins with an individual abstracted from social relations, as if individuals can exist prior to the conditions in which all human life takes place. In most cross-cultural psychology, even "social adjustment" refers to the individual's separated capacity for sociability.[58] It is a solely individuated notion. It is not a relational concept. The conception of individual identity in mainstream psychology is abstracted from particular locations. It shares that feature with the utopian "globalist" strand in social theory (see Chapter 3). Neither body of thought can successfully model an intercultural or cosmopolitan environment.

Fifth, as noted, international student adjustment is imagined in equilibrium models. For example, Ramsay and colleagues see sojourner adjustment as the successive removal of "psychological dissatisfiers" that generate "disequilibrium."[59] This suggests the objective is a stable personal configuration, with identity at rest. But what if identity is continually changing, and the individual drives and partly governs this process of change? Many international students reject not only the ethnocentric ideal imagined as the stasis at the heart of the equilibrium but any kind of equilibrium. Inescapably, many international students consciously seek *disequilibria*. Their purpose is to achieve personal change and to take some risks with themselves in doing so. Interview data reveal students undergoing rapid and destabilizing change. Many psychological researchers are indifferent to this.

Finally, the notion of self-formation focuses centrally on *self-determining* human agency. At the bottom of psychology lies the assumption that psychological researchers, counselors, and other professionals informed by psychology, such as teachers, know best—not the students themselves. Of course, it is true that most professionals working in education know more of the world and human behavior than do students in higher education. However, with the widespread availability of knowledge on the Internet, that is changing. And in one respect psychology-trained professionals do *not* know better than the students, that is, in relation to agency freedom and self-will. Only the individual student can say what she or he wants. The student is not an empty mind or a blank sheet of paper waiting to be filled. Professional strategies should not seek to make it so. That conception of the blank sheet does not derive from humanist democratic notions of education. It derives a more authoritarian approach. When practiced in English-speaking higher education institutions, in relation to nonwhite students from Asian nations, it connects directly to older imperial notions of educational and cultural superiority.

To argue that international students should be modeled as self-determining agents is not to argue that they do not need pastoral care. Higher educational institutions should fulfill a duty of care to all who work within them. Mobile persons face many difficulties in a new country, including information deficiencies. Some have more personal resources and are better at managing themselves than are others. Rather, it is to argue that such pastoral care should be extended to international students as thinking sovereign adults and not as dependent children.

CONCLUSION

The notion that students experience international education (and higher education as a whole) as a process of self-formation, drawing on a portfolio of strategies that include forms of multiplicity and hybridity, provides a richer basis for explaining international students, and for developing intercultural forms of teaching and learning, than the dominant interpretations used in cross-cultural psychology. Individuals evolve themselves in response to, and in engagement with, institutions, social systems, cultural objects, signs, and signals—and each other. *Here the animating vision of intercultural education is of self-forming individuals engaged with each other, within a common relational space criss-crossed by differences.*

The scope for forming identities and following different life paths is maximized when international students, along with local persons, share a social environment governed by cosmopolitan norms (Chapter 3). In short, the cosmopolitan relational environment nurtures a diverse set of individual cultural projects of self-formation.

Nevertheless, the orthodox approaches retain a grip on policy and professional practices. This can be attributed to a combination of path dependency and the embeddedness of applied psychology in government, economy, and institutional life. Too often counseling psychology assimilates individual difference and cultural plurality into an imagined social norm. The imagined final goal is smoothly functioning social equilibrium. This unrealizable utopia has obvious methodological attractions for those who manage large populations on a standard cost basis—including international students in those countries that run international education as a commercial industry, such as Australia, New Zealand, and the United Kingdom. A forward move toward more cosmopolitan international education requires a decisive break from these approaches. Above all, it is essential to set aside ethnocentrism and all other notions premised on the cultural superiority of "the West" (or "Britain" or "America") over "the Rest," to place the international students in the center of the frame, and to open the intercultural encounters to cosmopolitan relationships based on equal respect and appreciation of difference.

CHAPTER 8

---∗✖∗---

CONCLUSION 2
TOWARD INTERCULTURAL EDUCATION

WHY INTERCULTURAL EDUCATION?
ZHAO MEI'S STORY

Remember Zhao Mei, with whom this book began? The bright, personable student from Eastern China who found herself isolated and struggling in the English-speaking country, whose lecturers believed that it would be "inequitable" to offer international students any assistance additional or different from that received by their local Anglo-Australian classmates? Here is Zhao Mei's story as it should be.

When Zhao Mei first came to Melbourne to study for her master's degree in environmental management, she did not know much about the Australian education system and what the classroom experience would be like. She was confident about her English language skills. She had done well in the International English Language Testing System (IELTS) test in English language skills that regulated entry. She knew that she was a good student, she always worked hard, and she had won two subject prizes during her studies at Zhejiang University, one of China's top institutions. She was not bothered about the fact that environmental management had a strong emphasis on geology and climate science. Although she had not studied those particular applications before, her first degree had been in science and she had always done well in math. As a trainee manager in a construction company in Zhejiang, she also had some understanding of management issues. She had undertaken no special academic preparation before coming to Australia. Much time had gone into arranging the loan from her uncle's business and the paperwork for the application to the Australian university, the student visa, and the travel and accommodation arrangements, which had been booked in advance through a company based in Zhejiang that specialized in foreign student transfers.

But Mei had been totally shocked on arrival in Melbourne to find that her English language conversational skills were quite inadequate. This was a major setback. There had been little emphasis on English conversation at her school and in the university studies of English in China, in which she had always done well. Her communication difficulties on arrival had been the worst moment of her entire stay in Australia. During her first few days she seemed to understand almost nothing that was said to her. Accent, vocabulary, local references, speed of speech, a lack of care and patience from some local people—all compounded her communication problems. She couldn't seem to get into the rhythm of talking with people and felt very inhibited when she needed to initiate speech. Fortunately, the university environmental studies department had comprehensively tested her academic English skills in the first few days, as it did with all the students from non-English-speaking backgrounds. This had pinpointed her problem: her reading and writing skills were good, but her oral comprehension and to a lesser extent her speech needed intensive work if she was to participate effectively in the program, which at the classroom level was highly interactive in all units.

Immediately Mei was placed in a two-week withdrawal class devoted to conversation skill-building in English, using learning materials from the first stages of the master's program. Then she and the other students in that class rejoined the main program just as it began to get down to real work. After that she had attended two three-hour evening classes each week in speaking and listening, through the end of first semester. Some students took part in those classes and also did another set of classes in academic writing. Mei hadn't needed the second set of classes. Like the withdrawal class, the evening classes were provided by the department as part of the degree program. They were needs-based and covered by her tuition fees. Mei is pleased now that her mother had advised her to enroll in a high-quality university when she was considering another university with a cheaper tuition fee in order to save money. The extra help with English, at a crucial stage of her program, had been great and had made a lot of difference. Now she feels quite confident. When talking to local students she still has some difficulty, but even if she makes mistakes she isn't afraid to keep talking.

The lecturers place a lot of emphasis on English as part of the program. They ask students to give them feedback, even to stop lectures and classes, if students cannot understand what is being said. Best of all, the university provides an English as a second language teacher operating alongside the normal teachers in all first-year programs, which had been really helpful to Mei when she was doing her first assignments. Language skills are seen as essential to not only learning the material and talking in class and in work groups but also because the university makes high-quality English skills an explicit objective of all programs. Graduates are certified in English as well as their disciplines. After first semester the free evening classes in conversation had stopped, but Mei had been offered the option of subsidized fee-based evening classes in more advanced English skills. She had hesitated because of the cost, but fortunately she had been able to obtain a part-time job working in retail with her friend Mia, one of the Australian students in environmental management. The work has covered the cost of the extra classes and the rent on her apartment, which has been higher than she expected.

The development of her friendship with Mia was unexpected, but it was one of the best things that happened since she came to Melbourne. It started about five weeks into the first semester, when Mei was still struggling with English. Mei was trying to explain something in a tutorial, in fact it was she who asked the question, and then she had to give up because she just didn't have the words. She petered out while everyone was waiting for her to finish. The tutor was very nice about it though, and afterward Mia took Mei to the student lounge and gave her a cup of tea. Mia was very nice and asked Mei lots of questions about her family, her course in Zhejiang University, and what she hoped to achieve from studying in Australia. They also talked about climate management, which they both were interested in. After that, they started to hang out together. Mia said later that what she liked about Mei was that she wasn't afraid to speak up even if she didn't know what to say. And when she got it wrong, she just laughed at herself! "That was really random!" said Mia. Mei had to ask her what "random" meant. Sometimes Mei did things with Mia on the weekends, like go to the beach or the movies, though that was expensive. Also, twice she had gone for dinner with Mia and her boyfriend David, who was also in the master's program. Next time, David is going to bring one of his friends as well. Mia is one of Mei's closest non-Chinese friends in Australia. The other is Araya from Thailand, who is also in the program. Mei misses her family a lot sometimes, but she has good friends in Melbourne. She is lucky.

Mei also is lucky that she chose the environmental management course. The class is 45 percent international, and the lecturers provide what they call an "intercultural" program. In the first semester, where the subject matter was almost all in the core sciences, the examples were from many different countries and there had been a run of four weeks of classes devoted solely to common world environmental systems. The lecturers use a variety of teaching aids, with a lot of visual displays including slides and holograms and computer simulations. There is careful, repeated emphasis on the key facts and ideas using the different media. The lecturers also focus on teamwork and relationship building and making sure everyone is active. All of the work groups are mixed between local and international students, and the international students are often asked to report on behalf of their "teams." This had put Mei under a lot of pressure at first, but there's no doubt that her language skills improved in class and the work groups helped in making friends. Some group activity involves students located in the two partner institutions, one in Singapore and the other in Denmark. In the problem-solving section of the program that started in second semester, students talk about the way the issues and problems of environmental management are handled in their different countries. They are expected to keep researching and studying this during the program, often using Internet resources in the home language and resources from media and books from home. They are also expected to do two exercises that look at a problem from the standpoint of the culture of one of the *other* countries in the group. This was a "head-blaster," according to Mia, but it was quite fun, especially at class discussion stage. There is a lot of emphasis on comparisons between countries, taking account of different traditions, values, economies, government, and so on.

Sometimes two students swap countries and do a kind of reverse comparison on each other's countries. Mia had looked at water conservation in Eastern China, and Mei did the same thing in Australia. Again, Mei had to learn a lot very quickly for that assignment, but it was quite interesting. Melbourne has a serious long-term water problem. Doing the preparation for that class had made Mei think about working in Australia, something she hadn't considered before. Of course, all the assignments and the classes are in English. Sometimes non-English words and concepts are discussed in classes or lectures, though. Two of the lecturers worked in Southeast Asia, and one is from Europe. This probably helps.

Mei always has the feeling that who she is and where she comes from are recognized and respected. She also feels that no obstacle will stop her from learning what she wants to learn. The program is competitive—everyone wants to get high grades, get a good job, or get a PhD scholarship—but international students definitely have the chance to do well, even though it might mean taking extra language classes and spending more hours on assignments than local students do. Two years ago, the top two graduates from the program were international students. One was a woman from Norway and the other was a man from Shanghai. The Shanghai man is working for an international agency in Bangkok now. He came back to the university to give a guest lecture in the master's program. Mei talked to him at the special lunch arranged for him after the lecture.

This Chapter

Ideas for Intercultural Education argues that Zhao Mei can achieve this kind of education only when cross-cultural education is imagined as a relational zone in which all parties, and all cultures, are engaged with each other and open to change. The chapter begins by summarizing the case made by the book. It then proceeds to look at practical means by which intercultural education can be advanced. In turn it discusses changes in international student servicing, teaching, classroom learning, motivating local students, and language learning.

What Intercultural Education? A Summary

How do we make the transition from the international education currently offered in the English-speaking nations to the kind of program that is enjoyed by Zhao Mei? An intercultural education is a *relational* education in which all parties in the encounter open themselves to transformative learning and change, enabling them to see the world through each other's eyes and evolve new practices while interacting with each other. This close cultural engagement is lacking in most international education. How do we overcome the twin related problems of (1) unchanging local curricula and teaching methods and (2) entrenched separation between international and local student populations? These were the questions with which the book began. This section draws together and summarizes the main elements in its argument.

The First Key

Ideas for Intercultural Education has argued that the first key to the puzzle is knowledge about cross-cultural international education. Knowledge sets the horizon of our thinking and prestructures the systems in which international educators work. Both psychological knowledge and sociocultural knowledge tend to shape teaching, learning, and international student servicing. Each field of knowledge has a contribution to make, and they are potentially complementary. Psychology works best at the level of individual personality and behavior. Sociology and cultural analysis explain the larger relational settings in which individual learning occurs. But the relational context has been underplayed, while much of the psychology has constrained international education and international students, undermining the agency of the students by defining them as in learning and social deficit.

Often students are expected to "adjust" to local educational practices without regard for their own educational and cultural backgrounds, implicitly modeled as inferior, while local monocultural educational practices continue unquestioned and unchanged. "Culture" is modeled as fixed and determining, and often it is simply assumed that international students must move from old to new culture in order to be academically successful. These notions, embedded in the mainstream of educational psychology, play out in hundreds of classrooms. This is compounded by the fact that many educators lack the time or resources to do more than process students on a mass scale. That means treating all students as the same regardless of their learning needs. But whether the problem lies in certain strands of thinking in psychology or in economic pragmatics, it is vital to abandon Anglo-ethnocentrism and cultural essentialism—and the underlying assumptions about cultural and educational superiority that support both—so as to move forward. We live in a relational global setting in which many educational traditions contribute. International students, and their countries, are worthy of respect. Local students will not draw consistent intercultural benefits from the international students in their midst unless those students are valued systemically for who they are.

The strengths of Anglo-American education are reduced by ethnocentrism, which is the legacy of three hundred years of imperialism on the world scale, but are not abolished. The virtues of this educational tradition are many. It is important to understand those strengths while learning also from the strengths of other modern traditions, such as those of the Confucian education systems of East Asia, those of Latin America, and those of the German-speaking nations. Increasingly, in the global setting, these different traditions are rubbing up against each other. Globally, we need to negotiate between traditions on the basis of common ground rather than attempt to impose one or another way of seeing in blanket fashion. A relational cosmopolitan approach to international education fosters, in students and educators, understanding of multiple cultural viewpoints and the capacity to articulate between them, without losing one's own grounded standpoint.

The cosmopolitan relational environment nurtures a diverse set of individual cultural projects of self-formation. The social dimension makes individual action possible, but it is also continually in motion, being modified by the play of different identities. This picture of the relation between individual and social is substantially different from that provided by orthodox cross-cultural psychology, in which the individual in the foreground dominates the picture, the social conditions are obscured, and the fate of individuals tends to be seen as a matter for them alone rather than the joint product of social relations and individual agency.

A relational cosmopolitan approach recognizes that no one tradition or way of seeing provides "complete" knowledge. All traditions are worthy of equal respect, though not all are equally valued. In teaching and learning, this means the development of strategies that simulate the cosmopolitan relational environment inside the classroom and build the required global attributes.

Teachers and managers in international education programs do not have to look far to see what is wrong with ethnocentrism and deficit modeling. The evidence is the students themselves. International students are not simply objects imagined by psychology; they are subjects who manage their own self-formation. They have no intention of succeeding at the expense of who they are. They shape their own identities and life trajectories, often combining elements of old and new using strategies of multiplicity and hybridity. Empathetic educators can see this. Psychology is not inherently ethnocentric. The best cross-cultural psychology knows that "identity" and "culture" are not fixed and singular but change and evolve. Recent studies suggest that three interacting elements are instrumental in student success: language proficiency in English and especially communicative competence, the self-determining agency of students, and cross-cultural interactions under the right conditions. Each of these elements is both medium for the others and tends to combine with and produce the others in a complex set of mutually reinforcing feedback effects. This strand of psychology is centrally interested in enhancing the agency confidence of students, which is the driver.

The Second Key

"Under the right conditions" is a crucial caveat and a challenging one for international educators. For example, the "conditions" of international education are shaped both inside and outside the classroom. Given that communicative competence and cross-cultural encounters are at the core of student development, experience outside the classroom is as important as experience within it—and there are more problems in cross-cultural relations outside the classroom than inside it. This suggests a role for government, especially local authorities, who have the capacity to reach further than education institutions into life beyond the campus grounds.

There is overwhelming evidence that most students want to forge genuine friendships with local students and move freely between a mix of same-culture (and language) networks and local student networks. It is equally clear that most nonwhite international students are disappointing by the paucity of their local friendships and some have almost no contact with locals at all. The cross-cultural space is reduced by stereotyping and locally induced segregation practices and contaminated by episodes of discrimination and abuse. This "Others" international students as surely as does ethnocentrism and deficit modeling in psychology, and much more violently. There is clear evidence that while the students often learn to brush off cultural hostility—some are notably thick skinned to begin with—these episodic incidents are not rare. They are endemic in most locations. International student testimony shows that many students become partly or largely inhibited in cross-cultural relations as a result of these experiences. Language barriers are one trigger of discrimination, but communicative competence alone is not enough. At bottom the problem is lack of equal respect. Here host country governments fail to send out the right signals. Little is done to protect international students with antidiscrimination legislation or to reeducate local perpetrators.

Problems of discrimination and abuse largely arise in the community rather than on campus. Nevertheless, even though local students are not the main problem, they might be able to provide the main solution. Spontaneous segregation between locals and internationals *is* endemic on campus. If this could be modified or overcome, that would embed international students more deeply in the host society and enhance their development of relational skills. This brings us back to the day-to-day environment inside institutions and the classroom itself.

By and large, international students do a superb job in remaking themselves in the country of education. But relational cosmopolitanism cannot possibly take root unless it is built on more than international student adjustment. Local educators and local students must change. This is the second key to the puzzle. Locals, too, need to improve their skills of communication and interaction with people from other cultural backgrounds. The problem is that in the English-speaking systems, the local *motivation* to open up to cross-cultural encounters, the local willingness to change and to see this as a good thing, has been largely missing up to now. Institutional support systems attempt to structure interactions between local and international students, especially early in the sojourn, but the effort is not strongly grounded in local student motivation and soon peters out. The problem of inducing motivation among local students will be discussed again later in this chapter.

Notions such as deficit modeling and "cultural fit" retain a grip because they leave local complacency undisturbed and are functional means of managing large-scale encounters with the foreign student Other. The development of a relational cosmopolitan approach to international education means breaking with immediate utilities. It means making the educational task more complex and, in the short term, more expensive. In the longer term it creates economies by expanding productivity. It draws a much richer set of resources into cross-cultural education. It draws on the resources and energies released in the agency-driven creativity of international students and local students. The benefits of change are immense.

The next and final section looks more closely at the "how" of doing all this.

HOW INTERCULTURAL EDUCATION? SERVICES AND CLASSROOMS

Student Servicing

How do higher education institutions implement the kind of teaching and learning program that could provide Zhao Mei with an inter-cultural education? Institutional strategies for vitalizing intercultural education have three components. The first is to work on the attitudes and competences of international students. The second is structured mixing arrangments. The third, discussed in more detail in the fol-lowing section, is to work on the attitudes and competences of local students (and staff).

The threshold step is to secure institution-wide responsibility for augmenting cross-cultural relations.[1] The collective commitment should flow through the whole of teaching and service delivery. Lin and Yi suggest that programs to assist internationals should be conceived in four phases: (1) pre-arrival information and workshops; (2) the stage of initial adjustment in the first six months of the educational program, which includes meet-and-greet functions, help with housing, orientation programs, and advice about available services; (3) the facilitation of ongoing adjustment until graduation, including assistance with both same-culture and other-culture networking; and (4) assistance with return-home adjustment.[2] Schuerholz-Lehr[3] remarks that internationalizing the curriculum should not be done simply in response to the presence of international students. It should be seen as institutions' commitment to preparing students for a globalized world and routinely structured into the education of local students. This starting position is widely if not universally agreed upon in the English-speaking university world. It must be emphasized that in most institutions, it has yet to become associated with deep change in the local outlook. It is essential to move from statements of intentions to a thorough transformation. Here, international students can become the lever and the medium with which to secure intercultural sites. This is why it is vital to bring them in from the margins where adjustment and deficit practices have confined them. That is the first practical step in the transformation process.

Much can be done early in the academic program to provide international students with opportunities to develop cross-cultural skills, at a moment when students are most conscious of the need for those skills and have more time to acquire them than later in the program. Li and Gasser suggest that "international students' cross-cultural self-efficacy can be enhanced through actively engaging in controlled cross-cultural social interactions, watching peer performance in social contexts, soliciting feedback and encouragement for their own performance," and also through "focusing on their own performance instead of their emotional arousal in social interactions."[4] These strategies should be employed alongside careful monitoring of language proficiency, especially competence in spoken conversation—and, where needed, extra English learning of the type that was provided to Zhao Mei in the first year of her academic program.

Structured Cross-Cultural Mixing

Structured mixing arrangements have three aspects. First, there are temporary game frameworks, such buddy systems with host culture nationals, mentoring by local senior students, and semicompulsory mixed social activities. Second, there are combined student residences, as testified by Jabe from Singapore in Chapter 4. Third, there is structured cooperation in the classroom, which was first discussed in Chapter 6 and is explored further in the next section of this chapter.

Cross-cultural game frameworks are routinely used early in the international student's sojourn. In the literature there is much enthusiasm for them.[5] But the impact of such programs is limited in time and depth, and there is some evidence of relatively low student satisfaction with them.[6] In most instances this nominal cross-cultural contact fails to generate solid ongoing relationships. Recognizing this, Spencer-Rodgers and McGovern place greater emphasis on a mix of residential arrangements, longer-term recreational programs, intercultural training (especially for locals) and improved language competence (especially for internationals).[7]

Outside the classroom the most effective way to encourage deep intercultural friendship is by providing subsidized student accommodation with a population balance between local and international students. As discussed in more detail in the study of *International Student Security*,[8] cross-cultural student residences provide an especially favorable environment in which to develop cross-cultural friendships and cooperation. Residential living entails interaction in several spheres (day-to-day living, eating, recreation, dating, study). Contact is frequent. Interaction is spontaneous or easily initiated. Residences are open to rule setting and create "captive participants" who for the most part are readily persuaded to engage in structured mixing, especially in the first year of the student sojourn. A problem is that on-campus and near-campus residences are subsidized only in some countries. Subsidized accommodation is a feature of student life in many Asian universities, for example in China, Malaysia, and Vietnam. It is provided to a large minority of first degree students in the United States. It is not provided in Australia, where the cost of most student residences is higher than private rents.

CLASSROOM TEACHING

Leask suggests that teachers in higher education need to reflect on their own teaching to see whether their own culture and values influence their teaching practices. The students in front of teachers act as resources with which teachers can deepen their own intercultural competences, by engaging with the students and acquiring new cultural perspectives[9] and possibly elements of language as well. Teekens argues that teachers in higher education should develop a basic knowledge of the main features of the education systems from which their students have come, their prior educational preparation, and their expectations concerning the teacher-student relationship.[10] With intercultural knowledge from these sources, teachers are well placed to overhaul the curriculum to incorporate the students' cultural positions, which are one of the conditions of their learning. The first step is to respect and understand the cultures and educational traditions students bring to the classroom.[11] This is not to say the curriculum should reflect all these traditions equally. All effective learning programs embody a coherent pedagogical approach.

There is more emphasis on the need for prior knowledge of home-country systems in the literature from Australia than there is in that from the United States and United Kingdom, for example, the studies by Ninnes and colleagues[12] and by Ramburuth and McCormick. Robertson and colleagues find that "where there is a willingness within an institution to learn about the backgrounds of students from other countries, a process of intercultural learning can begin."[13] Dunn and Wallace argue for cultural reciprocity in transnational education, citing Leask, who states that "we could move towards a construction of off-shore teaching as an opportunity for 'us' to learn about and be more like 'them,' rather than as an opportunity for 'us' to teach 'them' about 'us' and how to be more like 'us'—as an opportunity for deep, transformational engagement with cultural others."[14] Prescott and Hellsten argue that international education should be conceived pedagogically as a process of "transition" from home-country education system to the education system of the host nation.[15] Whereas the concept of transition has long been used to facilitate local student movement from school to higher education, up till now it has not been widely used in the framing of international education. The conception of transition is very helpful.

In the United States, Wan's study of two Chinese students concludes that "educators can assist these students by becoming aware of their home culture, different learning styles [and] . . . frustrations in adjusting to school life."[16] Savicki and colleagues note the need for host educator awareness of "the personal resources and coping strategies" that international students bring with them.[17]

Some teachers are better placed to make these moves than are others. Clandinin and Connelly discuss the interconnectedness between teacher identity, including prior experience, and teaching practice.[18] Teachers with international and especially intercultural experience or knowledge of languages other than English tend to be more open to diversity and have positive attitudes toward plurality of cultures.[19]

This should be taken into account in the selection of academic staff to work in programs with large numbers of international students from nations in which English is not a first or widely used second language. But even regular travel abroad and participation in international conferences have the potential to augment intercultural competence. Anderson and colleagues note that all else being equal, travel in itself tends to have "a positive impact on the overall development of cross-cultural sensitivity."[20] Helms's study indicates that living in another country has a considerable impact on a person's cultural perspective. Teachers who have done so perceived themselves to be more interculturally sensitive.[21] Nevertheless, mobility alone is not enough to transform teaching to the level of cosmopolitan engagement. Green and Olson remark that teachers also need to work out how to apply their international experience to their teaching.[22]

Not all teachers have the opportunity to travel, but all have the potential to benefit from professional development activities. Schuerholz-Lehr suggests workshops on course design to help teachers to integrate their intercultural knowledge and competence into course design and classroom practices.[23]

Intercultural Learning

The essence of a cosmopolitan approach to teaching and learning is the development of deep cultural engagement on a mutual basis. This is very challenging because of the radical departure from established practice. A small history of examples shows that it *can* be achieved and can be highly beneficial.

At the most basic level intercultural learning in classrooms is facilitated by protocols of cross-cultural respect and the cultivation of communications and cultural awareness. These qualities were reviewed in Chapter 3 and are much discussed in the literature on international education. For example, Webb states that "internationalization of the curriculum therefore incorporates a range of values, including openness, tolerance, and culturally inclusive behaviour, which are necessary to ensure that cultural differences are heard and explored."[24] Gabb emphasizes the need for teaching to be enriched by cross-cultural communication skills; teaching materials "appropriate to a culturally diverse audience"; modifications to the curriculum to incorporate case studies from other cultures; clear explanations in English; "the use of language that is not based on local metaphor, slang or colloquialisms" and awareness of the teacher's own cultural identity. She makes a point similar to that of Leask, cited in the previous section of this chapter. "An awareness of our own ethnocentric tendencies and how they affect how we communicate and interact with others culturally distant from ourselves is a vital part of professional expertise," and has "a powerful influence on how students approach classroom interactions."[25] Local teachers are best placed to lead the opening of local students to intercultural interactions.

Some studies are based on empirical investigations into how intercultural learning is known and valued by students and staff and the extent to which it is promoted in the classroom; for example, see the research by Leask, De Vita, Chang, and Ippolito.[26] Teekens writes that creating a classroom with intercultural learning means "blending the concept of foreign, strange and otherness." These need to be instilled in teaching strategies in an effort "to integrate the cultural input of students, to use cultural background as a source of learning and to make an effort to see students from different backgrounds as resources in themselves."[27]

Mixing the Groups

In their 2010 report for the Australian Teaching and Learning Council, Arkoudis and her collaborators developed a portfolio of strategies that use small-group and peer-sharing frameworks to enable teachers to directly work on cultural competences, by stimulating the imagination and creating learning experiences involving new ways of seeing. This strengthens the capacity of both groups of students to initiate and engage in intercultural relationships. These strategies acknowledge and capitalize on student diversity as a learning resource; design the curriculum so as to draw "students from diverse cultural and linguistic backgrounds" into mutual engagement; and embed this interaction in teaching, learning, and assessment. Modes of interaction are nuanced for learning context.[28] There is an emphasis on sustainability, and some strategies focus on catalyzing longer-term associations that spill beyond the duration of the formal program.

Many of the learning strategies use small-group and peer-sharing approaches, and all are discipline-specific. Examples include the following:

- Problem-based learning projects in which the mixed groups are sustained over a protracted period (engineering)
- Team-based learning in "syndicates" selected by the lecturer, across a whole semester, including group presentations, with the

syndicates often generating mixed groups for exam preparation (law)
- Regular cross-cultural pairs for interactive learning tasks (several disciplines)
- Group work in which the participants all contribute examples of research problems from their home countries (business studies)
- Routine group-based assessment tasks with cultural contents in which the cross-cultural groups come to learn that as a group they can perform better than any one individual could (communications)

Arkoudis and colleagues also discuss several examples of the use of cross-cultural peer assessment, and the formation of longer term "communities of practice" using electronic and other networking media. They state that in order to overcome the tendency of most students to group with same-culture peers, if mixed groups are to be used as the principal medium for learning it is essential to structure these firmly from the beginning of the learning unit and to set clear expectations regarding cross-cultural interaction and the planned benefits. Interactive activities should be mainstream assessable work. It may be necessary to establish rules for cross-cultural peer interactions and to spend time on the development of skills in "focussed listening, turn-taking, questioning, negotiating and giving (and receiving) feedback." The first session is most important. It is vital to create a warm, welcoming, interactive atmosphere by generating peer-to-peer conversations. A useful early tactic is moving students next to unfamiliar peers.[29]

Cosmopolitan Simulations

As suggested in Chapter 4, relational cosmoplitanism is most effectively advanced in classroom strategies that simulate the diverse interconnected global setting and directly foster its relational competencies. Intercultural learning is more than a matter of acquiring new cognitive knowledge. According to De Vita, "it requires participation in social experiences that simulates learning also in the self and action domains. It involves the discovery and transcendence of difference through authentic experiences of cross-cultural interaction that involve real tasks, and emotional as well as intellectual participation."[30] De Vita also argues that forming such a group should be handled carefully. Allowing students to self-select the composition of groups may reinforce existing networks rather than build additional social cohesion. Like Volet and Ang he argues that teachers should be closely involved in the selection of groups.[31]

The literature on international education includes cases of advanced practice in cross-cultural simulation. For example, Chang mobilizes cultural diversity and the mutual development of cross-cultural comparative perspectives through what she calls a "transcultural wisdom bank" supported by group work.[32] Core objectives of the program are for students to learn to understand a range of cultures and situate their home culture within that range, to develop the capacity to make comparative judgments about what is valuable in cultures, and "to develop non-ethnocentric views about social issues in their own lives"[33]—in short, to value cultural differences and learn from them. The "wisdom bank" is the process whereby the class pools reflective insights and experiences in the study domain, which is sociology. The subject matter of the program enables the continuous development of examples in plural cultural contexts. "A 'wisdom bank' is the collection of the set of possible 'solutions' from many different cultures or societies to recurrent problems that are common to the human condition and that no one culture has (ever) managed to solve completely." This broadens students' views as to the range of possibilities in content areas such as, for example, transitions in life or in family.[34] On the first day of tutorial classes, students are required to form study groups of three members from different cultural backgrounds and differing characteristics in other respects, such as gender, religion, and sexual orientation. These groups, based on self-selection and supervised by the tutor, remain intact for the whole semester. The subject matter of the program also emphasizes cross-national data banks and survey data and also uses contrasting cross-national products, such as films and journalism on a common topic. In their assessed work, students are routinely required to utilize data from two or more countries.[35]

MOTIVATING LOCALS

On the face of it, the most important conditions for intercultural engagement are already in place. Those conditions, of course, are people. The large pools of international students now enrolled in many institutions in the English-speaking countries provide local students with a ready-made set of resources that can be utilized to devlop cosmopolitan perspectives and global competences—though this is more true of Australia, the United Kingdom, and New Zealand, and to a lesser extent Canada, than it is of the United States, where international students comprise less than 4 percent of students in higher education. Conversely, local students constitute for international students a large reservoir of resources for developing communicative skills and binational and hybrid perspectives. All that is needed is interaction.

How can local cohorts be motivated to engage in intercultural learning through their relationships with international students? Normative exhortation and appeals to self-interest alone are not sufficient. Claims that a "global outlook" and "global skills" are good for one's individual career are only partly true for most graduates from higher education and do not point the way to a common cosmopolitanism. A "global outlook" can be defined in relatively shallow terms and so acquired without engaging in active cross-cultural relationships. Calls for people to invest in one or another activity as a matter of self-interest are so common in Western cultures, being recycled dozens of times in an evening in front of the television, that each such call has little impact, unless the emotional resonances are very strong. Simply making such claims to local students cannot drive a large-scale shift in attitudes.

Assessment-based incentives (see the next section on language), rather than normative exhortations, are more likely to tap into the self-interest of local students to the extent needed to shift behaviors.

Indeed, at the level of norms and exhortations, more is to be gained by appealing to collective values than by appealing to individual self-interest. There is broad understanding among students of global interdependency and awareness of world issues and common public goods,[36] especially in the domains of ecology and poverty. This awareness alone will not carry students into intercultural learning with the international students alongside them, unless the global commitment is strong *and* they are able to connect particular issues or national sites to particular international students who are close at hand.

The main difference between international students and local students is that the latter have not placed themselves in settings in which cross-cultural learning has become essential to them. This suggests that the way to bring local students into the intercultural zone is to provide such experiences and mandate individual engagement. Throughgoing and sustained cross-cultural pedagogies such as those used by Chang can achieve this. Not all disciplines lend themselves to comparative and global approaches as readily as does sociology, but at least one intercultural unit of study of two semesters' duration during each student's degree program would have transformative effects on the scale required. More is to be gained by movement altogether out of familiar locations, whereby local students make geographical or intellectual journeys parallel to those of international students. As with academic teachers, so it is with students: transformative cross-cultural experiences such as a semester or more spent in study abroad, and learning a foreign language, make a lasting difference to cross-cultural capacity and orientation. Here the task for higher-education institutions is to develop the offshore experiences of local students.

Inescapably, this comes down to resources and investment priorities. Like cross-cultural student residences, large-scale study abroad programs cannot provide for intercultural learning in the breadth and depth required unless they are subsidized. Ultimately this means that higher education institutions share the cost with students, sourcing part of the resources from student tuition payments, as occurs to a lesser degree already in the United States; or that public authorities subsidize study abroad on a matching funds basis with student families, which in effect is what happens in Europe; or some combination of both approaches. These solutions are within reach. It is possible for higher education in the English-speaking countries to expand existing systems of study abroad to the point where 30 or 40 percent of the student body has spent several months of the program in another cultural setting. Once this level of engagement is achieved, cross-cultural learning becomes normalized. It gathers sufficient momentum to reproduce itself.

INTERCULTURAL LANGUAGE CAPACITY

Language proficiency and communicative competence are key elements of any strategy. Every advance in language proficiency is a potential advance in intercultural learning. Here, communicative competence has three aspects: the foreign language proficiency of local students, English language proficiency among international students, and bilingual education programs.

Foreign Languages for Locals

In English-speaking education systems, it has proven difficult to encourage foreign language learning by local students. This requires an infrastructure of language learning in both schools and higher education. In Australia, successive policies to enhance Asian language learning have been retarded by the paucity of qualified teachers. Because of training times, there are lags of half a decade or more in developing the necessary capacity and this has discouraged commitment. On the supply side, the evolution of multilinguistic education requires sustained investment by public authorities, of the kind that have already been implemented by many Asian nations in building their capacity in global English.

A large-scale expansion of study-abroad programs, as discussed in the previous section, would help. It would enhance the motivation of local students to learn other languages so as to facilitate cross-cultural ventures, driving the expansion of language programs from the demand side.

English for Internationals

As discussed in Chapter 6, the large-scale commercial international education programs in the United Kingdom, Australia, and New Zealand, particularly in business studies and technologies, have under-provided for English language support and skill development. Both higher education institutions and government policy makers have equated the maintenance and advance of language proficiency with the regulation of tested skills at the point of entry. Improvement in English is equated with raising IELTS or Test of English as a Foreign Language (TOEFL) scores. This enables the responsibility for language development to be transferred wholly from institution and teacher to student, and from host-country education system to the home-country education system. However, it neglects the literature on language development in higher education in which embeddedness in disciplinary learning contexts is seen as crucial.[37]

It is necessary to increase the level of resources provided in foundation programs and remedial support, but those steps by themselves are insufficient. Larger questions about the role of language need to be addressed. At present some teachers in higher education insist on an implicit standard based on native-level quality in students' written work and oral expression, while others vary the standard of expected English to fit the varied backgrounds of the students. In the first approach the development of language proficiency is rendered implicit rather than explicit and is thus neglected. But in the second approach the need for language proficiency is often underemphasized and retarded. We suggest that where a single common language is used in the cross-cultural educational setting, native language proficiency cannot be assumed and a commitment to language formation should be made integral to the program. For example, in large business studies classes in which a significant minority or even majority of the students are drawn from countries where English is a foreign language, institutions should provide specialist English language support teachers coordinating closely with subject teachers in the same classroom.

How can institutions be persuaded to make that kind of advanced resource commitment? As stated in *International Student Security*,[38] the vital step is to make English language standards an objective of all programs and to include them in the formal assessment of all students' work, local and international. Rochecouste and colleagues argue along the same lines: "Our team therefore recommends that assessments include marks for English. We are aware that many academic staff are reluctant to judge the quality of English in their students' assignment, feeling untrained to do so. However, the combination of clear organization, affective cohesion and coherent argumentation will render a better mark regardless of the assessor's skills and it seems that knowing this has a relationship with students' efforts."[39]

Mandatory English standards within the degree program—not just at the point of entry to or graduation from the program—would meet the expectations of international students and their families, for whom preparation in English is often as important as preparation in the discipline or occupation. As noted, there would also be many ongoing benefits in facilitating the student's communicative competence and underpinning cross-cultural interaction inside and outside the classroom.

Bilingual Education: The Next Frontier

Beyond the grounding of English language learning and the development of relational intercultural classrooms, the next step is bilingual education. This has two dimensions: the fostering of foreign language learning by local students, in which some work could be in another language of instruction, and the provision of international education in more than one language. Fridenberg discusses the potential of bilingual education programs,[40] and some Australian institutions have already explored this in practice, largely at offshore sites. For example, in a 2006 study of the financial effects of international education in Australian universities, an academic leader in business studies described the benefits of such a program:

> My view is that most Australian universities have got this wrong. We are trying to force an Anglo Saxon curriculum and an Anglo Saxon Celtic way of teaching people on a group of people that can do it only with difficulty. You get some very bland stuff out of them when you force them to do it our way. Sadly many of my colleagues believe that it's the only way to do it . . .

I was in [names place in China] recently with a group of students, the best group of students I had taken through in a long time. They then took me out in the afternoon to have a look at one of their projects, a $US 120 million tower that they were building. I thought to myself that their essays in English might be mediocre, but the quality of their strategic thinking, which was most objective, as expressed in their interaction in the classroom through an interpreter, could be very valuable. We don't have to curtail them because they can't reference properly. In my class we try to develop a much more inclusive approach. For example, when I set my exam this year, I gave a choice of two cases, the turn around of IBM, a study in English; or a Shanghai VW case that could be written in English or Mandarin. The students could choose. We have to get out of our parochial backyards and get into their incredibly world class front yards. You will not get proper educational outcomes from them unless you are flexible and you bend your rules to include some other rules.

There is a significant amount of institutionalized racism which says that if they are yellow or brown, they don't speak English and they have not been taught to reference in the Harvard manner, they cannot be as good as us . . . [A] student we have got here who is really bright, just enrolling in a PhD, said to me "the only way I can write this is that I have to think and write in Chinese first, make sense of what I think and then get somebody to help me translate my own Chinese back into English. Otherwise you lose the richness of it." When I was running the bilingual group in China I was so delighted to have good conversation, because they were thinking and talking in Chinese. A really classy interpreter was working with me and he understood my subject and we had fantastic interchange.[41]

This opens the way to a richer set of possibilities, where language is the door to agency, and students can mix and match their engagement in different cultures and languages to power their own intellectual evolution in the global setting. Then intercultural education is fully expressed as self-formation.

NOTES

PREFACE

1. Published as Marginson, Nyland, Sawir, and Forbes-Mewett, 2010.

CHAPTER 1

1. Sawir, Marginson, Deumert, Nyland, and Ramia, 2008; Marginson, Nyland, Swair, and Forbes-Mewett, 2010.
2. DEEWR, 2009.
3. OECD, 2008, 366f.
4. Dolby and Rahman, 2008.
5. See Preface and Marginson et al., 2010.
6. Marginson et al., 2010; Marginson, 2010a.
7. Appadurai, 1996.
8. Marginson and Rhoades, 2002.
9. Held and McGrew, 2000, 54.
10. Held, McGrew, Goldblatt, and Perraton, 1999, 2.
11. Cambridge and Thompson, 2004.
12. Crossley and Watson, 2003.
13. Schapper and Mayson, 2005.
14. Teekens, 2003.
15. Schuerholz-Lehr, 2007, 182.
16. Archibugi, 1998, 216.
17. Knight, 2003.
18. Knight, 2004, 10.
19. Knight, 2004, 6.
20. Marginson and Mollis, 2001.

CHAPTER 2

1. These concepts are discussed further later in this chapter.
2. Church, 1982, 541; Oberg, 1960; Adler, 1975.
3. Bochner, 1972; Furnham and Bochner, 1986.
4. Pedersen, 1991, 26.
5. Ibid., 26.
6. Ibid., 26.

7. Bochner, 1972; Church, 1982, 543–44.
8. Berry, Kim, Power, Young, and Bujaki, 1989, 186.
9. Berry, 1997, 13.
10. Berry, 1974; Berry, 1984; Berry, 1997.
11. Berry et al., 1989, 186.
12. For example, see the opening section of Chapter 7.
13. Berry et al., 1989, 186.
14. Berry, 1997.
15. Berry et al., 1989, 188.
16. Berry, 1997, 11.
17. Ibid., 10.
18. Ibid., 10–11.
19. Ibid., 14.
20. Berry et al., 1989, 186–88. Some of the terms have changed along the way. *Separation* is referred to as *rejection* in the early publications, and *marginalization* was once termed *deculturation*.
21. For example as discussed in Berry et al. 1989. See also Ward and Rana-Deuba, 1999, 425–28.
22. Ward and Rana-Deuba, 1999, 424.
23. Zhang and Dixon, 2003, 208.
24. For example Berry, 1997.
25. Church, 1982, 540.
26. Ibid., 562.
27. Ibid., 561.
28. Ibid., 542–43.
29. Ibid., 561–62.
30. Ibid., 563.
31. Ibid., 544–45.
32. Ibid., 550.
33. Ibid., 551.
34. Ibid., 551.
35. Ibid., 551–52.
36. Ibid., 557.
37. Ibid., 552.
38. Ibid., 552–53.
39. Ibid., 553.
40. Ibid., 553.
41. Ibid., 554; Gardner, 1962; Adler, 1977; Bochner, 1977.
42. Church, 1982, 558.
43. Ibid., 558.
44. Pedersen, 1991, 15.
45. Ibid., 26.
46. Ibid., 10.
47. Ibid., 19.
48. Ibid., 17.

49. Ibid., 18.
50. Ibid., 16.
51. Ibid., 20.
52. Ibid., 45; Lee, 1981.
53. Ward, Okura, Kennedy, and Kojima, 1998, 279.
54. Ward and Chang, 1997, 526.
55. Ibid., 525 and 530.
56. Ibid., 525.
57. Leong and Ward, 2000, 766–67.
58. Ibid., 771.
59. Ward, 2008, 107.
60. Ward, Leong, and Low, 2004, 137.
61. Ibid., 138.
62. Ibid., 140.
63. Ibid., 144. Emphasis added.
64. Ibid., 147.
65. Ibid., 144.
66. Ibid., 147.
67. Ibid., 145.
68. Ibid., 148.
69. See also Redmond, 2000.
70. Yang, Noels, and Saumure, 2006.
71. Sam, 2001, 318.
72. Ibid., 319–20.
73. Ibid., 331–32.
74. Anderson, 2006, 4; The quotations from Ward and Masgoret, 2004, are at pp. 42, 70, and 72.
75. Anderson, 2006, 4; Ward, 2005. Emphasis is in Anderson text.
76. Anderson, 2006, 4; Butcher, 2004, 274.
77. The writer was working in Japan while this was being written.
78. Hofstede, 2007, 411.
79. Ibid., 413.
80. Ibid., 416 and ff. On uncertainty avoidance and the masculinity/femininity binary, Hofstede states, "there is as much variation within Asia as between Asia and the West."
81. But see Hofstede, 1980.
82. Hui, 1988.
83. Hofstede, 1998.
84. Triandis, 1989a; 1994.
85. Hui, 1988.
86. Triandis, Bontempo, Villareal, Asai, and Lucca, 1988.
87. Gudykunts et al., 1989.
88. Hui, 1988.
89. Triandis et al., 1988.

90. For recent examples see, among others, Constantine, Anderson, Berkel, Caldwell, and Utsey, 2005a; Constantine, Kindaichi, Okazaki, Gainor, and Baden, 2005b. Constantine, 2005a, discusses gendered aspects of the cultural distinction. For an example of research on the workplace that uses these same these value distinctions see Siu, Spector, Cooper, and Lu, 2005.
91. Triandis et al., 1988, 333.
92. Siu, Spector, Cooper, and Lu, 2005, 277.
93. Yang et al., 2006, 496.
94. Marginson, Nyland, Swair, and Forbes-Mewett, 2010, chapter 13.
95. Triandis et al., 1988, 324.
96. Ibid., 324.
97. Ward and Masgoret, 2004, 140; Triandis, 1989b.
98. Stephens, 1997, 114.
99. Ibid., 113.
100. Ibid., 121.
101. Ibid., 120.
102. Constantine et al., 2005a; 2005b.
103. Leong and Ward, 2000, 765.
104. Ibid., 766.
105. Ibid., 771–73.
106. Ibid., 771.
107. Hullett and Witte, 2001, 125.
108. Ibid., 126.
109. Ibid., 129.
110. Ibid., 137.
111. Matsumoto, LeRoux, Bernhard, and Gray, 2004, 281–82.
112. Ibid., 299.
113. Savicki, Downing-Burnette, Heller, Binder, and Suntinger, 2004, 314.
114. Ibid., 321.
115. Li and Gasser, 2005, 563.
116. Ibid., 568.
117. Ibid., 563.
118. Ibid., 566.
119. Ibid., 569–70.
120. Ibid., 571–72.
121. Ibid., 570.
122. Yang, Noels, and Saumure, 2006, 490.
123. Ibid., 489.
124. Ibid., 489.
125. Ibid., 489.
126. Ibid., 491.
127. Ibid., 491.
128. Ibid., 496.

129. Ibid., 501.
130. Ibid., 500.
131. Ibid., 500.
132. Ibid., 498.
133. Ibid., 501.
134. Ibid., 501.
135. Ibid., 500–501.
136. Ibid., 500.
137. Ibid., 501.
138. Ibid., 502.
139. Ibid., 503.
140. The usable response pool was one hundred.
141. Kashima and Loh, 2006, 475.
142. Ibid., 473.
143. Ibid., 472.
144. Ibid., 471.
145. Ibid., 473–74.
146. Ibid., 478–79.
147. Some of whom might nevertheless share heritage, for example, Chinese background students from other parts of Asia.
148. Ibid., 480.
149. Ibid., 480–81.
150. Ibid., 481.
151. Foucault, 1977.

CHAPTER 3

1. Marginson, 2011.
2. Matthews and Sidhu, 2005, 49.
3. Immanuel Kant, 1960. Original published in 1795.
4. Rizvi, 2009, 261.
5. Hall, 2002.
6. Rizvi, 2009, 261.
7. Hall, 2002, 28.
8. Marginson, 2010c.
9. Yuval-Davis, 2006.
10. Allan, 2003, 84.
11. Bradley, 2000, 419.
12. Calhoun, 2002.
13. Stone, 2006, 410–11.
14. Olson and Kroeger, 2001, 118–19.
15. Bennett, 1993.
16. Olson and Kroeger, 2001, 119.
17. Ibid., 122; Bennett, 1993, 53.
18. Olson and Kroeger, 2001, 122–24.

19. Ibid., 122.
20. Gunesch, 2004, 251.
21. Ibid., 262.
22. Ibid., 254 and 263.
23. Ibid., 264–65.
24. Held, 2002, 49–50.
25. Yuval-Davis, 2006.
26. Ibid.
27. Marginson and Rhoades, 2002.
28. Rizvi, 2009, 253.
29. Ibid., 257.
30. Ibid., 258.
31. Rizvi, 2005, 337.
32. Sen, 1999.
33. Said, 1994, 336.
34. Vetovec and Cohen, 2002, 4.
35. Rizvi, 2005, 335; 2008, 30.
36. Rizvi, 2005, 334–35.
37. Rizvi, 2009, 262.
38. Held, 2002, 58.
39. Ibid., 17.
40. Rizvi, 2009, 256.
41. Ibid., 256.
42. Ibid., 256.
43. Rizvi, 2009, 255.
44. Ibid., 259.
45. Ibid., 260.
46. Ibid., 260.
47. Ibid., 261.
48. Anderson, 2006, 4. In Berry the term "adaptation" is used only in relation to the subaltern "minorities."
49. Ibid., 11.
50. Ibid., 1.
51. Ibid., 4.
52. Rizvi, 2008, 23.
53. Rizvi, 2005, 331 and 334.
54. Vertovec and Cohen, 2002, 3.
55. Hall, 2002, 30.
56. Rizvi, 2005, 332.
57. Rizvi, 2009, 263.
58. Vertovec and Cohen, 2002, 4.
59. Church, 1982, 554; Gardner, 1962; Adler, 1977; Bochner, 1977.
60. Church, 1982, 557.
61. Pedersen, 1991, 22.
62. Ibid., 17.

63. Ibid., 18.
64. Ibid., 18.
65. Church, 1982, 554.
66. Redmond, 2000, 153.
67. Leong and Ward, 2000, 765.
68. Ward, Leong, and Low, 2004.
69. Gunesch, 2004, 265.
70. Ibid., 256.
71. For example, Hannerz, 1990.
72. Gunesch, 2004, 262.
73. Rizvi, 2008, 21.
74. Deardorff, 2006, 243.
75. Ibid., 245.
76. Ibid., 247–48.
77. Ibid., 247.
78. Ibid., 251.
79. Vertovec, 2009, 69–73.
80. Schuerholz-Lehr, 2007, 183.
81. Olson and Kroeger, 2001, 117.
82. Fennes and Hapgood, 1997, 37.
83. Otten, 2003, 15.
84. Lasonen, 2005, 405.
85. Ibid., 400.
86. Pearce, 1998, cited in Otten, 2003, 13.
87. Ninnes, Aitchison, and Kalos, 1999, 323 and 324.
88. Ibid., 340.
89. Ibid., 337–39.
90. Ibid., 325. This passage contains a useful summary of the debate, including a list of the "cultural proficiency" literature with emphasis on Australia.
91. Doherty and Singh, 2005, 60–61.
92. Harkness et al., 2007, 113–14 and 131; Wang, Ceci, Williams, and Kopko, 2004, 227.
93. Teekens, 2003, 114.
94. Elliott and Grigorenko, 2007, 1.
95. Sternberg, 2007.
96. Singh, 2005, 16.
97. Ibid., 19.
98. Lee and Rice, 2007, 381 and 385.
99. Ibid., 388.
100. Selvadurai, 1991; Trice and Yoo, 2007; AEI, 2007a and 2007b.
101. Rizvi, 2008, 21.
102. Ibid., 31.
103. Ibid., 30.
104. See also the argument about global openness in Marginson, 2010b.

105. Rizvi, 2009, 264.
106. Rizvi, 2009, 263.
107. Rizvi, 2009, 265.
108. Ibid.
109. Sanderson, 2008, 288–89.
110. Ibid., 291.
111. Luke, 2004, 1438–39.
112. Sanderson, 2008, 296; Matthews and Sidhu, 2005.
113. Yuval-Davis, 2006.
114. Yuval-Davis, 1999.

Chapter 4

1. The summary report of that study is published as Marginson, Nyland, Swair, and Forbes-Mewett, 2010. Another book from the study, which includes data gathered in New Zealand and Australia and is focused on governance and regulation issues, was in preparation at the time of this writing.
2. Sen, 2000.
3. UNDP, 1994, 23.
4. In this segment fictional names are used, but all other details are correct.
5. Berry, Kim, Power, Young, and Bujaki, 1989; Berry, 1997. See chapter 2.

Chapter 5

1. In addition to those already cited, see Chang, Astin, and Kim, 2004.
2. Further discussion on the research follows. See among other studies Church, 1982; Pedersen, 1991; AEI, 2007a and 2007b; Marginson, Nyland, Swair, and Forbes-Mewett, 2010. For government views, see among others Bradley, 2008.
3. Volet and Ang, 1998.
4. Otten, 2003, 14.
5. For example, Marginson et al., 2010.
6. Berry, 1997.
7. Spencer-Rodgers, 2001, 642.
8. Ibid., 642.
9. Spencer-Rodgers and McGovern, 2002, 625–26.
10. Olson and Kroeger, 2001, 120.
11. Ibid., 120.
12. Spencer-Rodgers, 2001, 639.
13. Ibid., 642.
14. Ibid., 639.
15. Ibid., 647.

16. Ibid., 651.
17. Ibid., 639.
18. Ibid., 650.
19. Ibid., 650.
20. Ibid., 654.
21. Pritchard and Skinner, 2002, 324.
22. Leong and Ward, 2000, 766.
23. Otten, 2003, 15; Church, 1982, 552.
24. Church, 1982, 552.
25. Petersen, 1991, 45.
26. Volet and Ang, 1998, 14.
27. Ibid., 15.
28. Nasrin, 2001, 43; Spencer-Rodgers and McGovern, 2002, 613.
29. For example, Hayes and Lin, 1994, 5; Spencer-Rodgers and McGovern, 2002, 613; Sam, 2002, 315.
30. Leong and Ward, 2000, 766.
31. Perrucci and Hu, 1995, 502.
32. Ibid., 503.
33. Lee, 2005, 1.
34. Ibid., 4.
35. Ibid., 13.
36. Ibid., 11–12.
37. Ibid., 6; Spears, 1999.
38. Anderson, 2006.
39. Lee and Rice, 2007, 389–90.
40. Ibid., 381.
41. Ibid., 393.
42. Ibid., 394–95.
43. Ibid., 394–95.
44. Nasrin, 2001, 44.
45. Hanassah and Tidwell, 2002, 310.
46. Hannassah, 2006, 165. The study was conducted before the attacks on the Pentagon and the World Trade Center in September 2001.
47. Ibid., 161.
48. Constantine, Anderson, Berkel, Caldwell, and Utsey, 2005a, 60.
49. Ibid., 61.
50. Ibid., 62.
51. Solberg, Ritsma, Davis, Tata, and Jolly, 1994, 275.
52. McGrath and Hooker, 2006, 7–8.
53. Collins, 2006, 217.
54. Ibid., 221.
55. Schweitzer, 1996, 5.
56. Robertson, Line, Jones, and Thomas, 2000, 93.
57. Ibid., 96.
58. Ibid., 99.

59. Rosenthal, Russell, and Thomson, 2006, 57.
60. Ibid., 42.
61. Ibid., 28.
62. AEI, 2007b, 30.
63. Spencer-Rodgers and McGovern, 2002, 610.
64. Ibid., 609.
65. Ibid., 624.
66. Ibid., 621.
67. Ibid., 620.
68. Ibid., 624–25.
69. Wan, 2001, 34.
70. Mori, 2000, 138.
71. Ibid., 139.
72. Spencer-Rodgers, 2001.
73. Spencer-Rodgers and McGovern, 2002, 610.
74. Ibid., 610–11.
75. Lee and Rice, 2007, 389–90.
76. Nasrin, 2001, 43.
77. Perrucci and Hu, 1995, 491.
78. Ibid., 506.
79. Church, 1982, 552–53, summarizes the discussion to that point.
80. In addition to those discussed later in this chapter, see Constantine, Kindaichi, Okazaki, Gainor, and Baden, 2005b, 164.
81. Perrucci and Hu, 1995, 491.
82. Li and Gasser, 2005, 569–71.
83. Otten, 2003, 14.
84. Hayes and Lin, 1994, 5; Lee, Maldonado-Maldonado, and Rhoades, 2006, 552.
85. Li and Kaye, 1998, 44–47.
86. UKCOSA, 2004, 67.
87. Ibid., 68.
88. Ibid., 67.
89. Ibid., 67.
90. Ibid., 68.
91. Ibid., 70.
92. Lee and Rice, 2007, 397. See also Pritchard and Skinner, 2002, 345.
93. Bradley, 2000, 425.
94. UKCOSA, 2004, 69.
95. Rosenthal, Russell, and Thomson, 2006, 23.
96. There is ambiguity in the study data because the category "Australian" does not distinguish same-culture and other-culture persons.
97. Ibid., 23–24.
98. Ibid., 24.
99. Ibid., 24.

100. AEI, 2007a, 6 and 65.
101. Ibid., 33.
102. AEI, 2007a, 6 and 65.
103. Ibid., 68.
104. AEI, 2007b, 51.
105. Ibid., 31.
106. Ibid., 32.
107. Ibid., 32–33.
108. Ibid., 23.
109. Hullett and Witte, 2001, 137.
110. Gabriel and Gabriel, 1978.
111. This is a strong finding of Marginson et al., 2010, chapter 14.

CHAPTER 6

1. Church, 1982, 550–51.
2. Boyer and Sedlacek, 1989, 405.
3. For example, Perrucci and Hu, 1995, 491; Struthers, Perry, and Menec, 2000, 589–90.
4. For example, Birrell, 2006.
5. Lee, 1997.
6. Lin and Yi, 1997; Nasrin, 2001. See also Grayson, 2005.
7. Nasrin, 2001.
8. Trice, 2003.
9. Ibid., 387.
10. Ibid., 394.
11. For example, Cownie and Addison, 1996.
12. Spack, 1997.
13. Li, Baker, and Marshall, 2002.
14. Gonzalez, Chen, and Sanchez, 2001; Wilkinson and Kavan, 2003; Zhu, 2004.
15. Feast, 2002; Carroll, 2005a, 2005b.
16. Malcolm and McGregor, 1995; Gatfield, Barker, and Graham, 1999.
17. These include Pantelides, 1999; Robertson, Line, Jones, and Thomas, 2000; Hellstén and Prescott, 2004; Daroesman, Looi, and Butler, 2005; Singh, 2005.
18. Samuelovicz, 1987.
19. Ballard and Clanchy, 1997, 9.
20. Ryan, 2000.
21. See also Samuelowicz, 1987.
22. Tran, 2006.
23. Kember and Gow, 1991; O'Donoghue, 1996; Ninnes, Aitchison, and Kalos, 1999; and the collection edited by Ninnes and Hellsten, 2005.

24. Doherty and Singh, 2005, 67.
25. Dunn and Wallace, 2006, 359.
26. Hellstén and Prescott, 2004.
27. Ibid., 347.
28. Prescott and Hellstén, 2005. See also Sawir, 2005.
29. Singh, 2005.
30. Ibid.
31. Tran, 2006, 122.
32. Mulligan and Kirkpatrick, 2000, 311.
33. Borland and Pearce, 2002, 103.
34. Ibid., 122.
35. Pantelides, 1999; Carroll, 2005a.
36. For example, Dooey, 1999.
37. Asmar, 1999; Dooey, 1999; Stoynoff, 1997.
38. Elder, 1993; Hill, Storch, and Lynch, 1999; Poyrazli, Arbona, Bullington, and Pisecco, 2001; Feast, 2002.
39. Poyrazli et al., 2001.
40. Kerstjens and Nery, 2000; Bayliss and Raymond, 2004.
41. Rochecouste, Oliver, Mulligan, and Davies, 2010, 13.
42. Pantelides, 1999.
43. Ibid., 70ff.
44. Fallon and Brown, 1999.
45. Fallon and Brown acknowledge that treating non-UK students as a homogenous group was one of the limitations of their study.
46. Trice, 2003.
47. Trice, 2005.
48. Trice and Yoo, 2007, 53–54.
49. Olson and Kroeger, 2001, 116.
50. Schuerholz-Lehr, 2007, 182.
51. Doherty and Singh, 2005.
52. Ibid., 360.
53. Bartram, 2007, 210.
54. Ibid., 212.
55. Tatar, 2005, 343.
56. Ibid., 349.
57. Ibid., 347–48.
58. Zhang, 2006, 36.
59. Ibid., 37.
60. Pritchard and Skinner, 2002, 324.
61. Ibid., 323.
62. Carroll, 2005.
63. Ippolito, 2007.
64. Arkoudis et al., 2010, 6.
65. Volet and Ang, 1998, 8.
66. Volet and Renshaw, 1995, 407.

67. Ramburuth and McCormick, 2001, 333.
68. Ibid., 346.
69. Volet and Ang, 1998, 12.
70. Ibid., 12.
71. Ibid., 10.
72. Ibid., 13.
73. Ibid., 19.
74. Ibid.
75. Ibid., 6.
76. Ibid., 8.
77. Ibid., 10.
78. Ibid., 11.
79. Ibid., 12.
80. Ibid., 16.
81. Ibid., 20.
82. Ibid., 6.
83. Ibid., 18.
84. Summers and Volet, 2008, 357.
85. Ibid., 358–59.
86. Ibid., 362.
87. Ibid., 366.
88. Ibid., 363.
89. Ibid., 367.
90. Ibid., 363.
91. Ibid., 363–64.
92. Ibid., 365.
93. Ibid., 369.
94. Ibid., 368.
95. Ibid., 366–67.

CHAPTER 7

1. Castoriadis talks about "radical otherness or creation," in which "something other than what exists is bringing itself into being, and bringing itself into being as new or as other and not simply as a consequence or as a different exemplar of the same": Castoriadis, 1987, 184–85. Murphy (2007) remarks on intuitions of order in the act of creation. There are traces of the past in every innovation. Rose (1999, 96) makes the comment that "we do not know what we are capable of" but we do know that "our history has produced a creature with the capacity to act upon its limits."

2. And without wanting to overplay the point, no one is quite the same as anyone else. There is always newness in the distinctive application of another person's intellectual apparatus to a set of old knowledge. The intellectual apparatus might process what it knows in a new way

(rearrange the elements in the synthesis) or it might take in new thoughts (the stimulus of someone else's ideas in the mix), or take in new observable phenomena. Everyone perceives and knows distinctively, but some are more distinctive and more sustained in that distinctiveness than others.

3. Gould, 2002, chapter 9.
4. Sen, 2000, 19.
5. Ibid., 288.
6. Sen, 1985; 1992.
7. Sen, 1985, 169.
8. Ibid., 206. Emphasis in original.
9. Sen, 2000, 218.
10. Ibid., 295.
11. Newman, 1982 (1852).
12. Bourdieu, 1984.
13. Rizvi, 2009, 261.
14. Rizvi, 2008, 33.
15. Rose, 1999.
16. The point is also made by Ward and Rana-Deuba, 1999, 423–24.
17. Berry, 1974; 1984; etc.
18. Pedersen, 1991.
19. Church, 1982, 557; Pedersen, 1991, 22.
20. Church, 1982, 557.
21. Ibid., 558.
22. Volet and Ang, 1998, 8.
23. Hanassah and Tidwell, 2002, 313–14.
24. For example, the study by Butcher of 50 graduates going home from international education in New Zealand, 2002, 355.
25. Lee and Koro-Ljungberg, 2007, 97.
26. Rizvi, 2005, 336.
27. Anderson, 2006, 11.
28. Goldbart, Marshall, and Evens, 2005, 105.
29. Rizvi, 2005, 338.
30. See the discussion of Baumeister's notions of "identity deficit" and identity conflict in Leong and Ward, 2000, 764.
31. Doherty and Singh, 2005.
32. Leong and Ward, 2000, 771.
33. Yang, Noels, and Saumure, 2006, 490.
34. Allan, 2003, 83.
35. Cannon, 2000, 364–65.
36. Ibid., 373.
37. Matsumoto, LeRoux, Bernhard, and Gray, 2004; Savicki, Downing-Burnette, Heller, Binder, and Suntinger, 2004, 312–13.
38. Leong and Ward, 2000, 763.
39. Redmond, 2000, 153.

40. Ying and Han, 2006, 625.
41. Spencer-Rodgers and McGovern, 2002, 620.
42. Bradley, 2000, 419.
43. Pyvis and Chapman, 2005, 23.
44. Kettle, 2005, 45.
45. Ibid., 48.
46. Ibid., 51.
47. Singh, 2005, 10.
48. Kettle comments that the main focus of the literature in Australia on the academic performance of international students has been on the problems created for the universities by the difference between student background and host country academic requirements. Kettle, 2005, 45.
49. Asmar, 2005, 293.
50. Ward, Leong, and Low, 2004.
51. Yoo, Matsumoto, and LeRoux, 2006.
52. Chirkov, Vansteenkiste, Tao, and Lynch, 2007.
53. Savicki et al., 2004.
54. Ward, Leong, and Low, 2004, 138.
55. Perrucci and Hu, 1995, 506.
56. Marginson, 2007b.
57. This was Keynes's solution to the problem of complex nonhomogenous wholes, which combine normative and empirically verifiable elements with incalculable probabilities. See Carabelli, 1995, 140–41.
58. See Chapter 2.
59. Ramsay, Barker, and Jones et al., 1999, 130.

CHAPTER 8

1. Lee and Rice, 2007; Volet and Tan-Quigley, 1999; Bretag, Horrocks, and Smith, 2002.
2. Lin and Yi, 1997.
3. Schuerholz-Lehr, 2007.
4. Li and Gasser, 2005, 572.
5. For example, Bradley, 2000, 430; and the literature reviewed by Lee and Rice, 2007, 388.
6. AEI, 2007b, 21–22.
7. Spencer-Rodgers and McGovern, 2002, 627–28.
8. Marginson, Nyland, Swair, and Forbes-Mewett, 2010, chapters 7 and 15.
9. Leask, 2005.
10. Teekens, 2003, 117.
11. Teekens, 2004, 36.
12. Ninnes, Aitchison, and Kalow, 1999.

13. Robertson, Line, Jones, and Thomas, 2000, 89; Volet and Ang, 1998.
14. Leask, 2004, 4; Dunn and Wallace, 2006, 362.
15. Prescott and Hellsten, 2005.
16. Wan, 2001, 28.
17. Savicki, Downing-Burnette, Heller, Binder, and Suntinger 2004, 313.
18. Clandinin and Connelly, 1999.
19. Johnson and Inoue, 2003; Chang, 2006.
20. Anderson, Lawton, Rexeisen, and Hubbard, 2006, 457.
21. Helms, 2004.
22. Green and Olson, 2003.
23. Schuerholz-Lehr, 2007.
24. Webb, 2005, 110.
25. Gabb, 2006, 362.
26. De Vita, 2005; Leask, 2005; Chang, 2006; Ippolito, 2007.
27. Teekens, 2003, 110.
28. Arkoudis et al., 2010, 10.
29. Ibid., 11–20.
30. De Vita, 2005, 75–76.
31. Ibid.; Volet and Ang, 1998.
32. Chang, 2006.
33. Ibid., 370.
34. Ibid., 371.
35. Ibid., 372–74.
36. Marginson, 2007b.
37. For example, Arkoudis et al., 2010.
38. Marginson et al., 2010, 459–60.
39. Rochecouste, Oliver, Mulligan, and Davies, 2010, 4.
40. Fridenberg, 2002.
41. Marginson and Eijkman, 2007.

REFERENCES

Adler, P. (1975). The transnational experience: An alternative view of culture shock. *Journal of Humanistic Psychology, 15*, 13–23.

Adler, P. (1977). Beyond cultural identity: Reflections upon cultural and multicultural man. In R. Brislin (Ed.), *Culture learning: Concepts, applications and research* (pp. 24–41). Honolulu, HI: University of Hawaii Press.

Allan, M. (2003). Frontier crossings: Cultural dissonance, intercultural learning and the multicultural personality. *Journal of Research in International Education, 2*(1), 83–110.

Anderson, P., Lawton, L., Rexeisen, R., & Hubbard, A. (2006). Short-term study abroad and intercultural sensitivity: A pilot study. *International Journal of Intercultural Relations, 30*(4), 457–69.

Anderson, V. (2006, December). *Who's not integrating? International women speak about New Zealand students.* Paper presented at the ISANA International Education Conference. University of New South Wales, Sydney, Australia.

Appadurai, A. (1996). *Modernity at large: Cultural dimensions of globalization.* Minneapolis, MN: University of Minnesota Press.

Archibugi, D. (1998). Principles of cosmopolitan democracy. In D. Archibugi, D. Held, & M. Kohler (Eds.) *Re-imaging political community* (pp. 198–228). Cambridge, UK: Polity Press.

Arkoudis, S., Yu, X., Baik, C., Borland, H., Chang, S., Lang, I., Lang, J., Pearce, A., & Watty, K. (2010). *Finding common ground: Enhancing interaction between domestic and international students.* Canberra, Australia: Australian Learning and Teaching Council.

Asmar, C. (1999). Scholarship, experience or both?: A developer's approach to cross-cultural teaching. *International Journal for Academic Development, 4*(1), 18–27.

Asmar, C. (2005). Internationalizing students: Reassessing diasporic and local student differences. *Studies in Higher Education, 30*(3), 291–309.

Australian Education International, AEI (2007a). *2006 international student survey: Higher education summary report.* Canberra, Australia: AEI.

Australian Education International, AEI (2007b). *2006 international student survey: Report of the consolidated results from the four education sectors in Australia.* Canberra, Australia: AEI.

Ballard, B., & Clanchy, J. (1997). *Teaching international students. A brief guide for lecturers and supervisors.* Canberra, Australia: IDP Education.

Bartram, B. (2007). The sociocultural needs of international students in higher education: A comparison of staff and student views. *Journal of Studies in International Education, 11*(2), 205–14.

Bayliss, D., & Raymond, P. (2004). The link between academic success and L2 proficiency in the context of two professional programs. *The Canadian Modern Language Review, 61*(1), 29–51.

Bennett, M. (1993). Towards ethnorelativism: A developmental model of intercultural sensitivity. In R. Paige (Ed.), *Education for the intercultural experience* (pp. 21-71). Yarmouth, ME: Intercultural Press.

Berry, J. (1974). Psychological aspects of cultural pluralism. *Topics in Cultural Learning, 2,* 17–22.

Berry, J. (1984). Cultural relations in plural societies. In N. Miller, & M. Brewer (Eds.), *Groups in contact* (pp. 11–27). San Diego, CA: Academic Press.

Berry, J. (1997). Immigration, acculturation and adaptation. *Applied Psychology, 46*(1), 5–34.

Berry, J., Kim, U., Power, S., Young, M., & Bujaki, M. (1989). Acculturation attitudes in plural societies. *Applied Psychology, 38*(2), 185–206.

Bexley, E., Marginson, S., & Wheelahan, L. (2004). *Social capital in theory and practice: The contribution of Victorian tertiary education in the "new economy" disciplines of business studies and IT.* Draft report. Centre for the Study of Higher Education, University of Melbourne, Melbourne, Australia.

Bhabha, H. (1990). DissemiNation: Time, narrative and the margins of the modern nation. In H. Babha (Ed.), *Nation and narration* (pp. 291–322). London, UK: Routledge.

Birrell, B. (2006). Implications of low English standards among overseas students at Australian universities. *People and Place, 14*(4), December.

Bochner, S. (1972). Problems in culture learning. In S. Bochner, & P. Wicks (Eds.), *Overseas students in Australia* (pp. 65–81). Sydney, Australia: University of New South Wales Press.

Bochner, S. (1977). The mediating man and cultural diversity. In R. Brislin (Ed.), *Culture learning: Concepts, applications and research* (pp. 3–17). Honolulu, HI: University of Hawaii Press.

Borland, H., & Pearce, A. (2002). Identifying key dimensions of language and cultural disadvantage at university. *Australian Review of Applied Linguistics, 25*(2), 101–27.

Bourdieu, P. (1984). *Distinction: A social critique of the judgment of taste.* London, UK: Routledge.

Boyer, S., & Sedlacek, W. (1989). Noncognitive predictors of counselling center use by international students. *Journal of Counseling and Development, 67,* 404–7.

Bradley, D., Chair of Panel (2008). *Review of Australian higher education: Final report.* Canberra: Australian Government. Retrieved January 10, 2008 from http://www.deewr.gov.au/HigherEducation/Review/Pages/ReviewofAustralianHigherEducationReport.aspx.

Bradley, G. (2000). Responding effectively to the mental health needs of international students. *Higher Education, 39*, 417–33.

Bretag, T., Horrocks, S., & Smith, J. (2002). Developing classroom practices to support NESB students in information system courses: Some preliminary findings. *International Education Journal, 3*(4), 57–69.

Butcher, A. (2002). A grief observed. Grief experiences of East Asian students returning to their countries of origin. *Journal of Studies in International Education, 6*(4), 354–68.

Butcher, A. (2004). Educate, consolidate, immigrate: Educational immigration in Auckland, New Zealand. *Asia Pacific Viewpoint, 45*(92), 255–78.

Calhoun, C. (2002). The class consciousness of frequent travellers: Towards a critique of actually existing cosmopolitanism. In S. Vertovec, & R. Cohen (Eds.), *Conceiving cosmopolitanism: Theory, context and practice* (pp. 86–109). Oxford, UK: Oxford University Press.

Cambridge, J., & Thompson, J. (2004). Internationalism and globalization as contexts for international education. *Compare, 34*(2), 161–75.

Cannon, R. (2000). The outcomes of an international education for Indonesian graduates: The third place? *Higher Education Research and Development, 19*(3), 357–79.

Carabelli, A. (1995). Uncertainty and measurement in Keynes: Probability and organicness. In S. Dow and J. Hillard (Eds.), *Keynes, knowledge, and uncertainty* (pp. 137–60). Cheltenham: Edward Elgar.

Carroll, J. (2005a). Lightening the load: Teaching in English, learning in English. In J. Carroll, & J. Ryan (Eds.), *Teaching international students* (pp. 35–42). London, UK: Routledge.

Carroll, J. (2005b). Multicultural groups for discipline-specific tasks. In J. Carroll, & J, Ryan (Eds.), *Teaching international students* (pp. 84–91). London, UK: Routledge.

Castoriadis, C. (1987). *The imaginary institution of society.* Cambridge, UK: Polity Press.

Chang, J. (2006). A transcultural wisdom bank in the classroom: Making cultural diversity a key resource in teaching and learning. *Journal of Studies in International Education, 10*(4), 369–77.

Chang, M., Astin, A., & Kim, D. (2004). Cross-racial interaction among undergraduates: Some consequences, causes and patterns. *Research in Higher Education, 45*(5), 529–53.

Chang, T., & Chang, R. (2004). Counseling and the internet: Asian American and Asian international college students' attitudes towards seeking online professional psychological help. *Journal of College Counselling, 7*, 140–49.

Chirkov, V., Vansteenkiste, M., Tao, R., & Lynch, M. (2007). The role of self-determined motivation and goals for study abroad in the adaptation of international students. *International Journal of Intercultural Relations, 31*, 199–222.

Church, A. (1982). Sojourner adjustment. *Psychological Bulletin, 91*(3), 540–72.

Clandinin, D. J., & Connelly, F. M. (Eds.). (1999). *Shaping a professional identity: Stories of educational practice.* London, UK: Althouse Press.

Collins, F. (2006). Making Asian students, making students Asian: The racialisation of export education in Auckland, New Zealand. *Asia Pacific Viewpoint, 47*(2), 217–34.

Connie, F., & Addison, W. (1996). International students and language support: A new survey. *Studies in Higher Education 21*(2), 221–31

Constantine, M., Anderson, G., Berkel, L., Caldwell, L., & Utsey, S. (2005a). Examining the cultural adjustment experiences of African international college students: A qualitative analysis. *Journal of Counseling Psychology, 52*(1), 57–66.

Constantine, M., Kindaichi, M., Okazaki, S., Gainor, K., & Baden, A. (2005b). A qualitative investigation of the cultural adjustment experiences of Asian international college women. *Cultural Diversity and Ethnic Minority Psychology, 11*(2), 162–75.

Crossley, M., & Watson, K. (2003). *Comparative and international research in education: Globalization, context and difference.* London, UK: Routledge.

Daroesman, S. Looi, K., & Butler, D. (2005). *Survey of final year international students on their experience of the University of Melbourne.* Melbourne, Australia: University Planning Office, University of Melbourne.

Deardorff, D. (2006). Identification and assessment of intercultural competence as a student outcome of internationalization. *Journal of Studies in International Education, 10*(3), 241–66.

Department of Education, Employment, and Workplace Relations (formerly Department of Education, Science, and Training). (2009). *Selected higher education statistics.* Retrieved January 10, 2009 from http://www.dest.gov.au/sectors/higher_education/publications_resources/profiles/students_2005_selected_higher_education_statistics.htm.

De Vita, G. (2005). Fostering intercultural learning through multicultural group work. In J. Carroll, & J, Ryan (Eds.), *Teaching international students* (pp. 75–83). London, UK: Routledge.

Doherty, C., & Singh, P. (2005). How the West is done: Simulating Western pedagogy in a curriculum for Asian international students. In P. Ninnes, & M. Hellsten (Eds.), *Internationalizing higher education: Critical explorations of pedagogy and policy* (pp. 53–74). Dordrecht, Netherlands: Springer.

Dolby, N., & Rahman, A. (2008). Research in international education. *Review of Educational Research, 78*(3), 676–726.

Dooey, P. (1999). An investigation into the predictive validity of the IELTS Test as an indictor of future academic success. In K. Martin, N. Stanley, & N. Davison (Eds.), *Teaching in the disciplines/learning in context* (pp. 114–18). Perth, Australia: Centre for Staff Development, University of Western Australia.

Dunn, L., & Wallace, M. (2006). Australian academics and transnational teaching: An exploratory study of their preparedness and experiences. *Education Research and Development, 25*(4), 357–69.

Elder, C. (1993). Language proficiency as a predictor of performance in teacher education. *Melbourne Papers in Language Testing, 2*(1), 68–78.

Elliott, J., & Grigorenko, E. (2007). Are Western educational theories and practices truly universal? *Comparative Education, 43*(1), 1–4.

Fallon, G., & Brown, R. B. (1999). What about the workers? Academic staff opinions about working with non-UK postgraduate students in higher education. *Journal of Further and Higher Education, 23*(1), 41–52.

Fatima, N. (2001). *International female graduate students' perceptions of their adjustment experiences and coping strategies at an urban research university.* Retrieved June 20, 2011, from http://www.eric.ed.gov/ERICWebPortal/search/detailmini.jsp?_nfpb=true&_&ERICExtSearch_SearchValue_0=ED452336&ERICExtSearch_SearchType_0=no&accno=ED452336.

Feast, V. (2002). The impact of IELTS scores on performance at university. *International Education Journal, 3*(4), 70–85.

Fennes, H., & Hapgood, K. (1997). *Intercultural learning in the classroom.* London, UK: Cassell.

Foucualt, M. (1977). *Discipline and punish: The birth of the prison.* Harmondsworth, UK: Penguin.

Friedenberg, J. (2002). The linguistic inaccessibility of U.S. higher education and the inherent inequality of U.S. IEPs: An argument for multilingual education. *Bilingual Research Journal, 26*(2), 309–26.

Furnham, A., & Bochner, S. (1986). *Culture shock: Psychological reactions to unfamiliar environments.* London, UK: Methuen.

Gabb, D. (2006). Transcultural dynamics in the classroom. *Journal of Studies in International Education, 10*(4), 357–68.

Gardner, G. (1962). Cross-cultural communication. *Journal of Social Psychology, 58*, 241–56.

Gatfield, T., Barker, M., & Graham, P. (1999). Measuring student quality variables and the implications for management practices in higher education institutions: An Australian and international student perspectives. *Journal of Higher Education Policy and Management, 21*(2), 239–52.

Goldbart, J., Marshall, J., & Evans, I. (2005). International students of speech and language therapy in the UK: Choices about where to study and whether to return. *Higher Education, 50*, 89–109.

Gonzalez, V., Chen, C., & Sanchez, C. (2001). Cultural thinking and discourse organisational patterns influencing writing skills in a Chinese English-as-a-foreign-language (EFL) learner. *Bilingual Research Journal, 25*(4), 417–42.

Gould, S. (2002). *The structure of evolutionary theory.* Cambridge, UK: Harvard University Press.

Green, M. F., & Olson, C. (2003). *Internationalizing the campus: A user's guide.* Washington, DC: American Council of Education.

Gudykunts, W., Gao, G., Nishida, T., Bond, M., Leung, K., Wang, G., & Barraclough, R. (1989). A cross-cultural study of self-monitoring. *Communication Research Report, 6*, 7–12.

Gunesch, K. (2004). Education for cosmopolitanism? Cosmopolitanism as a personal cultural identity model for and within international education. *Journal of Research in International Education, 3*(3), 251–75.

Hall, S. (2002). Political belonging in a world of multiple identities. In S. Vertovec, & R. Cohen (Eds.), *Conceiving cosmopolitanism: Theory, context and practice* (pp. 25–31). Oxford, UK: Oxford University Press.

Hanassah, S., & Tidwell, R. (2002). International students in higher education: Identification of needs and implications for policy and practice. *Journal of Studies in International Education, 6*(4), 305–22.

Hanassah, S. (2006). Diversity, international students and perceived discrimination: Implications for educators and counsellors. *Journal of Studies in International Education, 10*(2), 157–72.

Hannerz, U. (1990). Cosmopolitans and locals in world culture. In M. Featherstone (Ed.), *Global culture: Nationalism, globalization and modernity* (pp. 237–51). London, UK: Sage.

Harkness, S., Blom, M., Oliva, A., Moscardina, U., Zylicz, P., Bermudez, M., Feng, X., Carrasco-Zylicz, A., Axia, G., & Super, C. (2007). Teachers' ethnotheories of the "ideal student" in five Western cultures. *Comparative Education, 43*(1), 113–35.

Hayes, R., & Lin, H.-R. (1994). Coming to America: Developing social support systems for international students, *Journal of Multicultural Counseling and Development, 22*(1), 7–16.

Held, D. (2002). Culture and political community: National, global and cosmopolitan. In S. Vertovec, & R. Cohen (Eds.), *Conceiving cosmopolitanism: Theory, context, and practice* (pp. 48–58). Oxford, UK: Oxford University Press.

Held, D., & McGrew, A. (2000). *The global transformations reader.* Cambridge, UK: Polity Press.

Held, D., McGrew, A., Goldblatt D., & Perraton, J. (1999). *Global transformations: Politics, economics, and culture.* Stanford, CA: Stanford University Press.

Hellsten, M., & Prescott, A. (2004). Learning at university: The international student's experience. *International Education Journal, 5*(3), 344–51.

Helms, S. M. (2004). The examination of cultural sensitivity and exhibition of cultural competence for faculty at liberal arts institutions within higher education. *Dissertation Abstracts International, 64*(10), 3609A.

Hill, K., Storch, N., Lynch, B. (1999). A comparison of IETS and TOEFL as predictors of academic success. In R. Tulloh (Ed.), *International English language testing system research reports,* vol. 2. Canberra, Australia: IELTS Australia.

Hofstede, G (1980). *Culture's consequences: International differences in work-related values.* Beverly Hills, CA: Sage.

Hofstede, G. (1998). Think locally, act globally: Cultural constraints in personal management. *Management International Review, 38*(2), 7–26.

Hofstede, G. (2007). Asian management in the 21st century. *Asia-Pacific Journal of Management, 24*, 411–20.

Hui, C. (1988). Measurement of individualism and collectivism. *Journal of Research in Personality, 22*, 17–36.

Hullett, C., & Witte, K. (2001). Predicting intercultural adaptation and isolation: Using the extended parallel process model to test anxiety/uncertainty management theory. *International Journal of Intercultural Relations, 25*, 125–39.

Ippolito. K. (2007). Promoting intercultural learning in a multicultural university: Ideas and realities. *Teaching in Higher Education, 12*(5–6), 749–63.

Johnson, K., & Inoue, Y. (2003). Diversity and multicultural pedagogy: An analysis of attitudes and practices within an American Pacific Island University. *Journal of Research in International Education, 2*, 251–76.

Kant, I. (1960). Perpetual peace. In L. W. Beck (Ed.), *On History* (pp. 3–13). New York, NY: Macmillan. Originally published in 1795.

Kashima, E., & Loh, E. (2006). International students' acculturation: Effects of international, conational, and local ties and need for closure. *International Journal of Intercultural Relations, 30*, 471–85.

Kember, D., & Gow, L. (1991). A challenge to the anecdotal stereotype of the Asian student. *Studies in Higher Education, 16*, 117–28.

Kerstjen, M., & Nery, C. (2000). Predictive validity in the IELTS test: A study of the relationship between IELTS scores and students' subsequent academic performance. In R. Tulloh (Ed.), *International English language testing system research reports*, vol. 3 (pp. 85–108). Canberra, Australia: IELTS Australia.

Kettle, M. (2005). Agency as discursive practice: From "nobody" to "somebody" as an international student in Australia. *Asia-Pacific Journal of Education, 25*(1), 45–60.

Knight, J. (2003). Updated internationalization definition. *Internationalization Higher Education, 33*, 2–3.

Knight, J. (2004). Internationalization remodelled: Definition, approaches and rationales. *Journal of Studies in International Education, 8*(1), 5–31.

Lasonen, J. (2005). Reflections on interculturality in relation to education and work. *Higher Education Policy, 18*, 397–407.

Leask, B. (2005). Internationalization of the curriculum. Teaching and learning. In J. Carroll, & J, Ryan (Eds.), *Teaching international students: Improving learning for all* (pp. 119–29). London, UK: Routledge.

Lee, D. (1997). What teachers can do to relieve problems identified by international students. *New Directions for Teaching and Learning, 70*, 93–100.

Lee, I., & Koro-Ljunberg, M. (2007). A phenomenological study of Korean students' acculturation in middle schools in the USA. *Journal of Research in International Education, 6*(1), 95–117.

Lee, J. (2005). *The influence of international student experiences on recommending study in the U.S.* Draft report. Center for the Study of Higher Education, University of Arizona, Tucson, AZ.

Lee, J., Maldonado-Maldonado, A., & Rhoades, G. (2006). The political economy of international student flows: Patterns, ideas and propositions. In J. Smart (Ed.), *Higher Education: Handbook of theory and research*, vol. 7 (pp. 545–90). Dordrecht, Netherlands: Springer.

Lee, J., & Rice, C. (2007). Welcome to America? International student perceptions of discrimination. *Higher Education, 53*, 381–409.

Lee, M. (1981). *Needs of foreign students from developing nations in U.S. doctoral universities.* Washington, DC: National Association for Foreign Student Affairs (NAFSA).

Leong, C., & Ward, C. (2000). Identity conflict in sojourners. *International Journal of Intercultural Relations, 24*, 763–76.

Li, A., & Gasser, M. (2005). Predicting Asian international students' sociocultural adjustment: A test of two mediation models. *International Journal of Intercultural Relations, 29*, 561–76.

Li, M., Baker, T., & Marshall, K. (2002). Mismatched expectations: A case study of Asian students in New Zealand. *New Zealand Journal of Applied Business Research, 1*(1), 1–23.

Li, R., & Kaye, M. (1998). Understanding overseas students' concerns and problems. *Journal of Higher Education Policy and Management, 20*(1), 41–50.

Lin, J., & Yi, J. (1997). Asian international students' adjustment: Issues and program suggestions. *College Student Journal, 31*(4), 473–80.

Luke, A. (2004). Teaching after the market: From commodity to cosmopolitan. *Teachers College Record, 106*, 1422–43.

Malcolm, I., & McGregor, A. (1995). *Worlds apart: An investigation of linguistic and cultural factors affecting communication between NESB and Edith Cowan University staff.* Perth, Australia: Centre for Applied Language Research, Edith Cowan University.

Marginson, S. (2007a). Global position and position-taking: The case of Australia. *Journal of Studies in International Education, 11*(1), 5–32.

Marginson, S. (2007b). The public/private division in higher education: a global revision, *Higher Education, 53*, 307–33.

Marginson, S. (2010a). International student security: Globalization, state, university. *Journal of the World Universities Forum, 3*(3), 49–58.

Marginson, S. (2010b). Space, mobility and synchrony in the knowledge economy. In S. Marginson, P. Murphy, & M. Peters, *Global creation: Space, mobility and synchrony in the age of the knowledge economy* (pp. 117–49). New York, NY: Peter Lang.

Marginson, S. (2010c). World. In P. Murphy, M. Peters, & S. Marginson, *Imagination: Three models of imagination in the age of the knowledge economy* (pp. 139–65). New York, NY: Peter Lang.

Marginson, S. (2011). Imagining the global. In R. King, S. Marginson, & R. Naidoo (Eds.), *Handbook of higher education and globalization*. Cheltenham, UK: Edward Elgar.

Marginson, S., & Eijkman, H. (2007). *International education: Financial and organizational impacts in Australian universities*. Report prepared for the Monash Institute for the Study of Global Movements. Melbourne, Australia: Monash University. Retrieved January 1, 2008 from http://www.cshe .unimelb.edu.au/people/staff_pages/Marginson/Marginson.html.

Marginson, S, & Mollis, M. (2001). "The door opens and the tiger leaps": Theories and reflexivities of comparative education for a global millennium. *Comparative Education Review, 45*(4), 581–615.

Marginson, S., Nyland, C., Swair, E., & Forbes-Mewett, H. (2010). *International student security*. Cambridge, UK: Cambridge University Press.

Marginson, S., & Rhoades, G. (2002). Beyond national states, markets, and systems of higher education: A glonacal agency heuristic. *Higher Education, 43*(3), 281–309.

Matsumoto, D., LeRoux, J., Bernhard, R., & Gray, H. (2004). Unraveling the psychological correlates of intercultural adjustment potential. *International Journal of Intercultural Relations, 28*, 281–309.

Matthews, J., & Sidhu, R. (2005). Desperately seeking the global subject: International education, citizenship and cosmopolitanism. *Globalization, Societies and Education, 3*, 49–66.

Mori, S. (2000). Addressing the mental health concerns of international students. *Journal of Counseling and Development, 78*(2), 137–44.

Mulligan, D., & Kirkpatrick, A. (2000). How much do they understand? Lectures, students, and comprehension. *Higher Education Research and Development, 19*(3), 311–35.

Murphy, P. (2007). The art of systems: The cognitive-aesthetic culture of portal cities and the development of meta-cultural advanced knowledge economies. In David J. Pauleen (Ed.), *Cross-cultural perspectives on knowledge management* (pp. 35–63). Westport, CT: Greenwood.

National Liaison Committee, NLC (2004). *Submission for the ESOS Act evaluation*. Melbourne, Australia: NLC. Obtained February 9, 2008 by writing to research@nlc.edu.au. Not posted on the NLC website, but other and related documents can be accessed at http://www.nlc.edu.au/main/ nlc_submissions.html.

National Union of Students/Unipol (2007). *Accommodation costs survey 2006/07*. London, UK: NUS.

Newman, J. H. (1982). *The Idea of a university*. Notre Dame, IN: University of Notre Dame Press. First published in 1852.

Ninnes, P., Aitchison, C., & Kalos, S. (1999). Challenges to stereotypes of international students' prior education experience: Undergraduate education in India. *Higher Education Research and Development, 18*(3), 323–42.

Ninnes, P., & Hellsten, M. (Eds.). *Internationalizing higher education: Critical explorations of pedagogy and policy* (pp. 141–58). Dordrecht, Netherlands: Springer.

Oberg, K. (1960). Culture shock: Adjustment to new cultural environments. *Practical Anthropology, 7,* 177–82.

O'Donoghue, T. (1996). Malaysian Chinese students; perceptions of what is necessary for their academic success in Australia: A case study at one university. *Journal of Further and Higher Education, 20*(2), 67–80.

Olson, C., & Kroeger, K. (2001). Global competency and intercultural sensitivity. *Journal of Studies in International Education, 5*(2), 116–37.

Organization for Economic Cooperation and Development, OECD (2008). *Education at a glance.* Paris, France: OECD.

Otten, M. (2003). Intercultural learning and diversity in higher education. *Journal of Studies in International Education, 7*(1), 12–26.

Pantelides, U. (1999). Meeting the language needs of tertiary NESB students. *The Australian Journal of Language and Literacy, 22*(1), 60–76.

Pearce, R. (1998). Developing cultural identity in an international school environment. In M. Hayden, & J. Thompson (Eds.), *International education: Principles and practices,* pp. 60–83. London, UK: Kogan Page.

Pedersen, P. (1991). Counselling international students. *The Counseling Psychologist, 19*(10), 10–58.

Perrucci, R., & Hu. H. (1995). Satisfaction with social and educational experiences among international graduate students. *Research in Higher Education, 36*(4), 491–508.

Poyrazli, S., Arbona, C., Bullington, R., & Pisecco, S. (2001). Adjustment issues of Turkish college students studying in the United States. *College Student Journal, 35*(1), 52–62.

Prescott, A., & Hellstén, M. (2005). Hanging together with non-native speakers: The international student transition experience. In P. Ninnes, & M. Hellsten (Eds.), *Internationalzing higher education: Critical explorations of pedagogy and policy* (pp. 75–95). Dordrecht, Netherlands: Springer.

Pritchard, R., & Skinner, B. (2002). Cross-cultural partnerships between home and international students. *Journal of Studies in International Education, 6*(4), 323–54.

Pyvis, D., & Chapman, A. (2005). Culture shock and the international student "offshore." *Journal of Research in International Education, 4*(1), 23–42.

Ramburuth, P., & McCormick, J. (2001). Learning diversity in higher education: A comparative study of Asian international and Australian students. *Higher Education, 42,* 333–50.

Ramsay, S., Barker, M., & Jones, E. (1999). Academic adjustment and learning processes: A comparison of international and local students in first-year university. *Higher Education Research and Development, 18*(1), 129–44.

Redmond, M. (2000). Cultural distance as a mediating factor between stress and intercultural competence. *International Journal of Intercultural Relations, 24*, 151–59.

Rizvi, F. (2005). Identity, culture and cosmopolitan futures. *Higher Education Policy, 18*, 331–39.

Rizvi, F. (2008). Epistemic virtues and cosmopolitan learning. *The Australian Educational Researcher, 35*(1), 17–35.

Rizvi, F. (2009). Towards cosmopolitan learning. *Discourse: Studies in the Cultural Politics of Education, 30*(3), 253–68.

Robertson, M., Line, M., Jones, S., & Thomas, S. (2000). International students, learning environments and perceptions: A case study using the Delphi technique. *Higher Education Research and Development, 19*(1), 89–102.

Rochecouste, J., Oliver, R., Mulligan, D, & Davies, M. (2010). *Addressing the on-going English language needs of international students.* Canberra, Australia: Australian Learning and Teaching Council.

Rose, N. (1999). *Powers of freedom: Reframing political thought.* Cambridge, UK: Cambridge University Press.

Rosenthal, D., Russell, V., & Thomson, G. (2006). *A growing experience: The health and the wealth-being of international students at the University of Melbourne.* Melbourne, Australia: The University of Melbourne.

Ryan, J. (2000). *A guide to teaching international students.* Oxford, UK: Oxford Centre for Staff and Learning Development.

Said, E. (1979). *Orientalism.* New York, NY: Vintage.

Said, E. (1994). *Culture and imperialism.* New York, NY: Vintage.

Sam, D. (2001). Satisfaction with life among international students: An explanatory study. *Social Indicators Research, 53*, 315–37.

Samuelowicz, K. (1987). Learning problems of overseas students: Two sides of a story. *Higher Education Research and Development, 6*(2), 121–33.

Sanderson, G. (2008). A foundation for the internationalization of the academic self. *Journal of Studies in International Education, 12*(3), 276–307.

Savicki, V., Downing-Burnette, R., Heller, L., Binder, F., & Suntinger, W. (2004). Contrasts, changes and correlates in actual and potential intercultural adjustment. *International Journal of Intercultural Relations, 28*, 311–29.

Sawir, E. (2005). Language difficulties of international students in Australia: The effects of prior learning experience. *International Education Journal, 6*(5), 567–80.

Sawir, E., Marginson, S., Deumert, A., Nyland, C., Ramia, G. (2008). Loneliness and international students: An Australian study. *The Journal of Studies in International Education, 12*(2), 148–80.

Schapper, J., & Mayson, S. (2005). Managerialism, internationalization, taylorization and the deskilling of academic work: Evidence from an Australian university. In P. Ninnes, & M. Hellsten (Eds.), *Internationalizing higher education. Critical explorations of pedagogy and policy* (pp. 181–97). Hong Kong, China: Springer.

Schuerholz-Lehr, S. (2007). Teaching for global literacy in higher education: How prepared are the educators? *Journal of Studies in International Education, 11*(2), 180–204.

Schweitzer, R. (1996). Problems and awareness of support services among students at an urban Australian university. *Journal of American College Health, 45,* 73–81.

Selvadurai, R. (1991). Adequacy of selected services to international students in an urban college. *The Urban Review, 23*(4), 271–85.

Sen, A. (1985). Well-being, agency and freedom: The Dewey lectures 1984. *The Journal of Philosophy, 82*(4), 169–221.

Sen, A. (1992). *Inequality reexamined.* Cambridge, MA: Harvard University Press.

Sen, A. (1999). Global justice: Beyond international equity. In I. Kaul, I. Grunberg, & M. Stern (Eds.), *Global public goods: International cooperation in the 21st century* (pp. 116–25). Oxford, UK: Oxford University Press.

Sen, A. (2000). *Development as freedom.* New York, NY: Anchor Books.

Singh, M. (2005). Enabling translational learning communities: Policies, pedagogies and politics of educational power. In P. Ninnes, & M. Hellsten (Eds.), *Internationalizing higher education: Critical explorations of pedagogy and policy* (pp. 9–36). Dordrecht, Netherlands: Springer.

Siu, O., Spector, P., Cooper, C., & Lu, C. (2005). Work stress, self-efficacy, Chinese work values, and work well-being in Hong Kong and Beijing. *International Journal of Stress Management, 12*(3), 274–88.

Solberg, V., Ritsma, S., Davis, B., Tata, S., & Jolly, A. (1994). Asian-American students' severity of problems and willingness to seek help from university counselling centres: Role of previous counselling experience, gender and ethnicity. *Journal of Counseling Psychology, 41*(3), 275–79.

Spack, R. (1997). The acquisition of academic literacy in a second language: A longitudinal case study. *Written Communication, 14,* 3–62.

Spears, A. (1999). Race and ideology: An introduction. In A. Spears (Ed.), *Race and ideology: Language, symbolism, and popular culture* (pp. 11–59). Detroit, MI: Wayne State Press.

Spencer-Rodgers, J. (2001). Consensual and individual stereotypic beliefs about international students among American host nationals. *International Journal of Intercultural Relations, 25,* 639–57.

Spencer-Rodgers, J., & McGovern, T. (2002). Attitudes towards the culturally different: The role of intercultural communication barriers, affective responses, consensual stereotypes, and perceived threats. *International Journal of Intercultural Relations, 26,* 609–31.

Stephens, K. (1997). Cultural stereotyping and intercultural communication: Working with students from the People's Republic of China in the UK. *Language and Education, 11*(2), 113–24.

Sternberg, R. (2007). Culture, instruction, and assessment. *Comparative Education, 43*(1), 5–22.

Stone, N. (2006). Internationalizing the student learning experience: Possible indicators. *Journal of Studies in International Education, 10*(4), 409–13.

Stoynoff, S. (1997). Factors associated with international students' academic achievement. *Journal of Instructional Psychology, 24*(1), 56–69.

Struthers, C., Perry, R, & Menec, V. (2000). An examination of the relationship among academic stress, coping, motivation and performance at college. *Research in Higher Education, 41*(5), 581–92.

Summers, M., & Volet, S. (2008). Students' attitudes towards culturally mixed groups on international campuses: Impact of participation in diverse and non-diverse groups. *Studies in Higher Education, 33*(4), 357–70.

Tatar, S. (2005). Classroom participation by international students: The case of Turkish graduate students. *Journal of Studies in International Education, 9*(4), 337–55.

Teekens, H. (2003). The requirement to develop specific skills for teaching in an intercultural setting. *Journal of Studies in International Education, 7*(1), 108–19.

Teekens, H. (2004). A description of nine clusters of qualifications for lectures. In H. Teekens (Ed.), *Teaching and learning at home and abroad* (pp. 35–52). Hague, Netherlands: Nuffic.

Triandis, H., Bontempo, R, Villareal, M., Asai, M, & Lucca, N. (1988). Individualism and collectivism: Cross cultural perspectives on self-ingroup relationships. *Journal of Personality and Social Psychology, 54*(2), 323–38.

Triandis, H. (1989a). Cross-cultural studies of individualism and collectivism. In J. Berman (Ed.), *Nebraska symposium on motivation* (pp. 41–133). Lincoln, NE: University of Nebraska Press.

Triandis, H. (1994). *Individualism and collectivism.* Boulder, CO: Westview Press.

Trice, A. G. (2003). Faculty perceptions of graduate international students: The benefits and challenges. *Journal of Studies in International Education, 7*(4), 379–403.

Trice, A. G. (2005). Navigating in a multinational learning community: Academic departments' responses to graduate international students. *Journal of Studies in International Education, 9*(1), 62–89.

Trice, A., & Yoo, J. (2007). International graduate students' perceptions of their academic experience. *Journal of Research in International Education, 6*(1), 41–66.

UK Council for International Education, UKCOSA. (2004). *International students in UK universities and colleges: Broadening our horizons—report of the UKCOSA survey.* London, UK: UKCOSA.

United Nations Development Program, UNDP (1994). *Human development report.* New York, NY: United Nations Development Program.

Vertovec, S. (2009). *Transantionalism.* Oxford, UK: Routledge.

Vertovec, S., & Cohen, R. (2002). Introduction: Conceiving cosmopolitanism. In S. Vertovec, & R. Cohen (Eds.), *Conceiving cosmopolitanism: Theory, context, and practice* (pp. 1–22). Oxford, UK: Oxford University Press.

Volet, S., & Renshaw, P. (1995). Cross-cultural differences in university students' goals and perceptions of study settings for achieving their own goals. *Higher Education, 30*, 407–33.

Volet, S., & Ang, G. (1998). Culturally mixed groups on international campus: An opportunity for inter-cultural learning. *Higher Education Research and Development, 17*(1), 5–24.

Volet, S., & Tan-Quigley, A. (1999). Interactions of Southeast Asian students and administrative staff at university in Australia: The significance of reciprocal understanding. *Journal of Higher Education Policy and Management, 21*(1), 95–115.

Wan, G. (2001). The learning experience of Chinese students in American universities: A cross-cultural perspective. *College Student Journal*, March, 28–44.

Wang, W., Ceci, S., Williams, W., & Kopko, K. (2004). Culturally situated cognitive competence: A functional framework. In R. Sternberg, & E. Grigorenko (Eds.), *Culture and competence: Contexts of life success* (pp. 225–50). Washington, DC: American Psychological Association.

Ward, C. (2005). Comments during plenary session *Internationalization III.* Annual meeting of the ISANA International Education Association Conference, Christchurch, New Zealand, November 29–December 2.

Ward, C. (2008). Thinking outside the Berry boxes: New perspectives on identity, acculturation, and intercultural relations. *International Journal of Intercultural Relations, 32*, 105–14.

Ward, C., & Chang, W. (1997). "Cultural fit": A new perspective on personality and sojourner adjustment. *International Journal of Intercultural Relations, 21*(4), 525–33.

Ward, C., Leong, C., & Low, M. (2004). Personality and sojourner adjustment: An exploration of the Big Five and the cultural fit proposition. *Journal of Cross-Cultural Psychology, 35*(2), 137–51.

Ward, C., & Masgoret, A. M. (2004). *The experiences of international students in New Zealand: Report on the results of the national survey.* Wellington, New Zealand: New Zealand Ministry of Education.

Ward, C., Okura, Y., Kennedy, A., & Kojima, T. (1998). The U-curve on trial: A longitudinal study of psychological and sociocultural adjustment during cross-cultural transition. *International Journal of Intercultural Relations, 22*(3), 277–91.

Ward, C., & Rana-Deuba, A. (1999). Acculturation and adaptation revisited. *Journal of Cross-Cultural Psychology, 30*(4), 422–42.

Webb, G. (2005). Internationalization of curriculum. An institutional approach. In J. Carroll, & J, Ryan (Eds.), *Teaching international students. Improving learning for all* (pp. 109–18). London, UK: Routledge.

Wilkinson, L., & Kavan, H. (2003). Dialogues with dragons: Helping Chinese students' academic achievement. *ATLAANZ Conference proceedings* (pp. 119–31). Waikato, New Zealand: ATLAANZ.

Yang, R., Noels, K., & Saumure, K. (2006). Multiple routes to cross-cultural adaptation for international students: Mapping the paths between self-construals, English language confidence, and adjustment. *International Journal of Intercultural Relations, 30,* 487–506.

Ying, Y., & Han, M. (2006). The contribution of personality, acculturative stressors, and social affiliation to adjustment: A longitudinal study of Taiwanese students in the United States, *International Journal of Intercultural Relations, 30,* 623–35.

Yoo, S., Matsumoto, D., & LeRoux, J. (2006). The influence of emotion recognition and emotion regulation on intercultural adjustment. *International Journal of Intercultural Relations, 30,* 345–63.

Yuval-Davis, N. (1999). What is transversal politics? *Soundings, 12,* 94–98.

Yuval-Davis, N. (2006). *Racism, cosmopolitanism, and contemporary politics of belonging.* London, UK: Lawrence & Wishhart. Retrieved May 28, 2005 from http://www.lwbooks.co.uk/journals/articles/yuvaldavis05.html.

Zhang, N., & Dixon, D. (2003). Acculturation and attitudes of Asian international students toward seeking psychological help. *Multicultural Counselling and Development, 31,* 205–22.

Zhang, Q. (2006). Immediacy and out-of-class communication: A cross-cultural comparison. *International Journal of Intercultural Relations, 30,* 33–50.

Zhu, W. (2004). Faculty views on the importance of writing, the nature of academic writing, and teaching and responding to writing in the disciplines. *Journal of Second Language Writing, 13,* 29–48.

Index

Japan and Japanese people, 37, 85–86, 105, 110, 120

Kant, Immanuel, 54–55
Knight, Jane, 15–17
Korea and Korean people, 37, 105, 110, 115, 120

language learning and language proficiency, 18, 23, 141, 182–85. *See also* communicative competence, English
learning, incremental, 30, 70, 140
learning, transformational or transformative, 30, 70, 137, 140–43, 169, 181–82
loneliness, 5, 83

Malaysia and Malaysians, 46, 77, 87, 95, 100, 109, 114, 117, 126, 141, 175
marginalization, 25, 71, 96
market competition in international education, ix, 8
Melbourne, 1–2, 75, 165–68
motivation of local students, 74, 99–101, 134–35, 147, 169, 173, 180–82
multiculturalism, 25, 28, 58, 63–64, 66, 124
multiplicity in identity, 28, 41, 48, 54, 58, 60, 65, 67, 150–52, 158, 161, 171
mutual learning between international and local students, 8, 9, 119, 130–34, 168, 178–79, 180

nations and nationalism, 14–17, 59–61, 63–65, 70
neo-racism, 105–6, 117
neoliberalism, 16, 63, 73
New Zealand and New Zealanders, viii, 6, 7, 12, 34–35, 89, 105, 107–8, 120, 122, 128, 163, 180, 183
noncitizen, 80–81, 86, 99–101, 102–3, 108, 110–12, 131, 173
nonwhite students, experiences of, 2, 5, 71, 79, 84, 88, 97, 105–6, 117
normalization, 22, 49, 158

openness, 17, 32, 42, 46–48, 49, 56, 60, 64–67, 72, 102, 117, 128, 129, 134, 140, 147–48, 149, 155, 161
oral communication in class, 8, 92–93, 121, 122, 123, 124, 126, 127, 128, 131, 166
Organization for Economic Cooperation and Development (OECD), 7
Other(s) and Othering, viii, 10, 22, 35, 40, 49, 54, 66, 67, 71, 78, 79, 95, 101–12, 119, 123, 161, 172, 173

Pedersen, Paul, 23, 29–30, 65–66
place and identity, 56–59, 60–61, 64, 73, 148
plural identity. *See* multiplicity
psychology, cross-cultural, 10, 11, 19, 21–51, 53–54, 74, 116, 135, 140, 150, 157, 158–63, 170, 171, 172

racism. *See* discrimination and abuse; ethnocentrism
relational cosmopolitanism. *See* cosmopolitanism
Rizvi, Fazal, 55, 60–61, 62–65, 72, 147

safety of international students, 12
same-culture relations between students, 5, 6, 24–25, 27–28, 31, 37–39, 42, 47–48, 78, 88,